Dear Reader

Farangi girl . . . foreign girl.

Ashley Dartnell's mother was a glamorous American, her British father dashing and handsome, each trying to shed their past and transform in the romantic and exotic setting of Iran. As the story begins, Ashley is eight years old and living in Tehran in the Sixties: the Shah is in power, life for Westerners is rich and privileged. But somehow it doesn't all add up to a fairytale. There are bankruptcies and prisons, betrayals and lovers, lies and evasions. And throughout it all, Ashley's passionate and strong willed mother, Genie.

Stories of mothers and daughters are some of the most compelling in contemporary memoir, from *The Liars' Club* and *The Glass Castle* to *Don't Let's Go to the Dogs Tonight* and *Bad Blood*. *Farangi Girl* deserves to be in their company. It's an honest and compelling portrait of a mother by a daughter who loved her (and was loved in return).

Ashley's journey into adulthood, against this extraordinary background, was more helter-skelter than most and this portrait of a bewitching and resilient mother is surprising and deeply moving.

Lisa Highton
PUBLISHER

FARANGI GIRL

TWO
ROADS

ASHLEY DARTNELL

FARANGI
GIRL

a memoir of my mother, parties with princes
and growing up in Iran

www.tworoadsbooks.com

First published in Great Britain in 2011 by
Two Roads
An imprint of Hodder & Stoughton
An Hachette UK company

1

A CIP catalogue record for this title is available from the British Library.

Hardback ISBN 978 1 444 71469 2
Trade Paperback ISBN 978 1 444 71470 8
eBook ISBN 978 1 444 71472 2

Printed and bound in the UK by Clays Ltd, St Ives plc

Hodder & Stoughton policy is to use papers that are natural, renewable
and recyclable products and made from wood grown in sustainable
forests. The logging and manufacturing processes are expected to
conform to the environmental regulations of the country of origin.

Two Roads
Hodder & Stoughton Ltd
338 Euston Road
London NW1 3BH

With love

to my mother, father and brothers

and

Bruce, Dylan, Kyle and Cara

Author's Note

Throughout *Farangi Girl* I have made frequent reference to Farsi terms and expressions from my childhood (as in the title, which means 'foreign girl'). I have included these references in order to illustrate the environment in which I was raised. While it is not necessary for the reader to understand the literal translations of these references, I have attempted, wherever possible, to make their meaning clear.

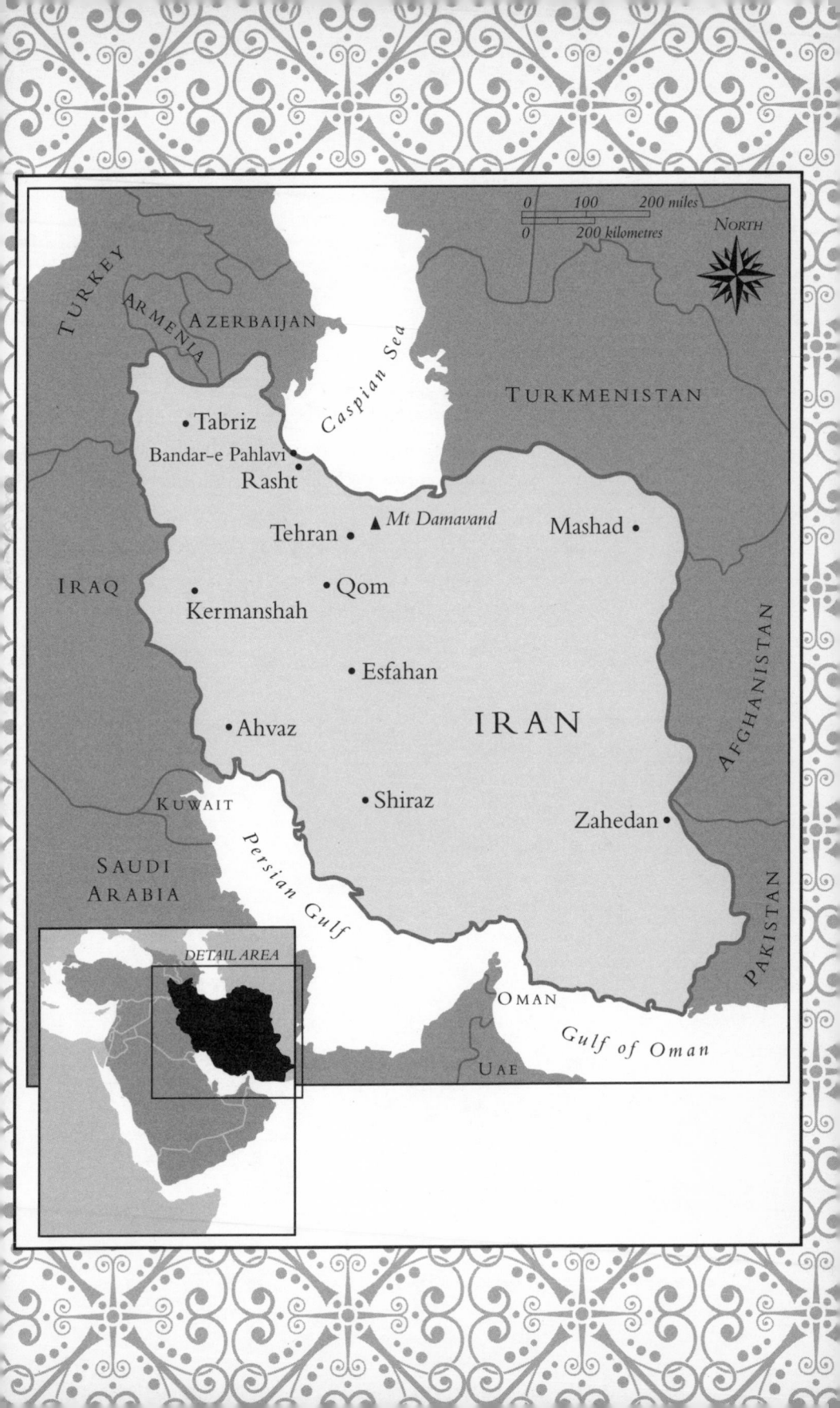

Contents

Iran, 1967–8

*my parents
young and in love*

I

The Chaloos Road

*my father with
Pakistani villagers*

'Get a move on, you donkeys! *Borro gomshoh olagh*!' my
father yelled, leaning on the horn.

All over the road lay watermelons that had fallen out the
back of a van. The driver struggled to gather them up as the
sound of horns grew louder. Behind us, I could see cars and
trucks strung like colourful beads around the mountain.
Realising it was futile, the driver stuck his head in the window
of each car, urging us to take some of the *hendevaneh*. Cameron
and I scampered out and each lugged one back. People stopped
to stretch and gossip as they picked up their melons, laughing
and joking, glad to take a break from driving.

But my father screamed from the window and waved his fist.
'*Borro, borro* – let's go!'

With a scowl, the driver hurled the remaining melons down the slope where they burst in a ragged explosion of scarlet. Cameron and I were happy because we both had a melon rolling around under our feet, and after weeks of not knowing when or even if we would see our mother again, we were on our way to pick her up from the airport.

My father wrestled our old grey Rover around one hairpin turn after another, pushing himself and the car, trying to make up for lost time. Even without the delay of the melons, we were hard pressed. We were on the dangerous Chaloos road that wound from the Caspian, making our way to Mehrabad Airport on the outskirts of Tehran. Cameron and I counted the lorry skeletons and car carcasses that littered the slopes. Earlier we had seen a dead man on the side of the road, a jacket flung over him, his car mangled on the boulders below. After a while we rolled up the windows. It had grown chilly once the fiery sun plummeted behind the peaks. Cameron fell asleep and I chattered away, terrified my father would go too fast and get us killed. The narrow road had just enough room for two cars to pass and he hardly braked at each blind corner.

As usual, my father had left too late.

*

I wonder whether I would have remembered any of this trip, that spring of 1967, if everything hadn't changed – and certainly not for the better. Some details are lost. I don't remember where we met my mother, whether she waited for hours at the airport or took a taxi back to the flat. When we did see her, she held herself away when I hugged her.

Over the days that followed, she seemed to come alive only when she told her friends about her adventures: how she and Nounou, the friend with whom she had gone to Europe, had stuck out their tongues and crossed their eyes when men flirted with them; how they had laughed; how

4

they had giggled; the fun they had; how much chocolate they had eaten.

At first I watched and smiled with glazed amazement. Soon, though, I found it hurtful. All that time I had been so worried: about her, about whether I would ever see her again, about whether she and my father would stay together. All that time she was central to my thoughts, while she had been chasing pigeons in piazzas across Europe.

Looking back at my parents, at the choices they made, I wonder what they would have done differently, had they been given a glimpse of the future. I suspect they would not have chosen the next five years of their lives, maybe even the rest of their lives. But then, no one wishes to have an unhappy marriage, just as no one elects to be ill, alcoholic or poor. Certainly, my parents' youthful expectations were, if anything, wildly exuberant and optimistic, and there was no couple with more potential. They were well educated, talented, charismatic and glamorous. But by the time we arrived, late, at Mehrabad Airport and after less than nine years of marriage, their lives were in turmoil.

Over a decade earlier, they had met in Kharian, a small dusty town near the Jhelum River and the North-West Frontier Province of Pakistan. My father, George Malin, (known as Lin or Malin), was thirty years old, a successful civil engineer building the Kharian army cantonment for the Pakistani government. How this Cambridge-educated young man from a respectable family ended up in a remote corner of Pakistan is a story of escape from the strictures of middle-class, war-depleted Britain. From the day he was born, my father had chafed against the narrowness of his society. He wanted adventure. He wanted excitement. He wanted to conquer new worlds, to climb the highest mountains, to explore the most remote regions. He had absolutely no desire to live in congested, grey, insular Britain.

His father, Arthur George Calbert Dartnell, was a man who had thrived following the rules, first as a regimental quartermaster sergeant in the Territorial Army during both world wars and then afterwards as a civil servant in South Wales. He was the epitome of respectability. By the time my father was born in 1927, Arthur, at forty, and Fanny, his wife of thirty-five, were upstanding members of their community. Always well dressed, always well fed, the family had a car, and my father and his younger brother spent happy days roaming the fields shooting birds with their air rifle. My father went to the local school, Whitchurch Grammar, played cricket and rugby, and held the UK Junior Discus Championship.

He attended Trinity College, Cambridge, the first member of his family to go to university. At Cambridge he escaped from his rooms by climbing down the drainpipes. His memories of the time were of cold quarters and inadequate food, with the entire university depressed and exhausted by the war. He graduated and joined the RAF, going to Germany to help build airfields. It was at this time, playing rugby, that he bit through his lip and someone took a chunk out of his neck during a scrum, resulting in the two distinctive scars that gave his handsome face a rakish cast.

After his military service, he joined Wimpey, the engineering company, to pursue his dream of going overseas: to Ethiopia, Aden and then Pakistan. He loved the scale of the landscapes, the freedom, and the impact that he could have as a young and ambitious civil engineer. When my mother met him, he was managing big construction projects with many workers. What my mother saw was someone respectable, well educated, well paid, from a solid family, with a Cambridge degree and an English accent. Importantly for my mother, he was tall and handsome.

My mother was born in a rocky, inhospitable corner of

Connecticut to an impoverished family with four children. Her father, Willy, who had only ever finished fourth grade, worked at the local sawmill where he made 50 cents an hour. Lilly, her mother, worked in a factory in East Hampton, known as Bell Town. To supplement their meagre salaries they kept a few goats, chickens and rabbits. From the earliest age, my mother and her twin brother worked chopping wood; feeding, killing and skinning rabbits; planting, picking, boiling, pickling and canning tomatoes, cucumbers and beans – from before dawn until they fell into bed late at night. They went to the local school where, even in a community of hard-up families, theirs stood out. Each week when the school nurse examined the children, my mother hid the holes in her socks between her toes and explained away the bruises from Willy and Lilly's beatings. My mother was always hungry, always cold and always in pain, as she had soft teeth and there was no money for a dentist or even for aspirin to deaden the ache.

In their house in Connecticut, it was so cold that the windows had icicles on the inside and snow drifted in through the cracks in the walls. There was no indoor toilet so they peed in milk bottles at night, which, by the time they awakened in the morning, had frozen solid. In one of those odd coincidences that shape a life, when she was little she read a *National Geographic* article about India. The dream of escaping to sun-drenched India took root and flourished.

At the age of twenty-three, having graduated from a teachers' training college and then taught first grade for a year, she boarded a ship and headed east to saris, curry, camels and sunshine. When she landed in Pakistan, seven years after partition, she said, 'I felt as if I had died and gone to heaven.' She was full of adventure: swimming in the muddy Jhelum River; riding camels; shooting guns at the Jamrud Gun

Factory; fishing; galloping on horseback along the Grand Trunk road; exploring the Rohtas Fort; and dancing and dining with the engineers – one of whom was my father. What my father saw in her was a courageous woman who didn't follow the rules. She seemed the opposite of the staid, middle-class, 'mumsy' women he had known as a child. When he described her to me years later, wistfully, he said, 'She was so strong and independent.' And, of course, there was her beauty.

As my mother told it, their courtship in Pakistan was completely one-sided: he caught a glimpse of her at a dance and was infatuated. She spurned him. He sent his houseboy with a posy. She spurned him. He called on her. She spurned him. She fled to America. He followed and begged her on bended knee to marry him. Finally, after hundreds of promises, including that they would always live overseas, that she would never have to work, that she could have five children and that she would live like a princess, she capitulated. My father told a different tale, a story of 'She chased me until I caught her.' They were married at City Hall in New York on 15 August 1958 with an Irish drunk off the street as their witness. They honeymooned in America. A month later, she was pregnant with me and three months later, they were on a plane to Iran.

The first years in Iran were heady. My father had a good position with IBEC, a Rockefeller company. They lived in expansive company housing, waited on by servants. In quick succession, my mother gave birth to two healthy babies: me and, just fifteen months later, my brother Cameron. She adored us and threw herself into the privileged life of the expatriate wife: the club during the day with the children; parties at night, where she danced with the princes of the Iranian royal family. Then things began to unravel: her pregnancies were difficult and she lost the next two babies, both at birth. She

8

was devastated by the deaths. My father, as always, wanted to move on. 'Don't think about it, look to the future. Have another baby.'

Meanwhile, against my mother's vehement pleas, my father set up his own business in partnership with two Iranians. They moved out of the grand house, gave up the big car, and fired the driver and servants. A tunnel near the Caspian was to be his first test.

2

Mr Engineer

en route to Iran

During those first months of 1967, my father took Cameron and me to live in a mud hut surrounded by rice fields, near the Caspian coast, while he built the tunnel. My mother, worn out and exhausted, had gone to recuperate in Switzerland with her friend Nounou, leaving our brother Rian, only three, in Tehran with another of her friends.

Every day we woke up to the sound of the village roosters crowing. We cawed back in high squeaky voices and tumbled off our low wooden sleeping platform to pee in the dirt next to the house. I squatted, trying not to wet my feet, while Cameron stood on the steps and aimed at the chickens and ducks. We thrust our hands into the straw where the ducks slept to collect the eggs, still warm, that an old village lady broke into a pan of sizzling ghee for our breakfast.

'*Beshin*,' she gestured to me to sit, a hand-rolled cigarette hanging from her toothless mouth. I crouched on the earth floor and dunked freshly baked *barbary* bread into the marigold egg yolk.

'*Cha-ee lotfan*.' I asked for hot tea from the pot on the top of the samovar and sipped the steaming brew through sugar lumps held between my teeth. Mummy never let us do that – our teeth would rot. Up here, without her, though, we ignored all the normal rules. After we'd eaten, Daddy, back from the job where he had been since dawn, would clomp up the wooden steps. While Cameron and I raced to pull on the muddy clothes we had left on the floor the night before, he drank a Nescafé.

'Have you cleaned your teeth?' he would ask, if he remembered.

Reluctantly, Cameron and I grabbed our toothbrushes and scrubbed, spitting from the porch into the yard where the chickens pecked at the blobs of toothpaste.

We drove to the job site, first on a paved road and then, as we drew closer, on rough gravel. On the way, my father made up stories of a mysterious world of elves and fairies, witches and goblins.

'Look, Asho, did you see that one? The old gnome with the red trousers and a beard?' he asked as I looked out the window.

I gazed out, searching between the twisting tree roots. I was pretty sure fairies didn't exist, but I played along with my father who was caught up in the mood of the dark forest, where the prehistoric trees embraced clumsily, their knotted arms grasping for one another in the shifting breeze. I tried hard to glimpse a magical creature, ignoring Cameron's taunts. Even though Cameron was a year younger, he didn't believe in Santa Claus or the Tooth Fairy. Sometimes I glanced at my father, his eyes intent on the road, to make sure he wasn't just pretending. I was almost eight years old and I didn't want him to think I was silly.

My father listed the trees as we drove: oak, beech, ironwood, hornbeam and chestnut. I asked him whether he thought any human being had been here before us.

He looked thoughtful and said, 'Maybe a few hunters or a villager collecting wood, but it's possible that no one has been here – ever.'

I thought about how we might be in one of the few places left on earth where no human had ever set foot and I smiled to myself. That was better than any gnome or fairy.

Passing immense trees that lay where they had been felled by my father's workers, their roots dangling small continents of dirt, we pulled up next to the camp where the labourers lived in ragged tents and huts of corrugated metal. The tangy, pickle smell of urine hung in the damp air. Workers gathered as we drove up and as soon as my father opened the car door he was off.

'*Aghayeh Mohandes, Aghayeh Mohandes,*' cried the men.

I had asked my father why the workers called him 'Mr Engineer' and he explained it was out of respect because, along with doctors, engineers were the most admired professionals in Iran.

Cameron and I knew most of the men by name and yelled out, '*Salam Agha Mostaghel! Salam Agha Sedegheh!*'

While my father got to work, Cameron and I walked around the site. The crew had already torn a huge red slash of clay out of the woods, but there was still more ground to clear. When the weather improved, they would blast the tunnel out of the mountain. My father was racing against time because here in the north, where the winters were snowy and bitter, and the rainy spring lasted for months and months, the most he could hope to work in a year was six or seven months.

The bulldozers and shovels nosed the trees back and forth, tearing them out of the bleeding clay. It was not enough to cut the trees; they had to remove the massive roots as well. The machines were like greedy prehistoric beasts as they crawled around, chomping the vegetation. I played a game in my head, grouping the machines into families: the yellow Caterpillar bulldozers with their headlight eyes and big smiling blades; the gangly loaders and shovels; the foolish-looking, sheep foot-rollers; and the fleet of menacing-looking Benz trucks. Each family had its own language and personality, and did its own special job. All around us big equipment was moving and grinding, and spewing the acrid smell of diesel and exhaust.

As I watched the big lumbering beasts and antlike men, picking and shovelling the tough clay, I chewed radishes and goat's cheese wrapped in flat *lavash* bread. Here in the clearing, away from the protection of the tall trees, it was soon warm, almost like summer. Sitting on a log, feeling its rough bark through my trousers, with the razed trees all around me, I saw a tree being wrenched from the earth, its roots snapping and pulling. I wondered how long it would take that tree to realise it had been killed. Would it know right away or would the water already in its roots continue to be drawn towards the branches, to the leaves that were still green, drop by drop, until there was no more?

Building this tunnel in the middle of the wilderness was my father's lucky break. To get this job and establish themselves with the royal family, who controlled many of the big earthmoving projects, he and his partners had underbid the competition. Daddy had explained to us that the tunnel was one of many of the Shah's undertakings 'to take Iran out of the dark ages'. He had told us how the Shah's father, Reza Shah, had overthrown the Qajar princes and seized huge tracts of land from them, including these forests. The Qajars, who had come from the north of Iran close to where we were living, had kept the peasants working the land, almost like serfs during feudal times in Europe. He told us that Reza Shah had taken the first step in giving some land to the people.

'Then only four years ago,' Daddy told us, 'in 1963 when you were both very little, the Shah launched the Enghelab-e Sefid,' or the 'White Revolution' to modernise Iran. It was called that because supposedly nobody was killed, but in reality many hundreds died. Since the Enghelab-e Sefid, everywhere across the country, engineers like my father were carving roads, bridges, tunnels, canals and dams out of the earth of Iran. Even if he hadn't told us all this, though, I would have known how important this tunnel job was to him because I had heard him say so many times, his voice high.

'I won't be just an employee. No more, "Dartnell, do this, do that." I'll be my own man.'

This was the first step in his dream.

Every day there were new emergencies he had to deal with: rock formations unexpectedly resilient to the dynamite, excessive water and seepage, workers ill, diesel shortages and equipment breaking down.

Cameron and I sat on our haunches near the generator hut, drinking hot, sweet tea out of tin bowls with the workers.

'So, are you going to dynamite today? Is the filter for the big bulldozer here from Tehran? How many trucks are they working? Has the diesel arrived?'

Six-year-old Cameron asked the workers every detail, copying my father almost to the word.

The men laughed and called him *Mohandes eh koucheek*, or the little engineer, and teased him with salutes and yes, sirs. Cameron was desperate to become an apprentice on the heavy equipment. He watched for hours as young boys clambered up and down the big machines, digging chunks of mud out of the treads, washing the windshields and tightening screws. I knew the workers tolerated us only because we were the *mohandes'* children, but we felt our father's responsibility keenly.

Only a few days before, we had gone to Bank Melli to collect the hundreds of soft worn notes and canvas bags of coins to pay the workers. My father had stashed the heavy bags underneath the car seat, where Cameron and I leaned to finger them, guessing how much money there was. When he told us, we were silent for we had never imagined such a large amount.

'Just wait, it will all be gone on Thursday night,' he said. He paid the workers before their day off on Friday.

That next payday, we arrived just as the men finished setting up a wooden platform where we sat cross-legged on an itchy Turkoman carpet. My father, seated on the only chair, carefully annotated the weekly account books with his gold-nibbed fountain pen. We were in a small clearing in a thicket of trees just coming into bud. The new leaves were a soft grey-green and their fresh growing smell whispered through the dusk. Dozens of labourers squatted around us, smoking roughly rolled cigarettes and hawking gobbets of spit.

'Ali Mostaghel.'

'Mamad Ali.'

'Khosro.'

One by one, he called each worker for his wages and Sammii, the foreman and the single fat man in the group, counted out each bill and coin. The worker double-counted his small pile: machine operators at the top end of the pay scale, common labourers who hewed the rock with pickaxes at the bottom.

The drivers and mechanics, who had worked with him for years, travelled with my father from job to job, leaving their families behind in their villages, and returned home only during the holiday month of Norouz. My father hired the manual hands from the nearby villages. Barefoot or wearing stiff cloth clogs, the men shuffled up, exhausted at the end of the long week, to mark the register, many with a simple X, which Sammii then witnessed. Their faces were brown and craggy, with creases running from eye to mouth. Harsh weather, injuries that barely healed and unset bones had left many painfully humped or bow-legged. There were men whose noses and cheeks were eaten away by the larvae of sand-flies, men with eyes clouded by blindness, men with missing teeth. Forty-year-olds were already old and wizened.

Cameron and I quizzed them, '*Chand sal daree?*' We found that boys a few years older than us were pushing heavy wheel-barrows and men who were in their late twenties had five children and had never travelled further than Rasht, a few miles away.

As my father paid the men, he handed the money bags to me, and I folded and stacked them, fingering the rough canvas. The air was cool and my stomach rumbled. Dark descended, and we packed up. A few stragglers approached my father.

'*Aghayeh Mohandes, pool lazem daram* – I need money,' one man begged. 'My child is ill and needs the hospital.'

Another entreated, 'My brother died and we need to bury him.'

In each case, my father authorised another couple of thousand rials or two days off.

As he did this, I imagined my mother saying, 'You have enough money to pay for *their* weddings and funerals and illnesses, yet *your* children need clothes, *your* children aren't in school, *your* children have never been to a doctor.'

When I asked my father about this, he explained that the amount of money the workers needed was small but that our school fees and our flat cost so much that no matter how much money he gave Mummy, she always needed more. 'Also, these men have no one else to turn to,' he said. I wondered what that said about us.

My father put the bags in the boot of the car and we piled in to go to the *hammam* for our weekly bath. As we entered, hot steam fingers tickled me and I broke out into a sweat. Suddenly the mud of the rice fields, the clay of the site, and the salty sea rime that had accumulated on my skin for the past week without my even noticing, were unbearably itchy.

'*Holeh daree?*' asked the attendant, wrapped in a grey chador.

Like a great toad, she crouched with her behind almost touching the concrete floor and handed us thin cotton towels in exchange for a few rials. The baths were segregated by sex, so my father rented a small cubicle just for the three of us. We sat on small wooden stools and he sluiced us down, hefting the large copper *satl* filled with silky warm water. As soon as he emptied the jug, our skin erupted in goose pimples. We shivered and begged for just one more *satl*, please, just one more. We laughed at our father for, naked, he was pure white except for his dark-brown arms and face. We wiggled the pellet lodged under the skin of his leg where his brother had shot him with an air rifle when they were boys.

My father teased back, 'How many trees can we plant in the mud coming off Cam this week?' and admonished me, 'Wash behind your ears and in all the nooks and crannies.'

We shared the sliver of Imperial Leather soap with its little foil stamp that he kept with his razor, wrapped as carefully as a memento, in the boot of the car.

On one occasion, when there was no cubicle available, my father and Cameron went into the men's area while the old lady led me to the women's baths. I stared at the squatting women, their breasts hanging almost to the ground. I had never seen a naked woman before. My mother would run squealing if any of us walked into her room when she was dressing. The attendant scrubbed me hard with a rough *kiseh*, checking every few seconds to make sure she had rubbed away all the dark wormy squiggles of dirt and skin. She muttered under her breath as she worked, and I felt my whole body flush with embarrassment. If my mother knew, she would have killed me – or, rather, my father.

The attendant walked over to one of the women and borrowed a large bar of white soap to wash my hair. Everybody stared at me, the thin naked *farangi* girl without a mother to take care of her. When she returned me to my father, she lifted up my tangled hair and shook her head, unhappy. I had forgotten my hairbrush in Tehran so I hadn't brushed my hair the whole time we'd been in the Caspian. He laughed and said, '*Eyb nadareh.*' But she clearly thought it did matter. Warm and scrubbed, I wriggled free and raced out into the nippy evening, looking forward to our big meal of the week at a *chelow kebab* restaurant.

The warm odour of cooking rice, raw onions and grilled meat engulfed us as we entered. We waited for our feast, tracing the designs on the oilcloth and examining the portraits of the triumvirate that ruled over almost every shop and restaurant in Iran: the dark-bearded and turbaned Ali, the first imam of the Shi'a Muslim faith; the implacable Shah in his military uniform; and the handsome American president, John F. Kennedy, in a suit and tie. I stared at Kennedy, high up on the wall of this *chelow kebabi* in a tiny village in Iran.

'Daddy,' I asked, 'why do the Iranians love President Kennedy so much?'

JFK's name had flown like the bright American flag during the conversations my father had with the other men when we visited friends in Tehran. Over and over, I had heard it mixed with words like 'cold war', 'atom bomb', 'communism' and 'red scare', as the men sat with their legs crossed drinking and smoking. I remembered the day when I was not yet five, standing at the door of my father's office to see him fiddling with the dials of the radio, trying to catch the squealing voices of the BBC World Service.

'Oh my God, the president has been shot. Genie, my God, Genie!' He called to my mother, 'The president is dead.'

My mother came running, a questioning look on her face.

'President Kennedy! Someone shot JFK in Dallas.'

When Kennedy died, all of Iran including my father went into mourning. Kennedy was a hero, the man who would fight the Russians, who would protect Iran from communism and whose goodness was visible all over Tehran: immense wooden crates from the US marked CARE were stacked in every bazaar. The food was supposed to go to poor people but when the ships docked in the Persian Gulf, the dried milk, baby formula, flour and rice were often stolen by *bazaaris*, the merchants who supplied the food shops. Bags of flour destined for schools and orphanages were emptied and then filled with sand.

Even we had benefited from President Kennedy's generosity. When we had money, my mother stocked up on peanut butter and cake mix from these shipments. She was always indignant, though, when she saw the American foods in the bazaar. 'These are supposed to go to the poor!' Also, she was disgusted with the foods the Americans sent. 'It's just the stuff they want to get rid of,' she explained. 'How in the world is some village woman going to know what to do with a five-pound can of chocolate pudding mix? If she can even get it open!'

In any case, we kids loved the cake she made, but I felt sad that something so hopeful, something that said CARE all over it, was stolen and the money pocketed by rich *bazaaris*.

After Kennedy died, from the roof of our building, we had watched the tribute in Amjadieh Stadium. Squadrons of soldiers, with rifles and bayonets balanced on their shoulders, officers in dress uniforms on horseback, jeeps, tanks and cannons paraded by in a long khaki procession.

'Maybe the Iranians love Kennedy because for one brief moment in history it looked as if there would be some hope,' he said.

At last the food was brought out on scarred tin plates: mounds of snowy rice, and *shishlick* and *kubideh* kebabs, wrapped in *lavash* bread. Egg yolks, on the half-shell; raw onions; fresh herbs; goat's cheese and grilled tomatoes all arrived in colourful plastic side dishes. Cameron and I piled our rice high with a brick of melting butter on top, mushed in the egg yolks, then smashed in the tomatoes and showered on the sumac. Our favourite by far, but something that my father strictly rationed because it was so expensive, was kebab from the tail of a fat-tailed sheep. Cameron and I could eat those little nuggets of charred fat all day and all night. We stuffed ourselves, using small pieces of the *lavash* to grab the rice mixture and kebab. The Canada Dry that we gulped to wash it all down turned our teeth orange and we grinned like clowns, making faces at each other.

'Can I just have one more kebab, Daddy?' pleaded Cameron.

'Me too, me too!' I begged.

'*Mash Allah*, *Aghayeh* Dartnell, these children can eat,' laughed the owner of the restaurant as he brought more.

We were the only children there. In fact, I was the only female. That's how it was in this part of Iran: men only, eating and talking, slurping glasses of hot tea, shovelling away big plates of food and smoking their hubbly bubblies. For dessert, Daddy opened a can of Carnation condensed milk with his penknife and swirled a teaspoon into a steaming glass of Nescafé. Cameron and I each filled a spoon, licking the sweet ivory cream with shivers of delight.

*

One morning I saw my father running across the site.

'*Yavash! Yavash!* Careful!' he screamed.

While uprooting a tree, the shovel operator had misjudged the slope and the shovel was leaning dangerously, the back of its treads suspended in mid-air many feet up and the front tipping forward.

My father called instructions to the driver, perched high above in his tiny glass cabin. 'Use the shovel arm to grip the tree!'

I held my breath; Cameron was beside me, mouth ajar. If the tree gave way now, the shovel would fall over, a giant mechanical praying mantis on its back. I stared at the driver, his face tight with fear and concentration, willing him to do what my father instructed. Sweat gleamed on his forehead. He pulled hard on his controls and held on, clutching the tree trunk with the shovel arm, while my father and the workers raced to throw wheelbarrow-loads of rock under the treads. Cameron and I heaved in chunks of clay, digging them out of the earth with our fingers. I looked up to see the driver high in the air and prayed that this would work, that he wouldn't fall, that he and the loader wouldn't end up mangled on the side of the hill. After many minutes, the treads no longer hung suspended, but rested on a pile of rocks, and the driver inched back to more level ground.

My father called, '*Barricalla!* Well done!' to the driver in his funny, English-accented Farsi.

The driver raised his fist in a cheer and went back to work.

'That was lucky!' said my father, turning to us. Perspiration poured down his face and his shirt stuck to his chest.

I looked up at him. 'Daddy, why do you have to do this? You're killing the trees and the driver could have died.'

I was also upset about the tunnel itself. Once my father finished blasting the enormous hole through the rock, the mountain would never be the same again.

'Bloody fool. He should have known better.' He disregarded my question and began walking back to what he had been doing. The workers all returned to their pickaxes and shovels.

'Daddy, tell me why!' I ran to catch up with him, angry that he was ignoring me.

He stopped, his hands on his hips, and replied sharply, 'Look, Ashley, stop all this.'

He scorned Cameron's and my sentimental efforts to rescue the turtles, frogs and snails that the machines squashed; my disquiet about the trees dying; the tunnel ruining the mountain 'for all history'; my tears when I heard about an injured worker. Only the day before, we had found a tiny brown and yellow duckling abandoned by the stream. It lay flopped over, peeping pathetically. When we begged my father to save it, he had bent down and turned it over, gently, with his forefinger. 'Its back is broken. I'm going to drown it,' he said.

But I was distraught. 'No, Daddy, please. No!'

He looked over at Cameron who was braver. 'It's kinder to kill it.'

But we were adamant we would save it. By the next morning, despite the soft bed of straw and the little bowl of water we had wedged in the crate, the duckling was a ragged wad of feathers, its neck limp and its eyes closed.

'If we don't build this tunnel, if I never built another road, if we had no big buildings,' he continued, 'we'd be living like cave people. Look at these villagers.' He pointed at the men pushing wheelbarrows full of rock. 'They live the way we did two thousand years ago: with cholera, smallpox, starvation. A few trees, a few turtles – it's a small price to pay to help these people. Ashley, don't you want them to live the way we do in England and America?'

I thought about it. I supposed so. Even though my father was British, I had been neither to England nor to Wales, where he was born. My memory of my grandparents' house in America, where my mother grew up and where I had spent a summer, was of an outdoor pump, a bathtub filled with mildewed newspapers and a yard full of rusting farm implements. So I wasn't really sure. Was it better there than in Iran?

In any case, did I really come from those places – from England, from America? Maybe my parents did, but I was different, surely; I came from Iran, didn't I? I was born in Bazarganan Hospital, and I had lived here all my life.

3

What Bad Luck

*my mother
and me*

'It was funny about the watermelons, wasn't it, Daddy?' I asked. It was a long drive to pick up my mother at the airport and I tried to slip in some questions.

'Umhm.'

'Daddy? Daddy . . .' I tried again, but he interrupted. He wasn't a talkative person like my mother.

'Asho, have a sleep so you're fresh when you see Mummy.'

He turned his head and, as always, I had a feeling of recognition. Everybody, but especially my mother, said I looked exactly like him. I knew she would have preferred a daughter like her, with blue eyes and curly blonde hair, because every time she did my ponytails she complained about my 'lank, lifeless, mud-brown hair'.

In the hushed, dark car, away from the job where he was surrounded by men asking him questions about the equipment, I had the courage to ask, 'Daddy, why did Mummy go to Switzerland?'

'Your Mummy needed a holiday. She was tired. She doesn't like being alone so much when I'm on the job.'

I nodded. It was true. My mother always said, 'I'm going to have a nervous breakdown raising three kids with no money and no husband in this godforsaken country.'

I leaned over the seat and spoke to the back of his neck. 'Daddy, why are you always on the job?'

There was a long silence.

'Asho, this is my work. Mummy doesn't realise how hard it is here. When we married, she thought we would live in a sultan's palace with lots of servants. She thinks that life is a fairy tale with streets lined with gold and money growing on trees.'

It was unfair of him to say that. My mother wasn't like the other foreigners who had lots of servants and went from the hairdresser to the dressmaker. Day after day, she washed clothes, scrubbed the floor on her hands and knees, cut the grass with hand clippers. My resentment on behalf of my mother made me bolder.

'Daddy, if you work so hard, why don't we ever have any money?'

'I give your Mummy money!' he snapped. 'In any case, soon we'll have plenty of money. This tunnel job is going to change everything.'

I had heard him say that many times. How *this* job was going to change everything. I had heard him say it when I lay in bed, pretending to be asleep, a few days before my mother went to Europe and we left for the Caspian. He had just come back from the job and she didn't even wait for him to take off his windbreaker or have a Nescafé before she started.

'Lin, where have you been? You told me you'd be home weeks ago! How do you expect us to live? On air? On my good looks?'

'Hello, Genie. It's nice to see you, too,' he responded.

'Malin, I need money!'

I had heard *that* so many times.

'Genie, I gave you money.'

That refrain. I had heard it so many times.

'Enough for a week. You've been gone *four*.'

Money. My mother's answer to me was always, 'No, I don't have any.'

Whether it was for an orange popsicle at the *kuché* store or petrol for the car, there was never any money.

'The kids have to go to school. You have to get the money,' screamed my mother, her voice like splintered glass. 'What kind of a father can't even feed his children and send them to school?'

'It will all be different now.'

'Stop lying to me! It will never be different in this GD country. You're a *farangi*. You'll only get the jobs that nobody else wants.'

'Genie, that's not true. I just have to work harder, invest more and buy more equipment.'

My father had been silent for many minutes now, concentrating on the impenetrable darkness ahead.

'If we have no money, how did Mummy go to Switzerland?' I pressed.

'Ah, well.' He hesitated, 'Nounou and Nasser helped.'

That reminded me. My mother always said that the reason she was so tired was that she'd been nothing but pregnant or nursing a child for five years straight.

'And also, Daddy, Mummy said she had five children . . .'

'That's not true,' he interrupted.

'But Daddy, Mummy said she had two babies between

Cameron and Rian, and the first baby died when it was born and the second one strangled on its cord when it was inside her tummy.'

'She's lying. Don't listen to her.' His voice was gruff.

'She said they were both boys.'

I carried on because it seemed that there were always two stories: my mother's and my father's, and they were always completely opposite.

'I don't know why she has to keep on about those babies. She should just forget them.'

'So there were two more boys?'

Not every day, but regularly, my mother told me how sad she was about losing those two babies. How difficult the pregnancies had been and how heart broken she had been when there was no baby at the end. How she had wanted five children. How if she had received proper medical care they would have lived.

'Just forget it, Ashley, and go to sleep.'

He stared at the road and shook his legs to get the circulation back into them from driving so long.

Lights blinded me as enormous Benz trucks roared past, squeezing us to the edge of the road. In between bursts, I peered into the darkness, my forehead pressed against the cool, gritty glass. Silence. Roar. Light. Dark.

'Daddy, do you *really* think it will be different now?'

'I hope so, darling girl, I hope so.'

As if reading my mind, my father added, 'But don't worry, I'll always take care of you and Mummy and the boys, I promise.'

I lay back on the seat, its skin smooth and waxy as tortoiseshell, and stared out at the barbed-wire stars strung across the black sky.

There was something else I had been worrying away at for months, like a hangnail or a scab: were Mummy and Daddy

going to get a divorce? I had heard whispering between my
mother and her friends, the word flying around frantically like
a bird looking for a roost in a storm. I tried to ask, tried to say,
'Daddy, do you think the reason Mummy went away is so she
can leave us for ever? Do you really think she's coming home
tonight?' I was quiet, though, for I knew he would answer me
the same way he had about the money and the dead babies –
saying enough to make me stop asking questions but not really
telling the truth. I had learned that if my father didn't want to
answer, he would just switch off. Sometimes he would walk
out of the room, or I'd even seen him get his car keys and leave
for the job. Anyway, we would be at the airport soon enough
and there was a part of me that didn't want to know.

I lay on the seat next to Cameron and wondered what it
would be like to see Mummy again. I wondered whether she
would be happier, whether she and Daddy would still fight all
the time, whether we would finally be able to go back to school
and to live in our flat with Araboochie, our dog.

*

I awakened to the honks and cries of Tehran. Dawn fought its
way through the dust and diesel exhaust, pausing briefly before
the attack of the desert sun. A poster of a kohl-eyed beauty,
advertising an Indian movie, loomed above the road. Men on
bicycles veered in front of our car. Donkeys, garlanded in blue
beads, yawned, showing enormous yellow smiles. A flock of
fat-tailed sheep and long-eared goats, bells around their necks
clinking and clanking, were shooed through the traffic by a
barefoot boy. At the side of the road, praying men bowed
rhythmically, like pigeons, knocking their foreheads on their
prayer stones placed in front of their mats. I knew that all over
the city, all over the country, men were bobbing and pecking,
up and down, up and down, saying their *namaz*. The familiar
calls of mullahs, swaying high above in their minarets, synchro-
nised their followers: '*Allah O Akbar.*' The jangled lullaby of

the city soothed me: we *really* were on our way to Mehrabad
Airport to pick up our mother.

But then, suddenly, the car slammed to a stop, tipping at a
crazy angle. Cameron and I slid over to one side. My father
pounded on the steering wheel.

'Oh God dammit, dammit, dammit! What bad luck!'

I rubbed my forehead where it had hit the back of the seat.

'Are we at the airport, Daddy?' asked Cameron, kneading
his sleepy eyes.

Craning out the window, I could see the back axle of the car
sunk in a hole in the road. After having successfully negotiated
the dangerous Chaloos road, my father, lulled by the familiar-
ity of the Tehran streets, hadn't seen, in the half-light of dawn,
the deep pit in the middle of the road. He rested his head
against the steering wheel, his eyes closed, breathing heavily.
After some time, he opened the door and peered under the
car. Weaving his way through the early-morning traffic to the
centre of the roundabout, he waved to the passing cars, his
arms flailing. A few stopped, but when he explained that he
needed help and showed them a rope and a jack, they shot off.
His face looked baggy, his shirt stencilled with dust. Finally,
holding up a fistful of bills, he flagged down an army jeep and
a group of laughing young soldiers leaped out.

'Ashley,' he said, 'take Cameron over to the maydan until
we get the car out.'

We dodged between the rushing cars and watched as they
tied the rope to the back of the jeep and the front of our car.
Then, with one soldier driving the jeep, the others pushed the
back of the Rover. My father lay on the road, practically under
the car, trying to lever the wheel out of the hole with the jack.
I felt my back grow warmer and then finally hot as the sun rose
behind us. Over and over the soldiers grunted and pushed, and
my father threw himself on the jack until, after what felt like
hours, I saw the tyre roll towards his face. I squeezed my eyes

shut and wiggled my fingers in my ears, humming softly, 'Don't run him over, don't run him over.'

'It's out!' Cameron shouted.

I blinked to see the soldiers grab their money and jump into the back of the jeep before speeding away. My father dusted off his trousers and we were off again, merging into the traffic of Tehran.

*

Over the next few days, when we were all settled back into our flat in Amir Abad, happy to see Mummy and Rian and our dog Araboochie, I tried to explain to my mother how hard we had tried, how fast we had driven, how much time the watermelons had taken, how we had neither eaten nor peed on that long overnight drive, how brave Daddy had been, lying under the wheel of the car. How it was all down to bad luck.

She just pressed her lips together while she unpacked. 'It's always something with your father, isn't it?' she said, finally.

That made me think: why hadn't we left a day earlier? Why hadn't we stocked the fridge and bought flowers and then met her at the airport and taken her home? Why did Daddy always have to be late when it came to Mummy?

4

Strangers in the Night

*my parents having
a contemplative moment*

As we zigzagged back up the Alborz Mountains later that month, we followed the silver ribbon of the Chaloos road, spooling our way up over the desert bowl. I had assumed that, once we got settled in Tehran, we'd go straight back to school. But when after a few days there was no mention of it, I asked my mother, who said there was no money for things like school and that, in any case, the school year was almost over. In fact, we were all going up to the tunnel job to live.

Our parents' tension inflamed us like a caustic, itching powder, and we pinched and scratched and hissed at each other as we passed the monumental, newly built Karaj dam, crawled up the mountain and then plunged through tunnel after tunnel, to emerge on the other side to what seemed to be another land, even a different state of being. Since we had left a few weeks earlier, summer had drawn up in a golden flourish of sunlight. The Caspian coast was a velvet emerald cloth flung carelessly over the foothills, spangled with citrus groves and tea plantations. Soft jade rice fields clothed the flat land between the hills and the inky sea. The air of Bandar-e-Pahlavi as we drove through was filled with the scent of orange blossoms, so different from the petrol-station atmosphere of Tehran. Normally we cheered as we came around the final curve to glimpse the Caspian because we all loved that dirty inland sea. Today, though, nothing was right and nothing had been right for a long time.

Wedged between the boxes of bulldozer parts, we wore ourselves out trying to distract our parents.

'Daddy, sing "Strangers in the Night",' we begged.

His tuneless rendition usually spurred our mother into singing songs from *The Mikado* – which she had learned when she understudied the entire cast her senior year at Bacon Academy – with all of us joining in on, 'Three little girls are weeheehee!'

Neither took the bait.

'Mummy, can you recite "Jenny Kissed Me" or "The Congo"?'

Silence.

'Can you tell us stories about when you were a little girl in Connecticut?'

No response.

'Tell us "The Turtle Farm" or "Blueberry Picking" or "Flying the Plane and Knocking Down Granny's Chimney" or when you were in Pakistan, "The Vulture Story", please, "The Vulture Story".'

My mother glared out the window, chain-smoking, lighting one cigarette from the stub of the last. She didn't fill the car with the sunny smell of oranges as she usually did when we went to the job – peeling them for my father and handing him the next section as he drove; she didn't pick the grit from raisins, saying to us: 'Eat them, they're full of iron.' Nor did she leap out a million times to take photos.

We turned to our father. 'Daddy, look at the clouds – are they cumulus or stratus? Are the rocks red because they are ferrous?'

Complete silence.

Usually my father expounded on the weather patterns or rock formations, or tested whether we could convert kilometres to miles or estimate the incline of a slope. Finally he snapped, 'Put out the bloody cigarette, Genie. Soon you'll be smoking two at once.'

She scowled at him and lit two, which she smoked at the same time, one sticking out of each side of her mouth.

We didn't sing. We didn't play I Spy. We didn't laugh and we didn't joke. We didn't stop and stretch our legs, my father and the boys having a contest to see whose pee stream went the furthest, with tiny Rian, 'The Jet', always winning. Once over the mountains, we didn't go to a *gaveh khooneh* for Mummy to have tea and Daddy Nescafé. On this trip, like the journey going down the mountain, we didn't stop at all.

When we finally arrived at the job site, we circled like dogs, waiting our turn at the toilet, and Rian cried with hunger. My father went straight to work and my mother lugged our suitcase into the quarters where we would live. The house was dark and damp, the small windows unblinking eyes staring into the identical cube across the road. We children were in one room, our parents in the other.

'Here.'

My mother threw the big *rakht-e-khab*, the quilts the workers had left wrapped with twine, into our room.

We squabbled over which one we wanted. 'I bagsy the red one!' and laid them out next to each other. I unpacked, folding clothes into piles. 'Mummy, there's no place to put anything,' I complained.

'Nobody gives a damn what we look like here, throw 'em in a corner,' she said. 'You didn't brush your hair for a month so a few wrinkles aren't going to hurt you.'

33

I patted my hair, which my mother had hacked short – as short as a boy's – because it had been so tangled. She hung some shirts of my father's in front of her window.

'Mummy, where should we put our toothbrushes?' called Cameron. The small bathroom with a hole-in-the-ground toilet, which was our third room, had no sink.

'And where are you going to make food?' cried Rian. There was no kitchen.

'We'll eat with the workers,' said Mummy. 'There's a canteen.' She turned to Cameron. 'Put the toothbrushes near the door and I'll get a Pepsi bottle of water when we eat tonight so we can brush our teeth.'

*

Cameron and I dragged Rian up the roughly graded road, our skinny legs flailing against the thick mud.

'Look.' I pointed at the dark forests around the camp, my arm encircling his small shoulders.

'This is what the bulldozers do,' Cameron explained, showing him the immense trees that lay on the ground.

'See.' We gestured to the area torn out of the woods by my father's machines.

'There.' We showed him the red rutted roads, the workers' houses, the long, low canteen and small medical station: an entire concrete village that had been built, like one of our school projects constructed of cardboard and toilet rolls, to house and feed the people running the site.

'Look.' We showed him the workers' camp behind the tunnel.

'Here.' We stopped at the canteen and begged the cook for bread, which we ate standing in the doorway, tearing off huge sheets of the *lavash*.

'Come on,' we called as we raced up the hill.

Martin, Brigitte and their son Mikey were the prize exhibits of our job-site life and we ran, each holding one of Rian's

34

hands and pulling him up the steep slope. Mummy may have been away in Switzerland, stuffing herself with chocolate and doing silly crazy things, and Rian may have been coddled in Tehran, sleeping in a nice warm cot and eating wiener schnitzel, but we had our own playmates. Martin's job was to help my father with the equipment and generators and the electrics for the dynamiting. Cameron and I adored him for, unlike my father who was always busy and worried, Martin was light-hearted and fun. I couldn't believe he was married, particularly to Brigitte who seemed so serious.

I asked him about it so often that he finally laughed and said, 'Why, Ashley, do you want to marry me?'

Like his glossy hunting dogs, Donna and Jolie, we fawned over him and followed him wherever he went in his neatly ironed shirt and tight khaki trousers. We jabbered on and on to Rian about how, at dusk, Martin entered the forest, gun cocked, bow and quiver on his back, to hunt. How he inevitably stalked a great shaggy bear or boar, piercing it through the eye and leaving it skinned for the villagers to collect for meat the next day. How he had whittled fishing poles and helped us dig for worms, enormous red fleshy ones that looked like writhing internal organs. How he leaped from hillock to hillock, singing '*Oh Sole Mio*' and gave us a tiny bear cub and a baby boar, after careless hunters had killed their mothers. Brigitte was nice to us, too, always finding us a scrap to eat or wiping our noses.

We found Brigitte dyeing Easter eggs. Mikey, who, like Rian, was almost four, jumped around, happy to see us, as he was the only other child on the site. We teased him about his Dutch accent, saying, 'Yah, hallo, Mikey!' A smile creased his face and he moved over to let us squeeze in around the table. Brigitte had furnished their quarters and stocked it with toys for Mikey. There was a little two-burner stove and a small icebox. She put more eggs on to boil and we set to work decorating them. At some point in the afternoon, my mother wandered in and settled down for a cup of tea.

I knew precisely the second, the moment, Martin entered the room from my mother's reaction. Until then, she had been sitting languidly, legs crossed, cigarette cocked, chatting with Brigitte as we painted the eggs. When Martin swaggered in, all snake hips and buffalo-shoulders, cigarette hanging, my mother was electrified, sitting up, patting her hair, lighting another cigarette and, abruptly, completely and totally engaged: in us, the Easter eggs . . . and Martin.

Martin lurked in the doorway, smiling. 'Ashley, you never told me you had such a pretty mummy.'

He asked her question after question and they exchanged witticisms in Dutch, French, Italian and Farsi. My mother broke into an Urdu love song. Martin apologised for his English, my mother for her Dutch. She quipped, 'Many languages I am schpeaking and Engleesh is my best,' and they howled with laughter. She told the joke about the Pakistani peasant on Jhelum Bridge. Martin asked whether she had bought herself a paper mini dress in Europe, like the ones he'd seen in an article about the 'Swinging Sixties'. She pretended to blush and told him to be a gentleman.

Meanwhile Brigitte mixed the dyes and boiled more eggs. I kept an eye on my mother. The fun had gone out of the afternoon. I was worried that her friendship with Martin would usurp ours. Sure enough, by the time we left, he had agreed to set up fishing tackle for her, lend her a bow, and buy her cigarettes when he went to Bandar-e-Pahlavi.

'No, no, of course, don't worry about the money,' he said.

'Oh, but please, I insist.'

She pushed bills into his hand and they touched for the first time.

5

Farangi Girl

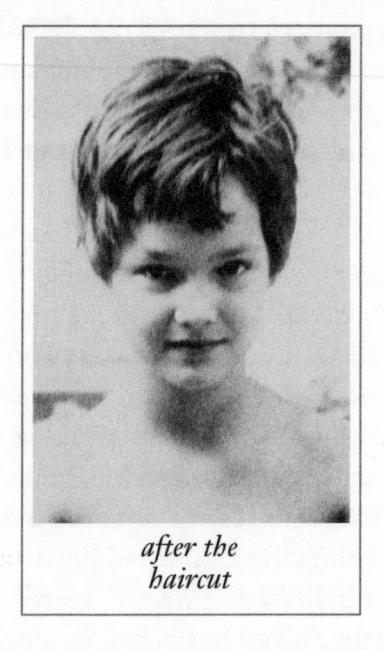

*after the
haircut*

T hat night my mother snipped off her curly hair, which she
had worn in a French roll since I was born, so that it blos-
somed into a dandelion furze around a face that was perpetually
in motion – talking, smoking, laughing, singing, whistling,
grimacing and flirting, flirting, flirting. Any minute that Martin
wasn't working, he was with her. Cameron and I both felt jilted.
Before our mother had arrived, we had been Martin's compan-
ions and Mikey's protectors. Now we were just 'the kids'.

We rarely saw our father. The unremitting kettledrum
rumble of the dynamite raised the tension. They were dynamiting every day. We would hear the boom boom boom of the
explosions and watch the men shovelling the broken rocks
into wheelbarrows or the backs of lorries. On days when they

ran out of explosives, my father was off site, trying to buy more. When we did see him, we asked, as persistent as gnats, 'Can we come on the job? Please?' for we felt ditched by our father, too. We had been relegated from being the Prince and Princess of the job site to viewers from the sidelines. And what we saw disturbed us: stubborn rock, dynamite shortages, an exceptionally high water table, mountains of rubble, trucks standing idle waiting for diesel, my father smoking after having quit years earlier.

*

Late one afternoon when Martin finished on the job, he hurried, the bottoms of his trousers stained red with clay, to our house and yelled, 'Let's get this show on the road!'

We piled into his Land Rover and bounced and jounced our way to a river he knew for sure was teeming with fish. On the way, we sang 'Guantanamera', and Martin bellowed, '*Yo soy un hombre sincero*,' with the rest of us joining in on the chorus. Mummy laughed and sang and waved her arm out the window.

We kids all dabbled by the side of a large stream while our mother and Martin moved upstream, baiting their lines, casting, reeling in and then casting again. I was looking for the bright-turquoise flash of a kingfisher. I had fallen in love with the gaudy birds and kept a running tally.

I heard my mother yell, 'I got one! A huge one.'

As we scrambled to see, slipping on the large smooth rocks, Martin ran over to pull in her catch, hauling it in, hand over hand, until finally, I glimpsed a pale belly.

I heard my mother's voice, shocked. 'Jesus Christ, it's a baby.'

Martin took it off the line and, with his back to us, threw it underarm back into the water, before rinsing his hands in the shallows.

My mother called to us, 'It was only a big catfish, don't worry.'

On the drive back, the conversation was subdued.

'Mummy, why didn't you keep the catfish?' Cameron asked. Normally they gave all the fish they caught to the workers to eat.

'Catfish are bottom feeders; they're not good eating,' she answered. 'Some religions don't even allow the consumption of catfish.'

'You said it was a baby, Mummy,' I said.

'I just said that because it was so big,' she answered, glancing at Martin.

'If it were a baby, Mummy, why would it be in the river?' I didn't believe that the white flash I had seen was a catfish. A fish would have been moving.

'Well, I thought it might have been, because sometimes the villagers in these remote areas will leave baby girls out to die. But it *wasn't* a baby!' She turned to me with a serious look on her face. 'It was a catfish.'

*

For the next few days, we didn't fish. Mummy said the giant catfish had spooked her. We were happy, though, because Mummy played with us instead of lying in a dark room and smoking all day, as she usually did when Martin was working.

One morning we climbed up the hill behind the site to a stream Martin had suggested.

'John Jacob Jingleheimer Schmidt, his name is my name too!' we sang as we stumbled across the bulldozer tracks, my mother dramatically whispering the final verses.

We walked a long distance up past all the men and equipment. Way below us, I could see my father and Martin unfurl their big rolls of drawings. From up here, I could see the tract that the men had cleared was vast. We followed our mother to a rocky, tree-shaded area with a stream. Once there, we paddled around the water's edge, sliding on the speckled rocks and catching the coin-sized frogs that lived in the cracks along the bank. My mother sat on a boulder, basking in the sun, a bandanna tied under her chin, with corkscrews of escaping hair gently lifting in the breeze. She looked young, the way she must have when she was a Connecticut farm girl, with her dark-blue dungarees and sneakers.

Some time later, out of the blue, screams ripped through the pastel fabric of the day: 'Ahhhhh, shit! Oh dammit to hell, God dammit!'

Where had Mummy gone? Why was she yelling? Downstream, frog hunting with the boys, I hadn't noticed her leave the boulder. We skittered up the rocky slope towards the screams, stumbling as the scree tumbled beneath our feet.

From above us on the slope, invisible to me, she cried, 'I fell down the mountain! I ripped myself apart! God dammit to hell!'

I didn't understand how she could have fallen when she had been sitting peacefully by the stream just a few moments earlier. I didn't stop to ask, though; my mother's hysteria was infectious, and instantly I was off.

'Get Daddy. Get Daddy,' I panted as I ran, stumbling and falling, towards the tunnel.

Mummy called out, 'Stop! Don't get your father!'

But I ran on, stumbling, falling, panting, until some workers in a Land Rover finally picked me up. They stared at me, their eyes bright white in the dark grime of their faces, looking like the pictures of Welsh coal miners I had seen in books and reeking of the raw onions they had eaten, wrapped in bread, for lunch. They watched me, the *farangi* girl, the *mohandes'* daughter. Silent, we all eyed each other as the driver bumped up and down the rutted road, backtracking to the site and towards my father.

I apologised. '*Bebakhsheed, shoma meetoneen harf bezaneen*

– you can talk.' These were not the friendly workers I had known for years, but villagers hired from the mountains surrounding us, villagers who might drown a girl baby because they didn't want it.

I tumbled out of the Land Rover and breathlessly explained what had happened. My father sprinted up the hill.

'Oh Jesus Christ, Genie, Jesus Christ. What are you doing?' he cried.

'Forget it, Lin!' She tried to pull away, to run to our little concrete house.

But he dragged her, struggling, to the clinic, where the medic examined her, asking her when and how *exactly* she had fallen and hurt herself.

My mother glared and puffed angrily on her cigarette. '*Dast nazan!*' she said, slapping away his hands. 'Don't touch me. I'll take care of it myself!'

'I need to know so I can treat you,' he snapped.

From the window where my brothers and I watched, I fumed. I had explained what had happened. I was the one who had been with her, hadn't I? I didn't understand his puzzled questions. I was also shocked that the medic, an Iranian man, indeed, any man other than my father, was allowed to see my mother's bare skin and that he addressed her in such a terse manner.

'How did you fall and scrape yourself, Genie?' my father asked, troubled. 'Your clothes aren't muddy or torn. There's no blood.'

Her only response was hair-raising yells as the medic dabbed at her with hydrogen peroxide. When they were done, she stalked out without giving my brothers or me a glance. That night I listened while she regaled the workers in the canteen with a dramatic retelling of her fall. My part in her rescue was left out entirely and, in fact, she cold-shouldered me for days.

*

She continued to sulk even when we went to a nearby village later that week. Normally she loved expeditions and meeting villagers: their work-worn hands fluttering to stroke her fair skin and fluffy golden curls, their cries of astonishment at her height and cloudy blue eyes.

On this trip, my father and Martin were meeting the village headman to recruit more labourers. Everything in the Caspian area happened in the summer, though: the tea, rice and orange plantations all required workers and men were in short supply. Higher and higher we drove up the mountain into the thick forest. I eavesdropped on my father's hushed story about a young woman who had been caught in these woods with a man and subsequently killed. Her body had been hung from a tree by the side of the road as an example to other village women. When the police questioned the villagers, they said she had hanged herself.

Cameron and I peered through the windows, looking for the body. 'Is it there?' I asked. 'There?'

My mother was furious with my father. 'Do you really think this kind of conversation is appropriate for children this age?'

By the time we arrived, my imagination was in a froth: the villagers were murderers; the curved knives hanging in their belts were used to cut throats; any shadow in a tree, a twisting body, and any log in the river, a dead baby. I entered the chief's mud hut with apprehension. His wife, emaciated and hugely pregnant, served us tea. Her belly fitted between the curve of her arms as she kneeled on the rush mat. Within a few minutes of whispered conversation, my mother learned she had been married at the age of ten and she hadn't met her husband before. Now twelve, almost thirteen, she was frightened about the birth and asked my mother if she could tell when the baby would arrive. Her own mother lived in a village on the other side of the mountain and she was worried that, if the baby was born after the snows fell, and the village and its inhabitants were shut off from the rest of the world, she would have no one to help her.

'If it is summer, *maman-eh man mee-ad*, my mother will come,' said the girl, 'but in the winter it is impossible.'

My mother questioned her and looked at the size of her belly, deciding the baby was due in the next month or two, before the snows fell.

I stared at the girl, serving her husband on her hands and knees, and thought that if I were her, I could be married in just a few years and having a baby. Her husband was old – older even than my forty-year-old father – with a short black beard and creased, worn hands.

The girl said to my mother, 'I pray it is not a girl. He has three girls with his other wife and he wants a boy.'

My mother responded, '*Inshallah*, it will be a boy, but it is in God's hands.'

I was angry at her. Why didn't she say girls were just as good?

The young wife made more tea as the negotiations continued, heating the water in the samovar, adding the tea leaves to the small tin pot, swishing each of the tiny glasses with boiling water, which she then flung out the window. My mother asked if the first wife was kind to her.

'*Akher marize-eh*,' was her answer.

From this I understood she was sick and old and a burden.

'*Si-o-panj sal dareh.*'

The other wife was thirty-five.

My mother said, 'Younger than me.'

The girl stared at her, incredulous. '*Nakher!* No!'

An Iranian village woman by the time she was in her thirties or forties was withered and faded.

The men's conversation progressed as the light coming through the open window turned from pale cream to purple-grey to abrupt dusky black. Sometime during the afternoon, my mother had excused herself, backing out the door and bowing politely. I thought she was waiting in the car, broodily smoking, but when we finally left the village chief's house, hungry and sleepy, she was nowhere to be seen. One, two, three, four hours later, she was still missing. The villagers were all asleep. The Land Rover's headlights made a feeble ghost circle in the clearing.

'Suh wee, suh wee.'

I could hear my father's trademark Welsh pig call as he searched the woods in one direction and Martin hunted in the other. Even though I had felt angry at Mummy for not talking to me for the past few days, for not taking any photos of me as she hungrily snapped Martin, for not helping me bait my fishing hooks, for not kissing me goodnight when she kissed the boys, I was terrified something had happened to her, that the villagers had kidnapped her, slit her throat, and hanged her from a tree. We would discover her body swaying from the high branches tomorrow or the day after.

Mummy had told me how, when she was a child, she discovered their next-door neighbour, Old Man Legumski, hanging in his barn after he had killed himself. 'The sight of him dangling from the rafters, his purple tongue sticking out, his eyes popped like a frog's and his shiny red shins jutting out from his trousers, was enough to terrify me for the rest of my life,' she said, shuddering dramatically.

I tried not to think about it, peering into the blackness outside. We were drowsy and huddled together for warmth. After an eternity, Martin's shout shattered the night. He pulled my mother, like a big child, by the hand. We ran out to hug her. Somehow, she was angry, furious in fact, and she pushed us away and refused to answer my father when he asked if she was all right. She got into Martin's Land Rover and slammed the door. They raced down the mountain, my father following slowly in their dust.

6

Killing for Sport

*a grass hut
at the Caspian*

It was a cool, grey morning on the Caspian coast and we rocked gently in a rowboat on the lagoon near Bandar-e-Pahlavi. The water sparkled around us, glinting shards of light. The early-morning sun turned the lagoon into an enormous pool of blood. Martin and Mummy were in one boat, with Rian sitting behind them, his curls shining softly. We had come here to Ramsar because my mother wanted to catch a big pike. In the streams around the job site, she had been catching lots of pickerel and bass, but Martin had told her how much fight a big pike, which could weigh ten or twenty kilos, would give her. He had shown us the scars on his fingers where pike had gnashed him as he removed the fish-hooks.

Martin and my mother were some way from our boat, smoking and laughing, periodically reeling in and recasting. Their lures zizzed into the water with comforting plinks and the air was filled with the whirring of their reels. The morning smelled watery clean, like a newly landed fish, before it began to smell fishy. Cameron, Daddy and I were spotting all the animals that filled the lagoon: snails and snail eggs, like tiny, pink sweetcorn for fairies; fish shadowy under the water; fluorescent dragonflies darting around like fighter jets; whimsical, prehistoric turtles and elegant egrets.

Cameron's eyes flitted around looking for the telltale swirl of a water snake. Soon he spotted one and, lurching to the edge of the unsteady rowboat, he threw himself, Tarzan-like, into the lagoon. The water crashed around him, splintering the morning's silence. Miraculously, it seemed to me, after thrashing about for a few minutes, he raised his arm aloft with a snake whipping around in his fist. He swam to the side of the boat and flung the snake over, before scrambling in himself. It slithered frantically while I squirmed as far away as possible. Grasping the snake behind the head, Cameron examined its yellow eye-slits, its flickering tongue and its writhing nickel body. If he had his choice, Cameron would have kept every snake for ever. My father gruffly told him to return it, though, 'Gently, gently,' to the water, whereupon it zigzagged into the reeds.

As the sun rose, the drowsy warmth penetrated at last and the lagoon turned from copper to pewter. Daddy urged us in for a swim but whereas Cameron leaped in, arms and legs spreadeagled, I shuddered with cold and inched my way over the edge of the boat. The icy water crawled up my legs as I tipped into the lagoon and I imagined the dangers that lurked beneath the molten surface: the blade-like water snakes, the leeches that sucked our blood, becoming big, fat wine gums that exploded scarlet when we squashed them, and the saw-toothed reeds that whipped long, deep, jagged cuts along our legs. Cameron swam across the lagoon, searching for more snakes, while I paddled around the boat. Finally, my father leaned over to haul me out and the water ran down my arms, the golden hairs catching the glistening drops. I shook, laughing and chatting, while Cameron clambered in, pulling himself up with his wiry arms.

'Look, look!'

Cameron spotted an egret, its wings serrated against the sky. It landed and busied itself, poking its rapier beak into the mud. Suddenly, we heard a blast so loud it sucked away all other noise. We sat stunned; even the sound of water lapping against the outside of the boat was momentarily arrested. In the aftermath, we heard something unnatural and imperfect. Flap, *flap-flap*, flap. We spotted the egret, struggling, pulling itself helplessly out of the water, its wings dragging as it tried to fly to the reeds.

'Daddy, what happened?' I cried out. Even as I asked, though, I could see Martin in the boat with his gun and I knew.

'Martin, you bloody bastard. Kill the bird and put it out of its misery,' barked my father. 'Kill it quickly.'

Martin, his rifle casually resting against his shoulder, smiled and fired. Again and again and again. Each time, the water erupted around the egret and the bird battled and rose, faltered and fell.

'Give me the bloody gun, you damn fool.' Rowing rapidly over to the other boat, my father grabbed the gun. He took aim, shot and killed the bird.

We rowed over to the egret and pulled it from the water. Cameron sat stony-faced, his lip jutting.

'Why did he do that? I spotted it. He shouldn't have killed my bird.'

We stroked the bird's wet feathers, stained now, its long neck snaking along the bottom of the boat, its pink skin showing through the damp, white down. The icy eyes quickly blurred.

'Daddy, can we at least give it to the villagers to eat?' I asked, tears pouring down my face.

'No, my darlings, there's no meat on an egret. This is what

you call killing for sport.' My father looked down, his eyes weary, and fingered the bird's feathers.

In the next boat, the conversation and the plink of fishing lures hitting the water resumed.

On the way back along the sandy road, Martin and my mother led the way, strings of fish dangling. They had caught a lot, but not the 'big pike' my mother coveted. We ran to catch up, to draw our mother away from Martin, to force her to walk with us, with our family.

'Mummy, how could he do that? It was cruel!'

She ignored us at first, finally responding, 'Well, you eat meat, don't you?'

We were shocked. Didn't Mummy, the tender-hearted saviour of kittens and frogs and even a fetid vulture in Pakistan, didn't she understand that killing something, just for the sake of killing, was wrong? The villagers ate the bear and boar that Martin hunted. But killing a beautiful bird just for the sake of it?

At the hotel, Daddy loaded the car for his trip to Tehran where he was going to meet his partners and the bank. Before he left, he took Martin aside and instructed him about what to do on the job over the next few days. My father's face was stern and Martin looked nervous, smoking his cigarette.

The moment my father left, though, a mood of abandon and glee overtook my mother and Martin. My mother joked that a friend of hers, upon visiting the newly built Ramsar Hotel, where we were staying, had told my mother, 'It must have been built on an old toilet.' My mother and Martin erupted into hysterical laughter. Cameron and I looked at them: everyone knew that toilets in Iran were smelly, so why did they think that was so funny? We were still smarting from the death of the egret and our mother's betrayal. We felt let down by Martin, too. He had been our friend, our playmate, and now all he did was show off for Mummy.

Later in the afternoon, Martin asked, 'You've never had crayfish, have you?' Cajoling me, he continued, 'Boiled in a big pot and then dipped in butter, it's the sweetest meat in the world – almost as sweet as Ashley here.' He grabbed my arm and pretended to nibble it.

I ignored him. They couldn't blackmail us with food and blandishments.

'You can get *balal* as well.'

Our mother knew that *balal*, ears of corn roasted on a charcoal brazier and dipped in salt water from the Caspian, was our favourite food.

'Don't want it.'

The fisherman who had caught the crayfish arrived and built the fire in the garden behind the hotel. Martin carried out a big pot from the kitchen. Dusk came and the two of them sat gorging, fingers dripping butter, cigarettes damp. When we didn't eat, they said we were spoilsports and sent us to bed in the twilight. We leaned far out of the windows to pick honey-sweet apricots from the trees outside and fell asleep to the drifting smell of cigarette smoke and the sound of our mother's laughter.

7

The Snake Dream

*our street and
apartment building in
Amir Abad*

The trees shivered in the wind and leaves skittered across our street. The cold and rain had driven us from the Caspian back to Tehran. The women filling their *satls* at the pump at the end of the road hurried back to their huts, careful not to slosh freezing water on their feet. My father rushed in and out of the flat, going from meeting to meeting and back and forth to the bank.

Then he disappeared.

Theresa, a friend of my mother's, came over with a flat brown-paper packet. Inside was a chador, the long black veil that traditional Iranian women wore in public. My mother's feet stuck out at the bottom when she draped it over herself.

'Wear trousers underneath,' said Theresa.

I sat on the edge of the conversation, absolutely silent, trying to glean some information: where my father was, when we would go back to school, why my mother was so nervous. Normally when someone visited, my mother sent me from the room, so I avoided making a sound.

'And proper shoes with socks – no high heels.'

'I'm going tomorrow. Sammii will drive me,' my mother said. 'I'm taking food, cigarettes, his razor. I'm sure they'll search me.'

'Put some money in the cigarette pack,' said Theresa. 'That way the guard can take it if he finds it and if he doesn't, at least Lin will have a few rials.'

She handed my mother some money. My mother slipped out the cigarettes and slid the notes in, before carefully replacing the cigarettes.

Later, after Theresa had left and we were sitting in the kitchen, eating chicken soup, courtesy of the bag of food Theresa had brought for us, I asked my mother why she had to wear a chador and where my father was. She lit a cigarette and drew deeply on it, filling herself up with smoke.

'Jesus Christ, I never thought I would have to tell my own children this.' She started to weep. 'Your father's in jail. Those bastards have put the bloody fool into jail.'

The light in the kitchen was dim. I gulped; the soup in my mouth barely made it down my throat.

'What did he do? Is he going to be all right? Will he die?' I asked. Rian began to cry and Cameron looked frightened.

'No! Don't be ridiculous,' she snapped, 'but how and when he'll get out of that place, I don't know.'

The following day we went to our friends the Selim's house and read comic books. When my mother came back from visiting my father in jail, she was subdued. I begged her to tell me what he had done and how he was and what the prison was like, but she just said, 'I pray to God that you never have to see a place like that. It is no place for a human being.'

Over time, gathering bits of information, I pieced together what had happened. The tunnel had collapsed, killing two men; the site had flooded and my father began to miss his construction deadlines. While there was cash still in the bank accounts, his partners cleared them out and fled to Germany, leaving my father no money to pay his men or his suppliers. He was arrested and put into jail. My mother frantically lobbied the British ambassador and the British consul, entreating them to intercede with the Home Office on behalf of my father. She borrowed money from her friends to pay people off to get him out of jail. For a brief period, my father, out of prison, tried to recover his assets, negotiate with his creditors, beg his partners to help. Then he was arrested again and thrown back into prison. His passport was taken away so he could not leave the country.

We didn't go back to school or pay our rent. When my mother's friends did their shopping, they bought extra, which they delivered to us on their way home. We would open the bags after they left, unloading the apples and bread and butter directly on to the table to eat straightaway. My mother sold her jewellery and won money playing gin rummy to feed us. While we still had one, I answered the telephone because she could not face the police and bill collectors. When the phone was cut off, creditors began appearing in person. After a couple of incidents when the man behind the glass door screamed at me so relentlessly that even my mother was afraid, we turned off the lights and pretended we were not there. Once they threw a large rock with a note tied around it through our window, leaving jagged shards of glass in the frame that rattled in the wind at night.

*

I leaped out of bed and raced into the hallway, tripping over my mother who was huddled on the floor behind the bookshelves.

'Mummy! They're going to break the door down.'

'Shush. Just don't let them see you.'

The silhouettes of two men wavered in the patterned glass. Typical of many Iranian apartment buildings, the inside doors to our flat were made of thick, opaque, floor-to-ceiling glass blocks.

'Dartnell, *pool eh mah ro bedeh*! Dartnell, we know you are there!' they yelled in a mixture of Farsi and broken English. They pounded the thick glass with pieces of brick they had picked up from the building site next door, fragments of which I swept up the next day.

'Mummy, if you tell them Daddy's not here, they'll stop,' I whispered.

Their cries became frenzied and the banging on the door louder.

'They're going to break the door, Mummy. They know someone's in here. Please!'

She put her finger to her lips to signal to be quiet. 'They'll get tired and go away.'

'Dartnell, *pool eh mah ro bedeh, pedar sag, pedar suckteh!* Give us our money, you bastard!'

When it seemed the glass couldn't last much longer under their onslaughts, my mother, as graceful as Venus, stood up in her nightgown and glided to the door. She pulled it open and the men tumbled into the front hall, like something out of a Marx Brothers film. I would have laughed if I hadn't been so scared.

'He isn't here. Why are you torturing me? I haven't seen him in months. I have no money. I'm desperate. Have pity on a poor woman trying to raise her children.'

Although her voice trembled, she spoke beautifully in Farsi and the men stood, respectfully listening.

'Come with me,' she cried pulling one man's arm. 'Come search my house! Look under the beds, wake my children.'

'Mrs Dartnell, he owes us money. We must find him.' The man spoke reasonably now.

My mother seemed to know them. I held my breath, trying to quiet my pounding heart, wondering how proper men who wore suits could almost break down our door in the middle of the night.

'On the life of my children, *Aghayan, beh janeh bacheyeh man,*' she said pulling me out from behind the shelves and holding me in front of her. 'On the life of my child, that bastard Dartnell is not here.'

I could smell the men's hot, smoky breath and their acrid sweat. I could see their eyes glittering in the faint hall light. I could feel my mother's soft breasts, moving raggedly against my back.

Abruptly, the men turned to go. 'Mrs Dartnell, when he comes back, please ask him to come see us.'

The door closed gently behind them.

My mother collapsed on to the hall carpet, sobbing. 'Oh dear God, what should I do? What did I do to deserve Lin Dartnell? He is a curse. I'm stuck here with three children and no money. I can't stay, but I can't leave. Dear God, what should I do?'

*

I was in complete darkness, crossing a huge field of deep wells filled with immense, writhing snakes. I had to get across to save my family, but I slithered and slid in faeces, almost slipping into the snake-filled wells. I crawled slowly, so slowly, from one well to the next, barely saving myself from falling into the roiling mass, from smothering in the disgusting stench. I had to keep moving, though. I couldn't turn back. I had to save my family. The hiss of the snakes slithering against each other filled my ears, the smell of excrement made me gag, and the thought of falling into the snake pits filled me with such terror that, shuddering, I awakened. Chilled, my chest a pounding drum, my ragged blue blanket churned into a wad, I slept and dreamed, awakened and slept.

*

My father, once again sprung from prison by my mother's entreaties and bribes went into hiding, holed up in the Rover. In the middle of the night, I occasionally heard the rattling glass panes of the front door and erupted out of bed to open it for him. He would creep in, smelling of dust and coffee, before leaving again before dawn. He spent that long winter on the run, living in his car with Araboochie.

8

Tea with the Queen

*my mother
with Prince
Mahmoud Reza*

My mother was thrilled: 'Oh Asho, how lovely! Tea with the Queen! You can tell your children about it when you grow up.'

I was going with my mother's friend Nounou to tea with Farah Diba, the Queen, at the Hilton Hotel, the only fancy hotel in the whole of Iran. Before that, though, Nounou was taking me with her to the beauty parlour to make the necessary preparations. We swerved and lurched in and out of blots of shadow where the *chenar* trees arched overhead high above Shemiran, one of the main roads in the north-western part of Tehran. The dead leaves eddied in the breeze, littering the street like dirty paper napkins.

I didn't know what to say to Nounou; normally, when she

57

was with my mother, the two of them ignored me – chatting, gossiping, laughing and giggling until tears dripped from the corners of their eyes and they gasped and hooted, clutching their stomachs. If ever I tried to creep into the conversation, my mother warned, 'Little pitchers,' and the rapid flow of words was suddenly dammed. Nounou had no children and, on the rare occasion she focused on one of us kids, it was with uncomprehending eyes.

When she had arrived earlier that day, the tone at the kitchen table was serious. I could hear 'Martin' and 'Brigitte' and 'That bastard Malin' and 'I don't know what the hell to do', as they filled and refilled their tall glasses with dark, woody tea and opened one pack of Nounou's Viceroys after another.

'Mummy, please tell me what you're talking about. I just want to know. I promise I won't tell anyone,' I begged, frantic to find out what was happening with my father.

'Go away, Ashley.'

'Please.'

'I'm telling a dirty joke,' said Nounou. 'A white horse fell in the mud!'

'No, seriously!' I was furious.

'OK, then, a white dog fell in the mud. Teeheehee.' Nounou laughed when I glared at her. 'Asho, darling,' she said, to placate me, 'how would you like to meet the Queen?'

A haze of fruity hair lacquer and nail varnish, mixed with the laundry smell of hair bleach and perm solution, hung over the beauty parlour. Hushed ladies in white tunics ministered to a few middle-aged *Khanoom*. Nounou, a dozen years younger, with her shrieky voice, geisha make-up and exotic clothes, flapped and fussed, a bird of paradise in a scatter of sparrows.

'*Salam, Golie. Salam, joonam!*'

She called her hellos to the beauticians before finally settling and resting her small round head in the sink while one of the aproned ladies lovingly shampooed her hair. A girl kneeled at her feet, transforming her toes into luscious scarlet berries, while at each hand yet another girl stood, snipping, pushing back cuticles and rubbing in cream, before turning the delicate ovals into matching delectable berries.

'May I get my nails painted for the Queen, too?' I asked her, my lips almost touching her glistening, wet ear.

'Ah, of course, my darling girl.'

This was something she understood – a little girl wanting to be pretty. She gestured to one of the Golies or Shirins and within minutes, I, too, had gleaming scarlet nails, although somehow they looked more like the broken ends of red crayons on me. Why was something that looked so beautiful on Nounou such a disappointment on my own fingers?

*

From behind, Nounou looked like a cello: golden brown, with smooth, gleaming swells, the tiniest of panties wedged between the sculptural curves of her buttocks.

I hesitated. 'May I come in?'

'Come help me choose my jewellery.'

Her breasts hung heavy and round over a glittering pile and her fingers dripped jewels as bright and pretty as boiled sweets – watermelon pink, cherry red, apple green and icy clear spearmint. Avoiding staring at her breasts, I considered each piece, looking over at the olive raw-silk dress that she had laid out to wear.

'The diamond earrings and the diamond ring and the diamond bracelet.'

'Perfect,' she cried, 'just what I would have chosen.'

She slipped the dress over her wobbly breasts and clipped on the earrings. She had backcombed her hair and painted her face white with black Cleopatra eyes and vermilion lipstick. Her high heels danced a flamenco down the stairs as she called instructions to the servants about dinner and what time to run '*Agha*' his bath. We were walking into the garage, ready to hop into her big white American car, when I finally had the courage to say what I had been planning ever since entering her room.

'I'm really sorry,' I said, 'I can't go.'

'What? What's wrong, my darling girl? Don't be silly. We're already late.'

'No, I can't. I can't meet the Queen.'

I had thought carefully about what I would say when I had realised, with stomach-plummeting dread, that I was meeting *the Queen*. The Queen! I was worried that she would know about my father and that she would have me put into jail – but I didn't want Nounou to know any of that.

'Why, my darling girl? Why?'

I shrugged.

'Come on, don't be silly!' She took my hand.

'Auntie Nounou, my nail polish doesn't match my dress,' I said in despair, hoping she would leave me behind.

She thoughtfully considered my scarlet fingertips against my white-and-lavender-flowered dress.

'Yes, you are right,' she agreed and marched me straight back upstairs where she removed the polish with small puffs of cotton wool dipped in yellow acetone. She then propelled me rapidly back through the house and to the car. I sniffed the ends of my fingers for as long as the chemical smell lasted, wondering whether I could introduce myself only as 'Ashley'.

We were late, but the Queen was even later. We all waited and waited, as ladies-in-waiting have done throughout history, stomachs whining, hairdos wilting and bladders pressing. The grown-ups took turns loitering in the lobby so they could warn us when the Queen arrived. When she finally appeared, I curtsied, the only child at the tea, and watched her, my eyes downcast, as I was introduced. She smiled and moved on to the next person, barely noticing me. Almost limp with relief, I stuffed myself with éclairs and *millefeuilles*.

*

My mother's friend Lisa popped in with some cartons of cigarettes. As she left, she fumbled in her bag and thrust a wrinkled
50-rial note at me: 'Buy yourself and the boys a little ice
cream, some sweets,' she said, stroking my cheek, 'you poor
children.'

Folding and refolding the note, I hid it. The next day I stole
out of the house on a mission. Earlier, from the car, I had
spotted a shop that sold flowers, and inside the doorway I
had glimpsed poppy-red bunches of tulips – tulips, a flower I
had read about in books about Holland but had never seen.
When I reached the store and asked the price, I found that, of
course, my grimy bill, enough for a few chocolates, was not
enough for flower-shop tulips.

The shopkeeper, seeing my sadness, wrapped me a small
bunch. '*Barayeh Madar-et?*' he asked.

When I nodded, yes, they were for my mother, he said,
'What a good girl. What a fine girl, who loves her mother so
much.'

Happily whistling and singing, buoyed by the shopkeeper's generosity, I trekked back through the streets of Amir
Abad. The tulips, tenderly clutched to my chest, transforming from glossy crimson to purple to black as darkness poured
into the bowl of Tehran. I imagined my mother's reaction,
the images unspooling in my head: her delight at the flowers,
her surprise that I was a big enough girl to walk all the way
to the flower store, the great big huggle buggle and kiss she
would give me.

Cameron answered the door and skipped to the kitchen. I
followed with the flowers behind my back and a smile waiting
to break out in a big grin.

'Mummy, I have a present for you.'

My mother was gaily frying French toast at the stove. She
and the boys didn't seem to have noticed that I had been gone
for hours and hours. Martin was sitting at the table. Here he

was, as if he had been sitting in our kitchen chair his whole life, instead of for the first time ever and after weeks, even months, of not seeing him.

'Say hello to your Uncle Martin, Ashley.'

'Hello, Uncle Martin.' I turned back to my mother. 'Mummy, I have a present for you.'

'What else do you have to say?'

'Daddy's not here?' I asked, bewildered.

A snort of laughter forced its way around Martin's cigarette. I wanted to give my mother her tulips, but before I could say anything, she said, 'Isn't it exciting? Uncle Martin has come back to Tehran. Go wash your hands for dinner, Ashley.'

'Mummy, I have a present . . .'

She turned back to Martin. It was the first time she had seemed happy in weeks. The house was noisy and alive. I left my tulips, wilting, a scarlet spot on the kitchen counter.

*

As usual the next morning, I was the first awake. Cameron and Rian were still asleep, their brown curls stuck sweatily to their heads. I peeked around the door, but Mummy's room was empty; dust motes, trapped in amber streams of light, eddied and swirled. In the kitchen, Six Pence our cat twined herself around the three tin canisters on the kitchen counter. Blue, red, and yellow, the large tins were filled with flour, sugar, and tea: the three staples. No matter what food shortages or how poor we were, we nearly always had flour, sugar and tea.

Six Pence jumped off the rickety kitchen cabinets, which were a hodgepodge of primary colours, the tag-end remainders from several other kitchens. As she wound around my feet, her cry insistent, I opened one cupboard door after another. They were almost all empty, with just the carcasses of a few bent pots, the scratched remains of a skillet. The little food we had was purchased on the day from the corner shop.

What funny things we ate in that kitchen: French toast, pancakes, raisin cake, lettuce with sugar, rice with ketchup.

I poured Six Pence some milk, wondering whether my mother would be angry that I had wasted it on the cat. She said Six Pence hunted for food at night when she was out prowling. The sink was full of last night's dishes. My mother's glass had a thick compost of tea leaves on the bottom.

I examined her mould collection, each growing on a different kind of food: a smudge of green, a beard of white, a soft velvet of mustard. She grew them in glass jars on the windowsill over the sink, sprinkling water on them and rotating them until she tired of them, at which point she chucked them into the rubbish bins in the alley behind the kitchen.

I unwrapped the tulips and put them in water, their heads drooping, soft and listless, against the vase. I thought it was strange that Mummy wasn't in bed because she was a night owl, wandering around the house during the hours of darkness and then sleeping the day away. Maybe she was in the living room. I tried the doors. How odd; I hadn't realised they could be locked. It dawned on me that Martin had stayed the night.

I rushed to wake the boys. 'Sh! Mummy and Uncle Martin are asleep in the living room; let's surprise them by making pancakes.'

We found a bit of flour, an egg, milk to make the pancakes. Then we poured tea for each of them.

A final flourish: 'Cam, get some of Mummy's cigarettes and matches.'

We each fought for a handhold on the tray. Surprised that the living-room doors were now unlocked, we entered, proudly carrying our tray. Martin lay smoking on the blue sofa, as relaxed as a lion after a feed.

'Uncle Martin! You spent the night!'

The boys jumped on top of him, making muscles, which he admired, squeezing their biceps with his fingers.

'Where's Mummy?' I asked, as he began eating.

'Isn't she asleep in her room?' He asked laughing, as Rian poked his hard bare stomach.

'No, she was here with you,' I said. 'No one slept in her room last night.'

'I was *not* here with Martin,' said my mother. 'I was in my room. Martin needed a place to stay and he fell asleep in here.'

She floated in behind us in a sea-foam nightgown, demurely covered with its matching robe.

9
Dirty Laundry

*in front of our
Amir Abad flat*

All the lights in the flat were on. Every single one. Everything was noisy and scrambled. Cameron had vomited in the front hall and the cidery tang filled the flat. Mummy was getting dressed, finding her shoes, teasing her hair. We were underfoot and in the way. All the adults milled about, dressed up, smoking, smelling of perfume and drinking whisky tinkly with ice. After weeks being away, my father was home. And despite this, Martin was also at the flat. There was a party, the lights were on, and Araboochie was barking and howling with excitement. When my mother appeared, beautiful in her sheath of gold-embroidered black wool, her hair a helmet of gold, she posed in the doorway and flung her stole aside dramatically. 'Ta-dah!'

'Darling!'

'You look lovely!'

She swept through the crowd, dispensing kisses and smiles. 'Asho, a tea please,' she asked.

The boys and I squirmed through the crowd, filling glasses and emptying ashtrays.

'We're off!' said my father.

It was then I realised.

'Mummy! You can't go! Who's going to take care of us? What if Cameron *estefraghs* another time? Who'll clean it up?'

I asked these questions aloud, while silently I wondered, what if the police came? Or the men who pounded on the front door, screaming? What if a rock flew through the window of the front room again, leaving its spoor of shattered glass? It seemed impossible that they leave us by ourselves.

After a pause, the men continued to put on their jackets and Martin wrapped Mummy into her stole, his hands lingering on her caramel arms.

'Don't leave us alone!' The scream wrenched out of me, unbidden.

The room grew quiet.

I shrieked and cried.

'It's not really my place to say,' said Helen, with the sly smile she reserved for comments like these, 'but don't you think they are a bit young to be here by themselves? You know, given the circumstances?'

'Stay out of my business, Helen,' answered my mother through gritted teeth.

My father put his arm around my shaking shoulders. 'What's wrong, Ashley? I thought you were a big brave girl?'

How could I explain in front of all these people?

'I'll tell you what's wrong, Malin, I'll tell you exactly what's wrong. What's wrong is that this little bitch is trying to keep me from going out for the first time in six months. After all I've been through.'

My mother grabbed my arm and yanked me into the air, pulling me into her bedroom and flinging me on the bed.

'How can you do this to me? You stay here and watch the boys. Nothing's going to happen.'

'No, no, no, please, Mummy,' I sobbed. 'Please, Mummy, please! Please let Daddy stay. Martin can go with you.'

The hairbrush rose above me again and again, hitting my back, my arms, my legs, my face, each bristle leaving a tiny hole to fill with blood.

My mother's voice was a jackhammer in my ear. 'You kids are killing me. You are sucking the life out of me. I am a prisoner in this goddam apartment. I am a prisoner in this goddam country. I have no life. I have no life.'

I bawled and cried, my face contorted and snotty. Finally, she broke off, flung the brush against the wall and, breathing harshly, smoothed her hair and reapplied her lipstick in the dressing-table mirror. I lay on the bed, spent, no more tears, no more cries. I could see each individual bobble on the white bedspread as I lay there plucking at them. She left the room without a glance. My father soon came in, soothing my back with a cool damp cloth and grazing my face with dozens of tiny whisky kisses.

'Darling Asho, stay here with the boys and take care of them for your mummy.'

'Why should I? Look what she just did to me.' I held up my arm. 'Daddy, stay with me, *please*.' I sobbed again, furious and helpless.

'No, Asho, I have to go.'

'Can you come back in the middle of the night to make sure we're all right?'

'Yes, yes, I promise you, I promise you. I'll take care of you.'

The door closed with a bang and I lay sniffling in the dark, clutching Araboochie, fat, doggy-smelling Araboochie.

When I finally heard the door click open, the dawn light had begun to nudge away the black of night. I turned to the wall and closed my eyes.

My father was up early the next morning, drinking coffee and reading the newspaper in his usual chair. Normally I would have been thrilled to see him, because I knew he would only be around for a few hours or a day before moving on again.

'You promised.'

I dragged past him, drained by sleeplessness and emotion, ignoring the photos of the night before that wandering photographers had sold them at the end of the evening. I knew, if I glanced at the pictures, I would see my mother, laughing, smoking and dancing, not at all worried about the boys and me alone in our flat.

*

Mummy came into the bedroom where I was reading.

'Helen wants to take you out for an ice-cream sundae.'

'No, thank you.' I had never had an ice-cream sundae before. 'Don't want to,' I said, suspecting there was a reason for this unprecedented invitation.

'Get up!' she said. 'She wants to talk to you about why you're giving me so much trouble. Why you behaved so badly the other night.'

'I won't.'

I couldn't believe she thought I was the one who had behaved badly. She had hit me so hard I still had marks.

'Yes, you will!' she hissed, pulling my arm. 'And remember, you keep our dirty laundry in our house. No talking about anything that happens here.'

When Helen came to pick me up, I wasn't dressed. 'Don't want to go.'

'Just wear your school uniform,' ordered my mother.

'Doesn't fit me.'

'Wear this.' She pulled out the dress I had worn to meet the Queen.

Maybe it was because the dress was now small and tight

around the chest, but eating my ice-cream sundae I couldn't draw in enough air to both speak and eat.

Helen asked, 'Now, Ashley, what's going on with you? It's not like you to act the way you did the other night.'

I took a tiny bite and slipped it into my mouth, hoping it would soften the concrete lump filling my throat. I just wished she didn't have to talk so I could taste the ice cream. My eyes filled and tears overflowed and dripped into the special sundae cup, on to the pretty balls of pink and white ice cream.

'No, Ashley, look at me. Answer my question!' she insisted.

I shook my head, hoping the lump would shift so I could breathe. I looked at her jolly, freckled face and I thought about what I could say. I knew she was just trying to be kind. In my head, I tried out response after response, trying to find one that would be truthful and still be all right – that wouldn't be 'dirty laundry'. That wouldn't get my mother angry. I knew I was taking too long from her sharp intakes of breath. Finally, I responded trying to smile, 'Thank you for the lovely sundae. It was so nice of you to bring me, Auntie Helen.'

'What! Ashley, that's not an answer. What's going on? I've known you since you were tiny. How can I help you if I don't know what's going on?'

I wanted to tell her, but what could I say? Should I tell that if my father wasn't in jail, he was living in his car and running from the police? That 'Uncle' Martin was always at our flat? That my mother was so nervous she smoked constantly and coughed so much she vomited every morning? That she screamed at us no matter what we did? That we had little food and if we complained we were hungry, she said, 'Drink a glass of water'? That we'd missed five terms of school? That all my clothes were too small? That every night I dreamed about falling into pits of writhing snakes? If I told her all that, what good would it do? What good could she do?

'Thank you for the lovely sundae,' I said, trying to eat the ice cream before it all melted.

'Ashley, now you're being disrespectful,' she said sharply. 'Is there a problem with Mummy? With Daddy? Uncle Martin?'

I was tempted. Maybe she knew. Maybe I *could* talk to her. I hesitated, remembering what my mother said about telling her secrets. About dirty laundry. Remembering the hairbrush.

Gulping, I repeated, 'Thank you for the lovely sundae.'

'Well, if that's how you're going to be, I can understand why your mummy is so fed up with you. Why she complains about you all the time. Just when your mummy needs you to be especially good, too, what's happened to you?' She grabbed me, pulling me out of the restaurant, leaving my lovely ice cream pooling in its tulip glass. 'And now you've made me waste all that money on the ice cream!'

My mother met us, a barefoot sentry, at the door.

'How did you like your first ice-cream sundae, honey?'

She smiled, leaning against the doorjamb in her pedal-pushers and striped shirt, barring the way into the flat. I knew it was because Martin was inside, working on her Pakistani stamp collection, magnifying glass in hand, and she didn't want Helen to come in.

'Well, what do you think, Ashley, did we have a nice time?' asked Helen, lurking at the door.

'Yes, thank you very much for the lovely sundae.'

I slid under my mother's arm and heard Helen saying, '. . . very difficult . . . wouldn't say a word . . . stubborn as a mule . . .'

*

Television had just been introduced to Iran and Mummy's friend had invited us over to watch. In the car, she tried to describe it: 'Imagine a film in your own house.' We were as jumpy and excited as frogs.

She added, 'If Vivienne offers you any food, for God's sake eat it. We have nothing at home.'

When we arrived, Vivienne gave her big, dimply smile and kneeled on the hallway floor to ask me in her heavy French accent, 'Asho, darling, where is your handsome daddy?'

When I shrugged because as usual, I had no idea where he was, she laughed and said, 'You funny girl, you can tell me. I know he has been in the jail.'

'It's not funny!' I said to Vivienne and turned to my mother. 'Mummy, why did you tell her? You told me about the dirty laundry and then *you* told!'

'Oh, just go in and watch television with the kids, Ashley. Why can't you be like other children?'

I sat on the sofa, squashed between my two brothers, the black-and-white images of a frantic cartoon cat blurred by my tears. I was worried my father was in prison again and I was furious that my mother's admonishments to keep our dirty laundry to ourselves referred only to things that could hurt *her*, not my father or us kids. She could say anything she wanted to Helen, Nounou, or Vivienne – she could tell them about my father being in jail or that I was a bad child. I realised that 'dirty laundry' was her way of describing 'her secrets', her way of saying I had to protect her when she did wrong things.

10

The Vulture Story

the famous vulture

'**G**ood morning, Uncle Martin.'
I bent shyly towards him to kiss his smooth cheek. His face was much softer than Daddy's, but it didn't smell of Old Spice. Once when he was shaving, I had tried to sprinkle some on him, but he had just laughed. 'Are you trying to make me into your daddy?'

Stamps were scattered across the table. I stood and watched while Martin catalogued them.

He explained the procedure: 'First, you take the stamp gently with tweezers.' Silent for a few seconds, he said, 'Then you slide it in.' He showed me the clear plastic envelope he had prepared. 'And then this is the fun part,' he continued as he identified the stamp using the fat Stanley Gibbons catalogue, counting the perforations, checking the ink colour and looking for rare over-stamps through a magnifying glass that made his eyes look monstrous, like a wasp's eyes up close. 'The last step,' he said, 'you glue the envelope in.'

I watched, my nose almost touching the paper as he stuck in the envelope and, in tiny writing, labelled the stamp. Over and over again, he selected a stamp from the miniature wax envelopes and went through these steps. Once in a while, he called out things like, 'Over-stamp from Lahore,' or 'Lovely, hand-stamp here!' My mother would come running and lean over his shoulder, gazing intently.

My father had bought my mother the stamp collection the previous year, before the collapse of the tunnel, when he still had some money. She was obsessed with everything about Pakistan and she loved collecting things. So, when Helen's husband, Faridun, who was a stamp dealer, told her that the best Pakistani stamp collection in the world was up for auction in London, she had begged my father for it. The stamps reminded her of Pakistan and Pakistanis; she didn't really care too much about the perforations and ink variations. She imagined the people who had bought the stamps, touched them and licked them. She commiserated with the Pakistani people, telling us about a village where the inhabitants lived by buying boxes of matches and then removing one match from each box, which they then sold.

'Imagine being so poor that one match makes a difference.'

She described how children collected cow-pats and dried them to use as cooking fuel because there was so little wood.

'The taste of chapatis cooked over a cow dung fire, my God, there's nothing better. You know,' she went on, 'most people in Pakistan can't read and in every bazaar a scribe writes letters for people for a few rupees.'

She made us close our eyes and imagine a mother writing to her child, a man to his beloved, a government official requisitioning supplies. Her favourite part of the collection was a small stack of flimsy blue envelopes, some of which had tissue-thin letters inside, which she read to us. 'Think about how important a letter would have to be for you to buy a stamp.'

Martin huddled over the catalogues and the stamps, counting perforations, while Mummy flitted in and out from mopping the floor, washing the sheets or cleaning the windows, telling us stories, urging him to have a cup of tea or a cigarette with her.

'Uncle Martin,' I asked, 'why do you love the stamp collection so much? You haven't even been to Pakistan like Mummy has, have you?'

'No, I've never been to Pakistan,' he said. 'I do this so I don't have to think about my life.'

I didn't understand him: surely just sitting there for hours and hours, he had nothing to do *but* think.

When we first met him, Martin had seemed to enjoy doing things with us – making bows and arrows, stalking animals, digging for worms. He had even mounted a set of tusks from a boar that he had killed just for me. Now he was impatient and said silly things like not having to 'think about his life', and he just wanted to be alone with my mother.

I wandered into the kitchen. My mother hadn't brought up my ice-cream date with Helen. Although I was still smarting from the whole incident, I was relieved that I hadn't said a single word to Helen about what was going on inside our house.

I asked my mother, 'Why isn't Martin on the job any more?'

'Well, your father ruined it for him, didn't he?'

'How?' I hated the way she blamed everything on my father.

'The way he ruins everything. The way he's ruined my life. Just being himself, George Malin Dartnell, is enough to destroy everything around him.'

'How Mummy?' It seemed to me that all my father ever did was work.

She shook her head and went back to her chopping.

I drifted back into the living room and flipped through my mother's Pakistani photo albums. She had stacks, each photo beautifully labelled, chronicling her happy years there. One album I particularly loved had dozens of pictures of her favourite animal, camels: camels in groups, camels ploughing, camels eating, mother camels, baby camels nursing, even an albino camel, all with their sardonic sideways mouths and floppy humps.

I pored over the pictures of my mother wearing a *shalvar kameez*, with a skinny man with glasses, with a tall man with wavy hair, with a dark Pakistani man, with a short older man with a beard, with my father, each of them wearing an Ali Jinnah-style hat and sitting cross-legged. My parents were as beautiful as movie stars. I stared at them as I turned the pages. In every picture, they were the life of the party. I glanced at Martin, who, even though he was much younger than Daddy, was not nearly as handsome – at least not to me.

Mummy came in from the kitchen and bent to look at the pictures in the albums.

'Mummy, please tell about how you went to Pakistan,' I begged.

At first she said no, she was too busy, but she loved to tell stories and there was nothing that we relished more. Finally she gathered us around her. Martin glanced up from the stamps with a smile and my mother performed for him across the room.

'Well, after I finished college, I worked for a year as a teacher to make enough money to go to India. You remember that when I was little, just a bit older than Rian, I read that in India it was warm and sunny every day. Where we lived in Connecticut, it was so damn cold and we were so damn poor that I was always miserable. Well, I promised myself that as soon as I was old enough, I would move there.'

She paused to take a deep draw on her cigarette.

'Anyway, as soon as I had enough money, I jumped on to a cargo ship. There were only two passengers on the whole ship and we had dinner with the Scottish captain every night. He was a lovely man and very taken with me.'

She glanced, smiling, at Martin.

'It took fifty-seven days, much longer than expected, because they closed down the Suez Canal. When we finally got there, we weren't actually in India because Pakistan and India had split during partition. But, I didn't give a damn, I loved it. I lived near the Jhelum River and had the most wonderful time of my life. I have never been happier. When I die I want to be buried in Pakistan . . .' She trailed off.

'Tell us about all the things you did in Pakistan, how you met Daddy and how Daddy built you a squash court.'

'Tell us about how you got malaria and how the Pakistani doctor saved your life.'

'Tell us about how you had to drink water with mosquito larvae in it.'

'Tell us about the prince who brought you chocolate-covered ants and honey locusts – did you really eat them?'

'Tell us how you saved the vulture.'

'Yes, the vulture story . . . please, the vulture story.'

We clamoured for all our favourite stories, but she wouldn't be drawn.

'No! Food . . . Jesus Christ, what the hell am I going to cook? Cam, run out to the *kuché* store and buy seven eggies.'

I went back to the albums, slipping the photos carefully from their paper corners and deciphering the writing on the back, sometimes borrowing Martin's magnifying glass.

'July 1957, Kharian, 105 Canal Street.'

'Dec. 1957, Road to Mangla.'

A funny picture of Mummy feeding a cow was labelled, 'Joan with a local belle.'

I knew that in Pakistan everybody called my mother Joan because that was her real name: Joan Patricia. When she married my father, he called her Patric and it was pronounced the same as the man's name 'Patrick' because he wanted her to have a special name, just for him. As soon as he named her Patric, though, everybody else began calling her that, too, which he said defeated the purpose. Then he started to call her Genie, short for genius. He claimed he called her that because she was so clever, but my mother said he was being sarcastic, as usual.

What puzzled me was that the photos labelled 'Me' were of the older, bearded man and what was even stranger was that in some of the pictures of him it said things like, 'Genius with the newborn camel.'

I asked Mummy, 'Who is this old man? Why is his name Genius? I thought that was your nickname.'

'He's not old! He's the same age as your father.'

She grabbed the album, slammed it shut and put it on the top shelf.

'He was the most wonderful, kind man. I let you look at these albums as a privilege, not so you can question me about every little thing.'

11

Rome is Burning

*Tehran Zoo in my school
uniform skirt and shoes*

Martin and all his things disappeared, erased completely like a shaken etch-a-sketch. I had realised by now that this meant my father would be back soon. How my mother and Martin knew he was returning, I didn't discover.

My father took me with him to the telephone exchange where he pleaded with his partners to return to Iran and bring back the money they had stolen.

'Please, I beg you, they have taken my passport, I have no money. I cannot work,' he whispered hoarsely, glancing around to make sure no one was listening.

My mother huffed around the flat, an angry storm cloud, prone to sudden outbursts.

'Malin, I don't care what you're going through.' Her scream was so penetrating, my ears rang. 'Look what I'm going through. When are you going to pay the rent? Ashley answers the door and says I'm not here. How long can that last?' Without waiting

78

for an answer, she continued, 'I've borrowed from Theresa, from Nounou, from Lisa. I even sold my diamond to Vivienne. That bitch always wanted my jewellery.'

I listened carefully, for eavesdropping was the only way I learned anything about what was going on.

Without waiting for an answer, she resumed, 'I don't care about you and your bloody problems. I spend my life alone in this cold apartment with the kids fighting from the time they get up in the morning: how long can I last?'

My father sat there, the newspaper draped across his lap. Finally he said, 'Genie, I don't know, I just don't know. Maybe it would be better if my wife helped me. This is difficult for me, too.'

Later, my father, sitting in the blue armchair, still reading the newspaper, said, 'Bring your maths book and come here.' He flipped through it, looking for problems. 'If a car is going at sixty miles per hour, how many miles will it travel in eight-five minutes?'

Standing before him, head down, bare toes digging into the Persian carpet, I mumbled, 'Don't know.'

'What do you mean?' he asked, incredulous. 'You're eight years old. Haven't you been doing your lessons with Mummy? What page are you up to?'

Months before, my father had visited our headmaster and persuaded him to lend us textbooks so that we could keep up with our schoolwork. It had been over a year since we had been in school and he was worried we would fall behind.

'What do you do all day?' my father asked.

Oh! How to explain our days? I wanted him to *know* so that he could change what was happening. What could I say, though, that would not reveal what our mother had forbidden: her face very close to each of ours in turn, 'Don't talk about Uncle Martin. Not a word. He hasn't been here.'

What could I tell my father about our days? That we awak-ened when the sun was already hot and thick in the room where the three of us slept all jumbled together? That we scrabbled through the pile of shabby clothes for something that fit? That we ate whatever stale bread remained from the day before? That we read, over and over, the half-dozen books we owned and that I was now reading all the books on the grown-up shelf? That we listened, over and over, to our three records, until Mummy snapped off the record player, the needle dragging across the grooves with an angry squeal? That we wandered up and down our dirt road, gazing longingly at the Iranian children, the fine dust like powdered sugar on their brown skin? That after trailing disconsolately back and forth, hungry and craving something sweet, we finally bought a head of wilted lettuce, bargaining vociferously with the shopkeeper, to eat it dipped in white sugar, sitting on the kitchen floor? That sometimes we ran the hose and wet each other on the long, soft grass of the untended garden outside? That we went up and down the stairs of our building, starting first on the scalding roof where we broke the melting asphalt bubbles with our toes, and watched the soldiers practising their drills in Amjadieh Stadium? That we then moved down from floor to floor, ringing each doorbell, yearning for company, food, anything to break up the monotony of our days?

Mostly, though, that our days, like our mother's, revolved around Martin.

'No, Daddy, I'm sorry. I haven't studied my arithmetic,' I said.

Soon he gave up, throwing the book on to the round brass table where bits of Mummy's stamp collection lay scattered, shouting at her: 'What the hell is going on here? Every time I come back, the children are thinner than the last time. I weighed Ashley this morning and she's lost three kilos since the summer. You haven't opened their books. What do you do with your life? It's bad enough you don't help me, but don't you even care about the children?'

'Go to hell, you bastard,' she screamed. 'I need money. How can I feed them with no money? How can I teach them when I'm on my hands and knees, scrubbing the floor and washing clothes in the bathtub?'

That night I heard the glass door rattle and I leaped out of bed, but by the time I got to the door, my father had gone, absorbed by the dark.

*

As suddenly as my father disappeared, Martin came back. Spring was spreading its creamy warmth over Tehran and, like a great hibernating bear, the city yawned, stretched and emerged from its winter cave. My mother and Martin were energised, too, and the stamp cataloguing of the winter months was put aside for a series of *gardeshes* or outings.

Our first trip was to the zoo. Happy to finally be out, my mother sang and whistled, ignoring her own admonishment about 'whistling girls and crowing hens'. In celebration, she wore her green towelling dress with the diamond pattern in purple, orange and yellow. She had bought the fabric in Switzerland with Nounou, and her friend Lisa had made the dress for her. Big yellow plastic sunglasses and matching dangling earrings completed her new look. When we had given her the sunglasses and the earrings for her birthday just after she returned from Switzerland, she had said to my father, 'Oh, Lin, how absurd! Rome is burning and you buy ridiculous trinkets like these.'

For months Cameron and I had saved any bits of change people had given us to help buy them. Now she wore them when we went out with Martin. The first time she sported them, Martin had grabbed them and tried them on, even the earrings, and she laughed so hard her stomach cramped.

The zoo was crowded, as always, with families from all over Iran. Mothers in their chadors carried babies slung over their backs; fathers held on to toddlers, and the rest of the family stared big-eyed at the creatures. This was an experience many of them would talk about for years after they returned to their villages. The sound of a lion, howling as loudly and plaintively as if on the African delta, drew an enormous crowd. The lion was the symbol of the Pahlavi dynasty and was revered by Iranians. All over Iran, on every official document, on signs, on the sides of buildings, you could see the symbol of the red lion and the sun.

'*Mash Allah, che dandoonayeh bozorgee!*' The crowd flinched as the lion bared his enormous fangs.

My mother laughed and pulled us away. 'Watch what he does now!' She smiled at Martin.

After drawing a huge crowd, the lion prowled swiftly to the front of the cage and lifted his leg, spraying a thick hot stream of piss all over the gawping people. Screams of disgust erupted from the victims and shouts of laughter from those of us who had escaped. The crowd quickly dispersed and the lion lay down, licking his flank.

'Come on, come on! Let's find Khersie!' cried Cameron, bringing us back to the point of our trip to the zoo on this fine sunny afternoon, and we skipped along, our feet crunching the sunflower seed husks littering the path. We were here to see the baby bear Martin had saved from the hunters the summer before and that my father had delivered to the zoo in one of his trucks when the tunnel job had ended.

'*Hallo, wie geht's?*' Martin spotted the dapper German who owned the Tehran Zoo, sauntering around the cages as if he were hosting a party, greeting and glad-handing the crowd.

'*Deine kinder?*' he asked, pointing at us.

'*Nein, nein,*' Martin laughed back, gesturing to my mother. '*Wir wollen uns den Bären ansehen.* The bear. Yah.'

'*Ach so, Komm mit,*' said the owner.

Suddenly we were royalty, accompanying the king in a procession. The owner summoned the handler with his pair of chimps, dressed like Hansel and Gretel, in Lederhosen and Dirndl. Cameron and I were each given a chimp's hand to hold and we ambled towards the bear cages, pulled along by their rollicking, powerful gait. As we walked, we fed them sunflower seeds that they paused to eat, delicately pursing their lips to spit out the husks. At one point, we stopped while the chimps begged a cigarette from a man, which they lit and then smoked, sharing it between them. We continued on past the mountain goats.

With a flourish of his arm, the German zookeeper presented Khersie. 'Well, children your bear is here.'

The stench of rotting meat and smeared bear excrement hit us as we rushed forward. Khersie, with a blank, nervy look, swung back and forth from one side of his cage to the other in the rhythmic, autistic way of imprisoned animals. His hair was bleached and matted like shredded bark. As we watched, a visitor poked him with a stick and he reared up, snarling viciously. The man jumped back, laughing.

'His cage is too small!' piped Cameron in an agitated voice. 'Daddy told us they would put him in a big cage and feed him.'

I joined in. My mother crouched down, squeezing my hands tightly. 'Be quiet! You'll insult the owner. At least he's alive.'

'We should have left him in the woods near Rasht. At least he would be free,' cried Cameron.

'Jesus Christ! What is that smell?' My mother grimaced, sniffing her hands and then bending to smell mine. 'Jesus, Maria, and Joseph! Your hands are covered with chimpanzee shit.'

The German owner shifted uncomfortably. 'Ah yah, the chimpanzees, they use their hands to clean themselves, you know. Ha ha ha. It is quite funny, no?'

He turned to Martin, laughing, but Martin's pugilist jaw was set. My mother threw the zookeeper a grim look and pulled us to the small stream of water, or *joob*, flowing next to the cages.

'Wash your hands.'

'Mummy, Cameron's right, Khersie's cage is too small. We have to get him out of here.'

'What the hell do you think you can do with a grown bear – put it in the garden?' snapped my mother.

Martin stalked away and my mother followed, her sandals slapping the sidewalk. We trailed after them, past the Brahmin bulls, their humps flopping over like tired laundry, the impala, the letter M emblazoned on their backsides, and the solitary chequerboard giraffe. Our gaiety had dissipated as rapidly as a balloon deflating.

'These damn kids, there's nothing I can do to make them happy, is there?' cried Mummy to Martin. 'There's nothing I can do right . . . They want to see their bear, we come to see the bear, but no, that's not enough.' Turning from Martin to us, she said, 'Say thank you to Uncle Martin for bringing you and for the lovely day.'

'Thank you, Uncle Martin,' we parroted in unison.

We sat silent on the ride back. Recently, after we had been to the stamp bazaar, my mother had taken me aside and said, 'If you aren't a little more enthusiastic with Martin, he won't take you any place. He's not your father, you know, he doesn't have to do these things.'

I mourned for our little bear, which, the previous summer, we had fed milk out of a Pepsi bottle. I could see that this past year hadn't gone so well for him either.

*

One daffodil-yellow spring day before the Norouz holiday, we drove out to a trout farm that had opened near Karaj. The trees were shot through with a sudden gold as the breeze blew sunlight through the leaves. Somehow, a long winter had passed between the wet and gusty autumn when we had arrived back in Tehran from the job and this warm spring day. I was groggy, as if I too had been hibernating. My eyes felt sensitive and my skin raw as if it had too many nerve endings. I jumped when my mother yipped with excitement.

When we got there, I stared at the trout pool, its skin rippling with the movement of the jostling fish beneath. The caretaker dumped a bucket of feed into the water and the fish boiled and thrashed. It reminded me of the roiling snakes of my dream.

Feeling edgy and fragile, I took off like a jackrabbit. In the fields surrounding the trout ponds, the bees chatted with each other, drunk on the nectar of sweet clover. I discovered a hobbled calf, which had fallen to the ground and was lying on its side, lowing mournfully. I tried to ease the rope that was tied so tightly around its back legs that its fur and skin had been rubbed away, leaving a bloody bald patch. The calf kicked out, surprisingly strong and angry for such a knobbly thing. Its eyes rolled back in its sockets. I searched for my mother and Martin to help with the calf and found them finally, lying together, in the clover, talking, talking, talking, and smoking, always smoking. Martin was lazily running his finger down her neck.

'Please, please . . . come help the calf, please? It can't walk and it's really hurt.'

'We will, we will,' came their dreamy reply. They too seemed dozy, basking in the new treacly sun of spring.

'Please, please . . .' I begged, as they smiled at each other.

'Oh, stop nagging, Ashley. Can't you just play like the other children?' snapped my mother as she lay soaking up the warmth.

They never saw the calf. Cameron and I struggled to help it for the rest of the afternoon. The calf was shockingly heavy and the rope thick and awkward for our childish fingers, although we finally released it to the point where it was able to stand unsteadily.

For many years, I thought that I had dreamed about these events. Then I found a packet of pictures, taken by Cameron with the Brownie camera someone had given him for his birth-day. There was the field, the other family that I had forgotten was with us, even pictures of the trout pool. He didn't take a picture of my mother and Martin in the grass, though. That, I have only in my memory along with the heat, the calf and the murmuring of the bees.

12

Ragg Mopp

my mother at sports day

Mummy called to us, 'Cam, Asho, come on, Uncle Martin's taking you for a drive.'

En route, we discovered that he was going to his flat to pick up some clothes.

'But I thought you didn't have a place to live – that you stayed with us because you had nowhere to go?' I asked.

He ignored me.

'Can we come in, Uncle Martin?' asked Cameron. 'Can we see your flat?'

'No.'

It dawned on me that Brigitte and Mikey were there. That this was where they lived. That when Martin wasn't with us, he was with them.

'Please, Uncle Martin, I want to see Mikey so much.'

'No.'

He parked and disappeared. We sat in the back seat of the car and grew listless.

'What should we do now?' asked Cameron.

'Say "Fish!"' I squealed, pinching his thin cheeks together so his mouth formed a gasping fish mouth.

'Fwith,' he lisped and we fell about giggling. This was one of the many games we had devised that required no toys or props and we played it endlessly.

Back and forth we went. 'Fwith.'

'Fwith.'

'Fwith,' until our faces were red and sore.

'You're doing it too hard.' I was always the one who backed down first.

'Not.'

'Can you believe that Mikey and Brigitte live here? Why does he stay with us then?'

'Open the windows.'

'We shouldn't, it might be dangerous here.'

We peered out at the hot, dusty street of this neighbourhood we did not know.

'I don't know,' I replied to his earlier question.

If we acknowledged to each other that Martin wasn't living with his family, that he was living with us, it would mean admitting what we both knew about our mother and father but didn't want to recognise.

I changed the subject. 'I'm going to die, it's so hot.'

Soon we had all the windows open wide. The sun hammered down. Our fingers burned when we rubbed the dirt off the chrome of the windows, which is what we did next, after finishing the 'fish' game. After that, we lay on the back seat, our tongues thick and our eyes dry and itchy.

How long had Martin been gone? It felt as if it had been for ever but our mother always said that we children thought everything took longer than it really did. Then the sun began to glide behind the hills to the west of the city and we knew for sure that we had been sitting in that little car for many hours. The slight cooling of the air and our hunger and thirst galvanised us into action.

'You know, Cam,' I said, 'Brigitte's probably forcing him to stay – or maybe they're having a fight and he can't tell her we're in the car waiting, can he?'

'He may never come,' said Cameron. 'We might have to sleep in the car.'

'Do you know how to walk home from here?'

'No, you?'

'No. Did you see which flat he went into?'

'No.'

We searched the floor of the car and in the cracks between the seats for lost coins.

'Come on, it's almost night.'

We got out and crossed the street to the *kuché* store, gazing longingly at the bottles of Pepsi and chocolate-covered marshmallow Negro Kisses.

'*Bebakhsheed Agha, ma komak lazem dareem.*'

The moustachioed storekeeper looked at us, astonished. Where had these two little *farangi* children asking for help come from?

We asked whether he knew Brigitte and could direct us.

No, he shook his head, bewildered. Unlike us, Brigitte must do her shopping at Iran Super, the expensive big supermarket where other foreigners bought their groceries.

Cameron and I searched, going from the tiny corner shop to the fruit vendor to the baker, who was pulling long, sweet-smelling sheaves of hot *sangak* from the yawning mouth of a domed oven. What we were searching for we didn't exactly know. Even if one of these shopkeepers had had a telephone, which was virtually unimaginable, our telephone had long ago gone dead, the bill unpaid. None of them knew Martin, Brigitte, or Mikey when we described them. We would never have rung their door bell, even if we had known which flat it was.

Were we hoping one of the shopkeepers would take pity and give us a glass of water or a scrap of bread? In our hearts we both knew that this whole search was just something to keep us occupied for a few minutes. Eventually we went back and sat on the dusty kerb next to the car, listening to the brassy cries of the birds as they settled for the night in the plane trees overhead.

'I told you not to get out of the car!' Martin barked. It was pitch black night. After hours of boiling, we were now chilled.

'Oh, Uncle Martin, you're back!' We jumped up.

'Get in the car.'

He didn't say a word as he jackhammered his way through the traffic. When we got home, he waited stolidly in his seat, staring straight ahead, for us to get out, then screeched away.

'Where were you? Where's Martin?' asked my mother from the kitchen where she was bathing Rian in the sink, her sleeves rolled up above the elbow and her cigarette hanging damply from her mouth.

'Home. He's gone to his home. To his family,' I answered.

*

Within a few days, my mother was calling us in our room. 'Hurry, hurry, *zood bash*! Kids, Helen is here to take you to sports day!'

Without Martin, my mother had dragged around the flat, her eyes grey and leached of vitality. Cameron, Rian and I had been lolling on the cool floor of our bedroom. If it were sports day, I did a quick calculation, that must mean it was almost summer. We had gone to the job with Daddy before the last sports day so that meant we had missed more than a year of school. Probably fourteen or fifteen months. It felt so long ago that I was in school, I could hardly remember it.

'Not going,' I said.

I couldn't go to sports day. That would mean explaining that we hadn't actually returned to the bucolic London suburb I had so carefully fabricated during my years at school. It was common for children to leave school to return home to England or to move on to another foreign posting, but it was definitely not normal to suddenly reappear and say I had just missed school for a year because my dad couldn't pay the fees.

During my years at the British School, all I had wanted was to fit in and be a proper little English girl. When classmates asked me, 'Why do you have an American accent?' I would hiss back, 'I don't!' I listened and imitated as precisely as possible the clipped accents of the children around me. I sounded just as English, didn't I?

'Where are you from back home?' they asked.

'Where did you go to school?'

'When are you going back?'

All innocent, normal questions, yet they plunged me into a deep, icy pool of insecurity. How could I confess to them I had been born in Iran – this country they reviled, that I spoke the language they imitated by hawking and spitting, that I played happily with the Iranian children they found so foreign, that I had never been to the UK, that my mother was an American, that we were poor and lived in a flat downtown in Amir Abad, miles away from their big villas with their well-watered gardens and aquamarine swimming pools?

No, there was absolutely no part of my life I could reveal. So I collected information from my classmates and teachers, and I frantically assembled what I thought was a normal, ordinary English background. My classmates sensed my desperation, though, and questioned me closely. Shards of made-up memories and images jammed my mind: which had I invented, and which were from another person's real-life story?

Judy came from Wimbledon, where she and her brother had played on the common. Andrew had attended a school for boys only (why only boys, I asked my father, who tried to explain about public schools and grammar schools and single-sex schools and boarding schools). Another classmate's home had attached to another house, which shared a communal garden where they roasted potatoes in the big bonfire on Guy Fawkes Night.

From these titbits, gathered at lunch and in the playground, from *The Secret Garden* and Enid Blyton, I constructed my own version of England. It was so hard to keep it all straight in my mind. I tried, but how could I, when I hadn't actually ever seen a common, a suburb, a semi-detached house, a pillar box, a bollard, a phone box, a bobby, a lane, or a hedge. I had never eaten fish fingers or sausages or jacket potatoes or beans on toast or even a Sunday roast. I had never worn a jumper or a pinny, and pants to me went over my undies, not under my trousers. I knew neither the words nor to what they referred. I literally spoke a different language. So I was always being caught out.

'There's no St Michael's in Richmond? Are you sure? I think there is . . .' I remembered saying once to a curly-headed boy.

'But St Michael's isn't the name of the shop; it's Marks and Spencer's,' he explained, his blue eyes troubled.

'Oh. Oh. I thought it was a store.'

I had seen the label in the school cardigan that Helen had brought me back from England. After these encouters, I felt shaken and I knew the other children were puzzled.

I tried hard to make friends at the British School. Judy, whose dark eyes under a short broom-like fringe seemed perpetually astonished, became my playmate. For a brief period, I was in a bright spot of happiness: I had a friend! I found the games she and the other girls played bewildering, though. Suddenly a virus would spread among the girls and none of them would be able to say a particular word.

'I can't say "scarecrow",' someone would squeal, skipping through the playground.

'But, you just said it,' I replied, confused.

'No, I didn't! I can't say it! I said "squarecrow".'

'Oh. Sorry. Sorry.'

I wandered away, disorientated by the exchange. What did it mean? Why was she saying it? What did it matter?

Nor did I understand the set of rules around the many notes that were passed back and forth. Why did they need to send all these tiny scraps of paper flying between them?

One day, Judy took me aside and told me that I had hurt Caroline's feelings by not answering her note.

'Oh, but she just told me to meet her in the playground and I did.'

'No, you have to write a note back. If someone writes you a note, you have to send one back.'

Visits after school and spending the night were another big hurdle. Once Judy invited me over, I gathered my courage to ask permission.

'So you would go over to her house and sleep there and do what?' my mother asked.

'Play?' I wasn't entirely sure.

'And then what happens after you've done that? They expect you to invite them back. We can't do that. You don't know how other people live. When her parents come over to pick her up, they would see this house.' She flung her hand wide to encompass our flat. 'They would see the way we live. No. No. No.'

On the last sports day we had attended two years earlier, my mother had stood with all the other mothers on the edge of the sandy track, against a background of dusty poplars. Her massive blonde beehive crowned her outfit. She chatted animatedly with her Greek friend Betty, staying well away from the proper British mothers in their prim cotton shifts.

She regularly made fun of them as she drove us home from school:

'Oh deah, hallo, Patricia darling, and how is that chahming husband of yours?'

We did not mix with these very English families, with their crisp accents, sunset drinks parties and weekend cricket matches. Each afternoon all the boys and girls of these families swam in each other's pools and ate sandwiches spread with the precious Marmite that their fathers brought back after visiting the 'home office' in London. We were never invited. We socialised with the Greeks, the Iraqis, the Syrians, the Armenians and the mixed British and Iranian families. Even in this group, though, we didn't fit in. We were the outsiders even on the fringe.

On that previous sports day, while my mother had stood smoking and chatting, I had done something that became part of the folklore of our family. Cameron won his race easily, tearing down the field, his teeth clenched and his arms pumping. Cameron had won every race he had ever run. He was fierce. When it was our turn, we girls loped along. My friends, Herman, Spiro and David, ran alongside the track, cheering me on, Spiro's polio-withered arm flailing. I was in the lead, but breathing down my neck was the tiny Caroline Grey who, despite suffering from asthma, skimmed along. Suddenly out of the corner of my eye, I saw a classmate fall – Judy or Amanda or someone, and I stopped to help her up. Caroline raced ahead and I came in a distant second. My mother watched, puzzled for a few moments. Then she began cheering.

'I'm so proud of you. You could have won the race, but you stopped and helped another child. You're like the Good Samaritan.'

She held up my arm, hailing me as if I had won.

'Mummy, stop, it's not fair to Caroline!'

I was conscious of the fact that Caroline's small mother, with her long old-fashioned braids and small hat perched on top, was not screaming and yelling – and Caroline had come in first.

Now after I had been out of school for over a year, having never fitted in even when I was there, my mother expected me to face my former classmates and teachers.

I stubbornly resisted. 'My uniform doesn't fit.'

'You don't need to wear a uniform, silly. It's sports day,' said my mother.

'If I don't wear a uniform, they'll know I haven't been in school.'

My mother kneeled down. 'Ashley, honey, do you really think that the other children haven't realised that you're not in school?'

I shook my head, mute, for it sounded ridiculous, even to me.

'Ashley, you just have to not care about other people. March to the beat of your own drum.' She looked at me intently.

'But what should I say?'

'To hell with them! Tell them it's none of their GD business.'

'I know, Mummy, I know. But what should I *say*?'

'Tell them all, every one of those bloody, snotty, British School brats *and* their mothers, to go to hell.'

Sports day was agony. I wore a red woolly jumper because it was the only item of clothing that I felt passed muster and I was almost driven mad by the itchy wool against my bare hot skin. I skulked around the edges of the crowd, and when my classmates and teachers approached me, I mumbled and tried to escape. Later that night, I wept.

'How could you make me?' I kept asking and my mother stared at me, perplexed by my upset, by my reluctance to join in.

'Whatever happened to my little Ragg Mop?' she asked.

Ragg Mop epitomised what I had been and was no longer. When I was four or five, we had taken visitors to the Caspian and were waiting in a restaurant for our sturgeon kebab lunch. The Caspian was famous for its sturgeon. After the black caviar was stripped out of the immense, prehistoric-looking fish, the thick slabs of white meat were marinated in oil, onion and lemon juice, and made into delicious kebabs. It was a big treat for us, as sturgeon was available only near the Caspian and expensive.

During the wait, I entertained ('Being the little actress that you were') the entire restaurant with a rousing rendition of Ragg Mopp ('Running around in front of everybody, singing R-A-G-G M-O-P-P, Ragg Mopp, at the top of your lungs'). I had fooled around and flirted ('Wiggling your little bottom and contorting your beautiful little face, dancing from table to table') until the entire restaurant was hysterical ('Grown men were crying with laughter – that is, of course, except your father'). For my mother, at that moment, I was the ideal child ('Cute as a button, with a little chup-chup nose. Lovely little legs. You were a doll. What a little Sarah Bernhardt'). To my mother's chagrin, that exuberant little girl had somehow disappeared. I had become so serious, so withdrawn, so overly sensitive and reproachful.

'I can't understand how you've changed so much,' she mourned. 'What happened to my little Ragg Mopp?'

13

Rice with Ketchup

at the
trout farm

'Come on, come on, take a bath and dress – we're doing something exciting tonight, kids! We're going to Shookoofeh-No.'

For the first time in ages, our mother was singing and dancing around the flat.

'Shookoofeh-No, Shookoofeh-No,' we chanted.

We had heard about Shookoofeh-No. Once we had even met two of the Shookoofeh-No dancers at Faridun and Helen's house. One, a tall brunette, had a mole on her cheek. For the other, a tanned blonde, it was her first trip away from England. Both wore miniskirts and go-go boots and had upswept hairdos and pale pink lipstick. They looked completely different from my mother and her friends, never mind the Iranian

97

women on the streets in their chadors and long trousers and baggy dresses.

'Who's taking us, Mummy?' we asked.

'A very nice American man.'

She asked us to open the door for Alvin and offer him a drink of whisky. We shook hands and sat him down in the grey chair, where he promptly crossed his leg over his knee. His hair was slicked back and his face pale. He was bony thin and with his white face he looked like the Joker in the Batman comic books.

In the car, my mother and Alvin held hands. Cameron and I caught one another's eye. Holding the steering wheel with only a few fingers, Alvin glanced back at us, smiling, his face mask-like.

'Your mama's a real lady, kids. You are very lucky, let me tell you.'

At the table that night, Cameron and I conferred under the cover of music.

'What about Daddy?' We hadn't heard from my father in ages.

'What about Martin?'

'Yes, even Martin's better than him.'

But, like my father, Martin had also inexplicably dropped out of our lives.

When the waiter came to take our order, we looked at our mother for guidance.

'Live it up, kids!' She ordered us rice and kebab with bottles of Pepsi.

'Well, Patric,' Alvin said, drawing out the first syllable with his cowboy accent, 'your children are certainly good eaters and very well mannered, too.'

Our mother beamed.

One day she had kneeled down and pulled us close. 'Do you know the most important thing to succeed in the world?'

We shook our heads.

'What do you think? Good looks, intelligence, luck, being a good sportsman?' she prompted.

We shook our heads again until finally I ventured a guess. '*Tarof?*'

Tarof was the self-deprecating form of flattery used by Iranians in social situations.

'Yes, kind of ... the answer is good manners!' she said. 'None of you three kids will ever be the smartest, the best looking, the most athletic, the best at anything. You can have the best manners, though. When I hear back from people about you, what they always say is, "Patric, you have the most polite children," and that makes me proud. Very, very, proud.'

We nodded miserably. Being well mannered had a high price: taking the smallest piece of anything offered; saying 'No thank you' when we really meant yes; setting the table and cleaning up while the other children played; having to be grown up when other children had fun.

We smiled politely at Alvin and turned our attention back to what was happening on the stage. Naked flesh jiggled and shook, high heels clicked and tapped, feathers waved, belly dancers' tummies gyrated, cymbals clinked and chinked. Our heads were on pivots and our eyes were on stalks. At the tables, the few Iranian women were wearing chadors, while on the stage the performers were wearing almost nothing. When the Iranian singers came on, the entire audience erupted, flicking their arms and shoulders back and forth, clicking their fingers and wailing along. For the finale, a clown shot off a dancer's bra using a cap gun. We were stunned and the audience went wild. The dancer clutched her arms across her breasts and ran off stage with her mouth in a pretend 'Oh'. Cameron and I spent the evening looking for the two English dancers we had met, but it was impossible; they were disguised by their make-up and costumes.

When we got home that night, Mummy had tea while Alvin had another glass of whisky. In the morning, we checked, but the living-room doors weren't locked and Mummy was fast asleep in her own bed.

*

One evening when Helen dropped us off, we found Martin sitting at the kitchen table.

Mummy called, 'Give your Uncle Martin a big huggle buggle.'

As I made my way around the table, he grabbed me playfully and I hit my knee against the fridge. Tears flooded out of me. 'I hate you,' I muttered.

'So this is the welcome I get!'

Martin stomped out and my mother followed, spatula in hand.

'Oh Martin, she didn't mean it. She hurt her knee.'

'No, it is not just that. I know Ashley. She is not . . .' He waved his hands around. 'It's something else, there's someone else, isn't there? Helen told me that you've been leaving the kids there for hours. Tell me the truth! I'm going through hell. For what, for what?' He shook his head, his shoulders slumped.

'No, Martin, I promise.'

He glared at me. My mother wouldn't allow me back in the kitchen, banishing me to the little hallway next to the kitchen where I reluctantly ate what was normally my favourite dinner of rice with ketchup. Despite the ketchup, the rice was dry and hard and each grain seemed huge going down my throat.

14

Mehrabad Airport

*watching the
planes land
when I was little*

Crowds of people jostled, shoving us from one place to
another.

'Ashley, you watch Cameron and Rian. No, you stay with
me. Boys, go with Lisa.'

My mother leaned down and gripped Cameron hard by the
arm.

'If you give me any trouble, *any* trouble on this trip, I will
kill you. I swear to God, I will kill you.'

People crushed together. The sound of babies crying
mingled with the loudspeaker system feedback. The stink of
sweat saturated into thick woollen jackets, the sting of hot
dust blowing in through the open doors from the parched
runways outside, the sheer weight of the sun flowing hot and

heavy into the crowded noisy building assailed me. Mehrabad Airport was not the friendly place Daddy had brought us, over the years, to watch planes land and take off, where we waved to Barbie-doll stewardesses from England and Switzerland as they sashayed through the marble terminal. No, the airport felt alien, like a film, with people I didn't recognise. It felt just like my dream, the one that inevitably followed 'the snake dream'. In this dream, it was night and I was falling, falling, my white nightgown billowing around me like a beautiful medusa jellyfish, breaking my fall as I landed with a bang on to a grate above a crowded room. Through the grate, I peered down at a party of glamorous men and women, all jostled together, laughing and drinking, ice tinkling crazily in their glasses, cigarette smoke spiralling into grotesque arabesques over their heads.

'Help! Let me in! Help!' I called.

None of them noticed. Their voices babbled on, in a language I didn't understand. No, wait! I strained, listening hard: I recognised the cadence, the inflection, the sentence structure, but the words ran unintelligibly together . . . Finally, I recognised they were speaking English, disturbingly speeded up to 78 rpm, just like Alvin and the Chipmunks when we switched the speed on the record player. I struggled to make out what they were saying, struggled to make them hear me . . .

*

What were we doing at Mehrabad Airport that June day in 1968? At the time, I didn't know. As ever, my mother hadn't told us. What does surprise me is that I hadn't gleaned it, given how adept I had become at tuning in to whispered conversations and offhand remarks. The feeling remains that I had no idea we were leaving until early that morning as we were bundled out of bed by our father who had suddenly reappeared. He whispered, 'Get up, Asho darling. Quickly now, and quietly. We're going to the airport.'

I still don't know what precipitated our sudden departure. Given that my father's passport and residence documents had been confiscated, and he was always in danger of being arrested, my mother must have decided she was better off in America. Maybe she just couldn't ask her friends for any more money. Later, I learned that over the course of the prior year she had borrowed $7,000 from friends to help pay my father's way out of jail. Given that in 1960, my father was making $4,000 as a senior engineer, the magnitude of those borrowings was huge. Meanwhile, we still weren't paying our rent, hadn't been to school in over a year and a half, had grown out of almost all our clothes, the phone had been cut off and we had no money for food. We were virtually hermits in our flat and when we came out, we were awkward, like moles above ground.

When I think back to whether anyone missed me after we left, whether anyone said to their mother, 'I wonder how Ashley is? Does she like her new school? Where are they living now?' in the way my children would wonder about a friend or classmate, I doubt that anyone noticed. There was no one who would have followed up on our disappearance. We were like fish gliding, without a trace, through the sea.

*

My mother's friend Lisa bustled about the airport, her Austrian accent zinging around. 'Na yah, Patric, take the money!' She pressed into her hand bags clinking with currency left over from trips to Beirut, Paris and Vienna.

I reached over to touch them. It was the first time I had ever seen a plastic bag.

'It's nothing, na yah, take it.'

My father was dealing with the tickets, passports, airport taxes and whatever bribes were required to get us out, for our visas had expired or, in the case of Rian who had never previously left the country, were non-existent. I was distracted; my mother declared suddenly that she needed my little blue valise for all our documents – her pocketbook was too small. On to the dirty airport floor she dumped my collection of dolls from Greece and Spain and Switzerland that I had hurriedly packed that morning. These were my prized possessions, this handful of small dolls that my mother's friends had brought back for me from their journeys.

'Genie, why didn't you think of this before?' snapped my father, kneeling down, holding the boys and then me. When he took me in his arms, I could feel his itchy, whiskery chin. 'Asho darling, no matter what anyone tells you, I love you more than anything in the world. Don't believe what they tell you about me,' he whispered. He stood and tried to kiss my mother goodbye, but she turned her face away. As she strode out, pulling Rian by the hand, he called to her, '*Ap saay pi hai*, Genie.'

It was the Urdu expression that he always used when he left, the one that meant 'I love you'.

'*Ap saay pi hai*, Genie.'

I turned to wave to Daddy, who clutched my treasured dolls, all muddled together, against his chest.

America, 1968–71

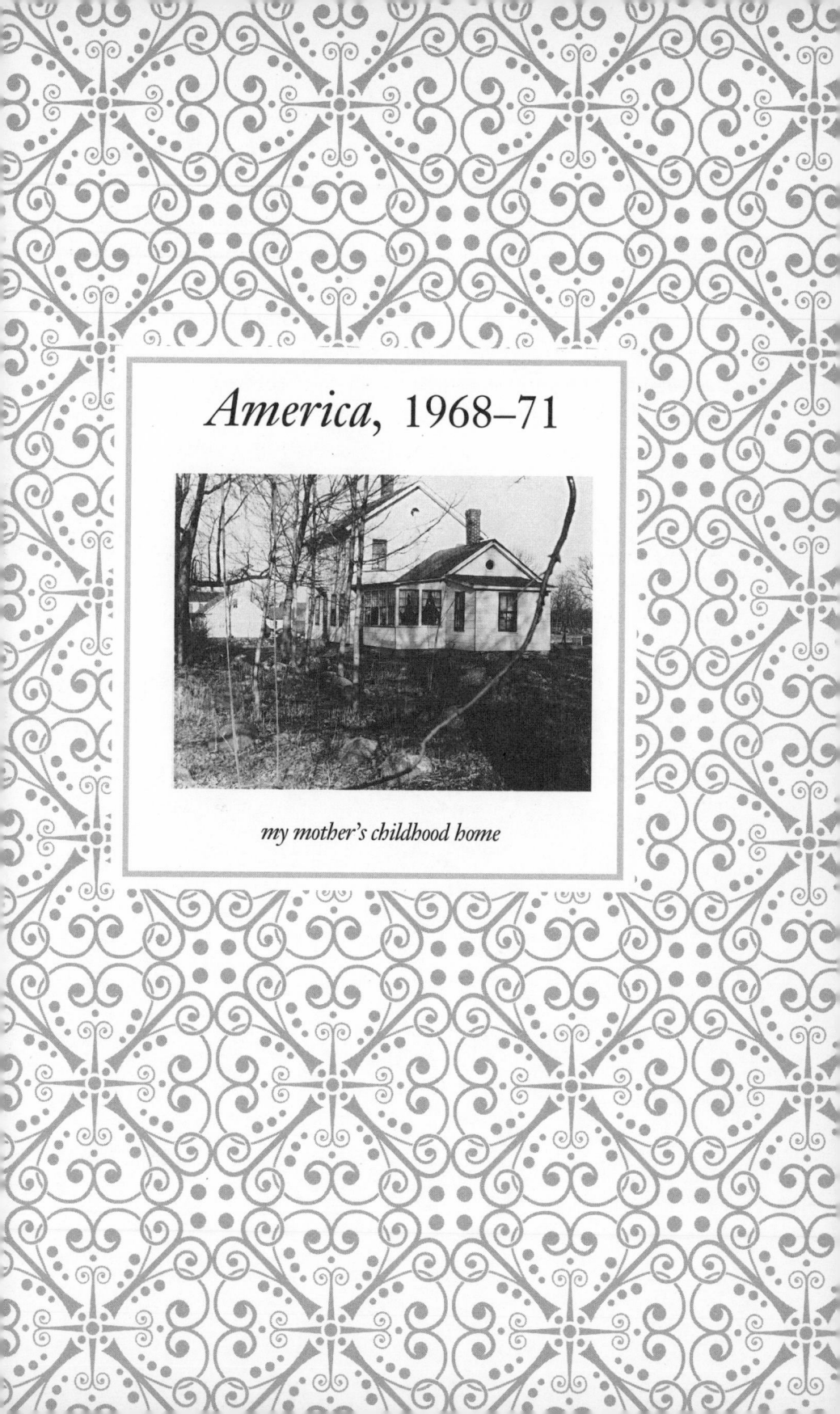

my mother's childhood home

15

Halls Hill Road

my mother
aged fifteen

My mother smoked continuously from Tehran to Cairo. When the stewardess asked us whether we would like a Pepsi, she blinked open her eyes, barked 'Milk!' and closed them again.

She traded the fought-over bags of coins for a couple of cartons of Viceroys at Cairo Airport, where we laid over for a few stifling hours. I looked out the window of the small terminal at the turbaned men wheeling barrows of sand and thought that I had to remember being there.

'I don't understand. I didn't realise ...' sputtered my mother, leaning over the counter at International Transfers at Heathrow.

'Madam, it says right here on your ticket that you leave at

oh-nine-hundred hours,' said the man at the ticket counter, where we were checking in for our onward flight to New York.

'Nine o'clock. He said nine o'clock. I thought it was the same night. That bastard didn't tell me . . .' She drummed her fingers. 'Jesus Christ, he didn't give me any money to feed these bloody children. Where will we sleep?'

She said this as if we were not hers, as if she were merely accompanying us and would drop us off with our real mother when we got to our destination.

She turned to the man. 'Where's the lounge, sir? We'll wait in the departure lounge.'

'Wait one moment, madam.' He disappeared.

We sat on the floor, leaning against the counter while my mother buried her head in her hands. Finally, the man emerged to say he had arranged to put us up in the airport hotel and give us some dinner vouchers, compliments of the airline.

'Thank you, thank you!' My mother shook his hand. We three kids jumped up and down and thanked him some more.

'It's no problem, madam,' he said. 'Enjoy your dinner.'

That night we gorged on spaghetti and meatballs and thick, creamy English milk from fat English cows fed on lush English grass. We scrubbed our teeth with soap on the corner of a towel and slept in our underwear, the boys together in one bed and me in the other. My mother sat up all night, propped up in the armchair, smoking and waiting for dawn; we had no alarm clock and if wake-up calls existed, she did not know about them.

*

International Arrivals at JFK was huge. Absolutely enormous. My eyes flew around the terminal, taking in all the new sights, the most surprising being that everybody looked like me. Not *just* like me, of course, but similar. In Iran, where almost everybody had black hair and dark eyes and wore Iranian clothes, we had always stood out. Here, though, nobody noticed me.

My eyes hopped from person to person, checking to see whether they were eyeing me in any special way. But no, I was just a little girl and if someone did glance at me with a smile or quizzically, it was just because I was staring at them.

Then suddenly, my eyes came to rest on someone who looked as different as different could be: a gigantic black man in brightly coloured robes whose hair stood out from his head. Massive necklaces coiled around his neck.

'Mummy, Mummy, it's an African chief!'

'*Sh*! Ashley, don't point. In America you can't say that, they are called "negroes".'

Soon I would know that negroes now called themselves 'black' and that this black man, the first I had ever seen, was probably not an African chief, but just an ordinary American. He seemed as out of place in this terminal as we had at Mehrabad Airport.

Everything at JFK was different from Iran and it wasn't only the way the people looked. The terminal was enormous, clean and white. The floors were sparkling, the windows shiny clean. The bathrooms were white and clean, so sparkly, whitely, cleanly clean. When I walked in, holding Rian's sweaty little hand, I smelled a hospital kind of a smell. No wet piles of excrement to step over, no swarms of flies to brush out of my eyes and mouth, their tiny feet covered in the faeces they had been hungrily climbing over. The airport was quiet, the murmur of talking people interrupted occasionally by the loudspeaker announcing flights. At the airport in Iran, people yelled over each other's heads, '*Agha beeya baba!*'

It took us a long time to go through passport control and get our bags. By the time we had collected our suitcases and dragged them to catch the coach to Connecticut, the arrivals area was emptying. By the time we had found the right queue and explained our destination, the runway lights were shooting their sterile rays up into the purple haze. By the time the coach had collected its full contingent, a thin cool breeze had displaced the thick muggy air. In our summer clothes, crumpled after two days' travelling, we huddled together on the suitcases. Even if we had had money to buy food, there was no place to buy it.

'OK, kids, up you get, gotta get them suitcases put away.'

The driver's chin wobbled and he sucked his teeth. His glasses were filmy and the top of his trousers folded over his belt buckle. Once in the coach, Cameron, Rian and I fell asleep instantly and awoke much later to see early-summer light creeping around the old oaks in my grandparents' yard.

'What! They said at the airport it would be twenty-eight dollars from Idlewild!' said my mother.

'They may have said that, but you didn't tell him you were going to some podunk place out in the woods. You said it was just outside New London. And it's called JFK now, in case you didn't know.'

'It *is* just outside New London,' she insisted.

'Fifty bucks!'

'I don't have it. I've given you all I have.'

'Go get it from them,' said old Wobble Chin, jerking an elbow at the silhouette of a woman in a flapping nightgown, her skinny pipe legs barely supporting her immense bulk, and a bald man, his palsied hand shaking in the porch light. I didn't remember them from the last time we had seen them when I was four and Cameron three. Rian hadn't even been born.

'Joanie? Is that Joan?' A high shrill voice pierced the night. My mother flinched.

'Nah, come back to bed, Lilly, it can't be her. She didn't tell us she's coming.' Turning towards the car, the old man yelled, 'Go away, you're at the wrong house.'

'Ma, Pa! Willy, Lilly! It's me. Have you got twenty bucks?' She marched to the front door where she waited while the fluttery old man retrieved cash from the depths of the house.

'Here.' She pushed the money at the driver. Helping us out of the car, she said, 'Go kiss your grandparents hello.'

There were no kisses to greet us, though, nor a 'Hello, how are you?' They just moved aside as Mummy herded us through the door.

'Ya got anything to eat, Lilly?' asked my mother. 'These kids haven't eaten.'

There was no kiss for her either. I noticed that my mother's voice had become rougher and her accent had changed. Lilly thrust her arm into the fridge and brought out small bowls of food: blueberries and sour cream; a pork chop, dried out like a piece of bark; tuna fish with the mayonnaise liquefying in a beige puddle around it; some scummy hot dogs and beans. She threw these willy-nilly on to the small table and flung a pile of spoons and forks next to them.

'So eat already if you're so hungry,' she said.

'Lilly, when is this food from? Is it fresh?' asked our mother, sniffing each item.

'Fresh? Waddya think, I eat rotten food?'

Our grandmother tottered around on her popsicle-stick legs, screeching instructions at my grandfather and berating my mother.

'Why didn't you tell us you were coming?' Turning to four-year-old Rian, 'Is this the baby? How do you say his name? How long you here for? You shoulda told us you were coming. Why don't you write? You never write. You're still smoking. Put that filthy thing out in my house. Disgusting. You hungry? Eat something! Eat!'

I had never seen anyone like her before. Her body was huge, like an enormous pumpkin, and all the bits stuck to it were too small: her head and fine-boned face as delicate as a porcelain doll's, her arms and legs so slim they seemed to be from another species entirely, her tapered feet and hands worthy of the most delicious leather and precious jewels.

We tasted the food, leaving most of it. She put it back in the fridge. Soon we heard earth-shattering snores, next door.

'That's Willy, the silly old schmuck.'

'Lilly, sh, they don't know words like that.'

We peeked around the corner to see my grandfather barricaded behind boxes piled up in the living room, covering every available surface. Glittering necklaces hung like trailing Amazon vines. Hundreds of pairs of earrings sparkled on the tops of cartons. Mannequins sporting colourful hats stared out at us, smiling. Silk scarves and flowered fabrics twined out from cartons and drawers. Narrow aisles led through the stacks. When we finally went upstairs, my mother had to move boxes from one pile to another to get our suitcases through. Upstairs, in the dark, jacket sleeves slapped our faces and trouser legs kicked out at us as we slid through the doorways, whose every lintel precariously supported dozens of hangers laden with clothes. Bare light bulbs hung down over urine-stained mattresses covered with squirrel droppings.

My mother gestured from the hallway. 'Find a mattress, lay some sheets on it and get to sleep.'

Many hours later, the boys and I crept downstairs. Our grandparents rocked on the front porch. Grandpa had bought jelly doughnuts and milk, which we crammed down standing in the small kitchen. He joined us, choking, gulping and sputtering, his shaking hand splashing brown puddles of coffee on to the counter.

'So, uh, how you kids doin'? Ya sleep good?'

'Yes, thank you, Grandpa,' we chirruped, smiling, but I was shocked that Americans lived this way; that song about everybody being rich in America wasn't true.

'Grandpa, are you sick?' I asked.

'No, why, uh ahg, do you ask that?'

'Why are you coughing and choking like that?'

Grandpa glanced, with a frightened expression, at Granny.

'Go out back and play. Don't touch anything in the house,' screamed our grandmother.

We soon learned that she very rarely spoke; mostly she shrieked. My mother slept through that day and night. We found her the next morning lying on her mattress and staring at the ceiling.

*

'What does she do up there all day?' my grandmother asked.

We were hanging sheets on the clothes line.

She didn't wait before continuing, 'The damn birds drop their cherry pits on the clothes and stain them. She knows she can't smoke up there, doesn't she? It's a fire trap. She'll burn the house down. She'll stink up my stuff. Tell her not to smoke. When she sends you out to buy cigarettes, tell her no.'

'OK, Granny. She's just writing letters.'

I was glad Granny couldn't see grey smoke seeping out into the humid summer breeze from my mother's window and was so fat she couldn't climb the stairs and discover the mason jars full of cigarette butts.

'Who's she writing all those damn letters to? Clatter clatter clatter all the time on that damn typewriter of hers.'

I shook my head. I had tried to look, but my mother covered up the top of the letter with a blank piece of paper whenever I came near, and she closed the typewriter and put it away whenever she wasn't using it.

*

I skipped down Halls Hill Road to the thrift shop my grandmother managed. We left the door ajar to diffuse the musty smell of second-hand clothes and books. She sat behind the counter, an embroidered handkerchief tied around her neck, and directed me.

'Give me that bag and I'll price it.' Or 'Bring all the glasses over here and I'll dust them.'

After an hour or two, I sat and read the donated Reader's Digest Condensed Books: the world's classics in a hundred pages. After having been starved of books for years, I gorged on the volumes cramming the thrift shop, chomping down hundreds of pages a day, day after day. My book life became my real life and my real life just something to live through until I could read again.

Each day, Granny sat at the counter and I sat on the floor, both of us reading. She commented non-stop about the people who walked past. 'Damn bitch,' she said about a tiny old lady with two braids who looked like a wizened prairie girl. Or, looking up from her book, 'Schnookie Schuster this, Schnookie Schuster that . . . Why all the time with the Schusters . . .'

At first I thought she was speaking to me but soon I realised she would have kept up the same running stream of invective if I weren't there. When customers occasionally came into the shop, she sold them a shirt for a quarter, a stuffed animal for a dime, a tumbler for a nickel.

Later, we struggled up the hill towards home, laden with more things for the already overstuffed house.

'Hide the bags from Willy! Stupid idiot,' Granny ordered as we made slow progress up the long incline. She called hello to the people sitting on their porches and as soon as we passed she said things like, 'Retarded child,' or 'Husband killed himself. Hanged himself, disgusting old fool,' or 'Stupid woman. Dog barks.'

If Willy caught us with the bags, he nagged. 'Uh huh huh, Lilly, we got too much stuff. We ain't got no place to put it. We ain't got the money. Stop with all the buying.'

'Shut up, you stupid old fool! It's my house and my money, you dummy!'

One day I asked my mother why Granny berated Grandpa

so much. To me, my grandfather seemed nicer than my grand-mother – he rarely shouted at us and generally said good morning when we came downstairs.

My mother warned me though, 'He's a bastard. He used to beat us until we bled. Be careful, he's not as nice as he looks.'

'But why, Mummy?'

'There's a lot you don't know, Ashley,' my mother shot back. 'There's a lot more than meets the eye.'

*

We discovered the Turners, the black family next door. The Turners were the all-American family with their shiny appli-ances, polished car and three intricately braided daughters. Like animals homing in on warmth, we sought the normalcy of their household and sidled into it, creeping as close as we could. Mr and Mrs Turner didn't scream at each other. If the girls needed new sneakers, they bought them *new*, and no one argued about how much they cost and why they needed them and couldn't they make do with what they had. I never heard any of them say shit, damn, or bastard, and no one smoked.

I watched the election campaign on TV with Mr Turner, who explained the electoral college, voting, Democrats and Republicans, and what it meant to be an American. He told me about the civil rights movement and how much America had changed in the last few years – especially for black people. He was the one who told me that I shouldn't use the word 'negro' and that 'black' had replaced it. He informed me that even though blacks had technically received the vote at the end of the nineteenth century, in reality very few were able to vote and that most blacks, especially in the South, were preju-diced against in all kinds of ways. He let me know, shaking his head sadly, that Robert F. Kennedy had been assassinated just a few days earlier on 6 June, and Martin Luther King in April. I couldn't believe that important men were gunned down in the streets of America.

'Honey,' said Mr Turner, 'this country is going through some big changes.'

On the news, I saw war protestors yelling and marching, pictures of teenagers burning their draft cards, and mothers crying when their sons died in Vietnam or went to Canada to avoid the draft. I learned that my mother's youngest brother, who had joined the Merchant Marines so that he could escape the war, had been drafted as soon as he came back. In the little town of Colchester, though, it was peaceful and buzzing with bees. Newly cut grass scented the breeze all summer long. American flags flew on the town common.

*

One bottle-green day we visited Mummy's first boyfriend, Joe Green. His parents came along as well to see 'their Joanie'. The two tiny old people sat on the couch and told all of us, including Joe's wife, 'Boy, we loved Joanie. What a good girl. Look at her – she's gorgeous. We wanted our Joe to marry her, but she wouldn't have him – would you, Joanie? No!'

Without stopping for an answer, they continued together, as if they had rehearsed, 'No! Joanie was too beautiful, too smart, too good for our Joe. You wanted more than our old Joe, didn't you?'

I looked at my mother, smiling happily as she regaled the group with her escapades in Pakistan and Iran. She was charming and witty. Joe's wife stood quickly and began collecting plates and cups.

'Go outside and play.' The wife shooed us out.

'Watch this!' said one tow-headed daughter as she ran screaming through a barn full of fluffy white chickens.

Like a carnival game, the chickens rose in front of her, clucking and cackling, sputtering white feathers all around. We followed, aeroplaning around the barn in circles and loop-the-loops, the chickens rising and scattering around us. Climbing the ladder to the hayloft was easy for the Green kids and Cameron, but Rian struggled up the steep, splintery rungs, his fat brown legs straining from one distant step to the next as I pushed him from behind. We balanced high up in the eaves on uneven boards pocked with knotholes, chasing each other and throwing clumps of dusty hay.

'Now watch this,' said another of the girls as she squatted over a hole in the planks. Her bottom was as smooth and white as a kitchen bowl. The chickens erupted beneath, fighting to eat the turds as they dropped.

'That's disgusting!' we cried. 'Can we do it?'

And we took it in turns to poop on to the chickens, which gabbled and gobbled greedily beneath us.

16

Push-Me Pull-You

*New York City
with Yosy*

'Kids, wake up! We're here!'
We found the buzzer with 'R.E. Jones'.

'It stands for Rosemary Elaine. I know because she told me,' I informed the boys. I wanted them to understand that she was *my* special friend.

She came running down. 'Hello, hello, hello!'

I threw my arms around her waist. We had met Yosy, which was what we called her because Rian couldn't say 'Rosemary' when he was little, when she moved on to the fourth floor of our Amir Abad apartment building in 1966. From her balcony she had seen my mother hanging laundry in the garden below her.

'Yoo-hoo,' she had called down, tipped off by my mother's Yale sweatshirt, 'are you an American?' Yosy too, had grown up in Connecticut, and after she graduated from college she had worked in New York in publishing. During the year she had been in Iran, we had become best friends and I had written to her after she left.

'I'll pick you up from the train station at four o'clock on Sunday,' said Willy to my mother.

He had belted his baggy grey suit trousers high up, almost under his armpits, and he wore a grey felt hat on his pink speckled head.

'Drive carefully, Willy. Do you have money for a coffee? Do you want to come in and use the bathroom?'

'Nah, nah, don't worry about me. I got money. I'll stop on the road and get a doughnut.'

We kissed Grandpa's bristly cheek and ran up the stairs, in front of Yosy and Mummy, who dragged our suitcase between them. We buzzed around the apartment like flies in a hot jar.

'Can I see your bedroom, Yosy?'

'This is it, kids! I do everything in this room. That's my bed.'

She pointed at the couch, covered in a block-printed spread that she and I had bought together at the Iranian handicrafts store. When she had found out that she wasn't able to renew her visa to stay in Iran we had spent hours choosing mosaic boxes and painted leather picture frames for her to bring back.

'You live in here? Just in this tiny room?'

'I told you that my apartment in Amir Abad was a palace. Now you believe me.'

I had spent days in Yosy's Amir Abad flat, reading, sketching and just chatting with her. Often when I came home from school, I would run straight up to the fourth floor and only go back home for dinner.

In New York, we slept at her friend's apartment. Mummy took the bed and we kids sprawled on blankets on the floor. We awakened early to the budgie chirping and scattering birdseed as it fluttered around its cage.

*

Flower power. Dashikis. Afros. Miniskirts. Maxi skirts. Long hair. Shaved heads. Beads. Beards. Music. Dancing. Drumming. People kissing on the street. I had never seen two people kissing like that before, not even in the Doris Day movies we had seen at the American Club in Tehran.

'Mummy! Look!'

The couple was entwined on a bench, faces melded together, their eyes closed. For minutes they never moved, statues with ecstatic faces, almost religious in their intensity. All of the sunshine and colour and music and happiness of New York City was pouring out of their mouths and into mine and then back again in a sizzling loop.

'Come on!' laughed Yosy as she pulled me away down the street. 'We're going to be late.'

We were on our way to see *Dr Doolittle* at Radio City Music Hall.

'It's five bucks a ticket. Even for the kids,' said Yosy, coming back from the ticket booth.

'I don't care how much it costs, these kids need a treat. I'll treatcha, kiddo!' said my mother, taking bills out of her wallet. I wondered where she had gotten money.

Entering Radio City was like landing on a cool dark planet in a different galaxy. I was transported when Dr Doolittle and the Push-Me Pull-You walked and talked with the animals. After the film ended, the feeling of being outside reality continued: New York City danced and swirled around us in a colourful tie-dye rainbow.

I remembered back to the street outside our flat in Tehran. It felt so long ago that I had seen the Iranian women scouring their pots with sand in front of the tap they shared at the end of our street, smelled rice cooking, soft and warm, mixed with the tangy meat smell of *khoresht eh bademjoon* or the grassy smell of *ghormeh sabzee*, felt the first slight breeze of dusk waft the scent of the honeysuckle outside our bedroom window as we drifted off to sleep. And then, in the morning, but only in June, which was strawberry season, we'd hear the yell of the strawberry seller leading his donkey, panniers full of gleaming red, as he called, '*Toot farangi! Toot farangi!*'

We would gather around the donkey, scratching its stuffed-animal face as the strawberry man weighed the crimson berries on scales he held aloft, adding or subtracting the lumpy lead weights he carried with him.

'Hare Krishna, Hare Krishna, Krishna Krishna, Hare Hare.'

I came back to New York City with a jolt as a procession of orange-robed dancers whirled through the park, eyes trance-like, feet moving nimbly. I stood staring, clutching Rian's damp hand, but my mind had leaped back to Iran.

'Hossein, Hossein.'

'Ali, Ali.'

'Mohammad.'

'In the name of Allah, most gracious, most merciful.'

From inside the flat we had heard the rhythmic chanting, the sound of feet pounding, the clink of chains swishing and hitting, and the cries of men coming closer and closer until they were on our road and the sound had become a roar. A procession of men marched, beating themselves with chains. Some of the marchers had attached razor blades to their chains and blood ran down their backs and congealed, jelly-like, on their shoulders. A man with a gleaming shaved head swung a curved silver sword and led the chanting in a rising and falling crescendo. The crowd was lamenting the death of the proph-et's descendant, Hossein, when hundreds of years ago Yazid's army had lured him and his followers into a trap at Karbala and slaughtered them.

Cameron and I had stood in the darkness, peeking out the corner of the window from behind the curtains. Some of the men looked familiar, like the owner of the *kuché* store across the street, but in the flickering light it was hard to tell. Suddenly there was a growl as the crowd surged towards us and smashed the window with the butts of their whips and chains. The glass splintered and men rattled the bars, screaming. We ran, leaping into the hallway and slamming the door. Our hearts beating wildly, we clutched each other, wondering whether they would break through the bars. Our mother came running, wrapped in a bath towel, her hair in tendrils around her neck.

'How dare you?' she shrieked while we huddled in terror, waiting for the procession to go by.

Later in the week, on the street, I found the baby doll that in my haste I had abandoned on the windowsill, stripped of her clothes, beheaded and covered with bloody fingerprints.

I came out of my reverie as one of the last Hare Krishnas grabbed my mother's hand and pulled her into the procession. After a few minutes of dancing along, she laughed and came back to us. We followed the throng moving slowly towards Central Park. All over the lawns, couples lay on blankets and towels, radios blaring.

New York was just as Mummy had described as there really was money lying in the streets. Rian found $3 rolled up in a tight tube under a tree and that began the reputation that would precede him from then on: that he had a nose for money. The rest of us had uptilted, ski-chute noses, but Rian's pointed delicately down, designed to sniff out any glinting coppers or folded bills.

*

Going back to Granny and Grandpa's after the carnival weekend in New York was like the minutes after *Dr Doolittle* had ended and the magical Doolittle world had gone black. My mother went straight back to lying in her room, smoking all day, calling down, 'Willy, has the mailman come yet?'

'No.'

A little later, 'Mailman come yet?'

Then, calling out the window to the back yard where I sat reading, my back against a tree trunk, and the boys were digging tunnels and canals in the mud, 'Asho, Cam, Rhidi, come here, I want you to do something.'

'Yes, Mummy?'

'Can you check to see if the mail has come yet?'

We would run to the front yard and check the mailbox. Once in a while, we found thin blue airmail letters with my father's spiky handwriting on them. When we asked how he was, she would snap that he was fine, just fine, wasn't he? He wasn't stuck in this house with Lilly and Willy and three goddam children. The letters Mummy was looking for, though, were in a different handwriting that we didn't recognise and had Iranian stamps and an Iranian return address but no name. Sometimes the letters turned her eyes a light milky blue and she lay on her bed, pensively thinking and smoking. Other times, she leaped up and said, 'Come on, let's go pick blueberries!'

Our days continued as formless as the clouds that drifted overhead that warm, humid summer. We continued to sleep on the mattresses. Where we bathed I don't remember because the only tub, downstairs off the kitchen, was filled with World War Two flour sacks, each printed with a different design. We were happy to have regular food: hot dogs and beans, canned soups and Spaghetti Os – whatever my grandmother picked up in the dented-can bins.

*

'Isn't she beautiful, kids?' asked my mother, rubbing the car's warm smooth flanks. 'Jessie. I am going to call her Jessie. The first car I've ever owned myself.'

'A Ford Fairlane Station Wagon. Nice car, Joanie. I think it's just what you need,' said Joe.

She had bought Jessie at the used car dealer with the giant American flag whipping and flapping high in the sky and the rows and rows of cars that had signs on them that said: 'Deal of the Week' and 'One Year Guarantee' and '$999.99!' Joe had checked the engine to make sure she was getting a good deal. I never thought to ask where she had found the money.

My mother baked Joe a pie to say thank you and he ate two pieces standing up.

'I'd never forget the taste of one of your lemon meringue pies, Joanie,' he said. 'I dream about your pies.'

'Blueberry, Joe! Her blueberry pies are the best. And her chocolate pudding, now that's real good,' said Willy. He stood next to the kitchen counter, eating his pie and drinking his coffee.

Lilly was always happy to see Joe. 'He was a good boy, Joan. Maybe if you had stuck with him, you wouldna had all of these problems.'

'Yeah, Ma, and lived on a chicken farm and been a goddam chicken farmer's wife. No thank you.'

After we had admired and stroked Jessie, my mother and Joe started loading the big trunk area in the back.

'Sheets, Lilly, sheets and towels. Willy, tell her not to give me any rags. Decent ones,' my mother called from the car.

'Dishtowels? Ask her does she need dishtowels!' screamed my grandmother.

We kids ran up and down the path, delivering whatever Granny unearthed from one of her many stacks. So it went, back and forth, as the car filled up. As we worked, we asked, 'Where are we going, Mummy?'

'Surprise,' she said. 'How much for the sheets, Lilly?'

'Take it, take it. Get it the hell out of the house. We got too much stuff,' said Grandpa.

'Fifty cents each.'

'Are you keeping track? Jesus Christ, I can't believe you're charging me for this crap,' said my mother.

'Lilly, just give the gal the stuff. You've got so much and she's got nothing,' said Joe. 'It's all second-hand already. She's your daughter.'

'And who gave it to me? I paid good money for it. If she don't want it, she don't have to take it,' said my grandmother, mopping her face.

Once or twice, I ran to the thrift shop down the hill to check – was there a frying pan? A can opener? As I ran, I puzzled about where we were going or what we were doing. My mother seemed to spend most of her days lying in bed, but I knew she was up prowling around during the night, unable to sleep. She must have been planning our escape then.

Sweat dripped down my mother's nose on to the pillows she wedged between pitted aluminium pots and rusted cast-iron skillets. Her hair clung in damp, dark snakes. Soon she jammed in the last items and tested to see whether the door would close.

'We'll keep all the stuff we need for the trip on the floor under the kids' feet,' she said.

'Fine, Joanie. You know what you're doin',' said Joe. 'You sure you don't want to stay? At least you have Lilly and Willy . . . and you have me, Joanie. You know you can always count on me.'

'Joe . . .' said my mother, stabbing her cigarette towards me.

Once again, 'Little Miss Pitchers'. She never told me anything and then she blamed me when I tried to find out.

'You see how Lilly and Willy are to me? Why would I stay in this cold place and freeze my ass off? No thank you. I left here a long time ago and I'm never coming back.'

*

With one hand on Jessie's red steering wheel and her other arm out the window with her cigarette, my mother said, 'Willy, tell me how to get to New York.'

'Go down Halls Hill, turn left, turn right at the gas station . . .'

At the gas station, she asked the attendant, 'How do you get to New York? Listen, kids, so we know the way. Uh-huh, left, right, straight for two miles.'

Her eyes glazed over. Right, straight, ask again, until many hours and many wrong turns later we were in Manhattan, asking how to get to Yosy's.

'Are we going to live in New York?' I asked.

'No.'

'Where are we going?'

'We're going to the only state in America I haven't been with your goddam father. Maybe that will give me some luck.'

When they had married, my father had answered an advertisement to drive an old lady's car from New York to California. This was the perfect honeymoon – they would be paid to holiday. The woman expected her car five or six days later with 3,000 miles on the odometer. When my mother and father arrived almost a month and many thousands of miles later, they had visited forty-seven of the forty-eight states. Hawaii and Alaska became states in 1959, the year after. During the trip they had fought relentlessly: my mother was distressed by his stinginess; his hygiene, for he showered in the morning and came to bed at night unwashed; and his manners – he read the newspaper at breakfast and went to the bathroom with the door open. Also, after only a week of marriage, he was putting pressure on her because she wasn't pregnant. Within a month of their marriage, there was almost no dimension on which she felt they were compatible.

One evening, after a long day's drive, they had stopped at a grocery store to stock up on food for dinner. At the checkout, my father had paid and walked out, leaving the bag for my mother to carry. My mother, furious, had also walked out and the two of them sat in the car in a stalemate, neither willing to carry out the bag of groceries. She left him in Texas, running out into the parking lot and down the highway in her night-gown where she was picked up by the police. She relented, though, because she discovered she was pregnant after all. Somewhere between the Big Apple and the Lone Star State, I was conceived.

*

I stared out the window, thinking about the trip I had taken to so many states in America when I was in my mother's belly. I wish I knew which one we had missed because then I would know where we were going.

'Stay here while I get Yosy.'

Our mother had revealed as we reached New York that Yosy had quit her job and was moving with us.

'Anyone need the bathroom?' she called as she ran up the stairs.

A few minutes later she came grumbling down, carrying two heavy suitcases, followed by Yosy lugging a carton and a small TV.

'Rosemary, there's no room in the car for all this crap. You told me you were bringing two suitcases and I only left room for that.'

After pushing, tugging and rearranging, we were off.

'You know the way, Rosemary? You've been there before?' my mother asked, as if we were driving around the corner to 48th Street.

'Patric, I've flown there. You know I'm hopeless with direc-tions.'

Cameron, now almost eight, took over the navigation. We still didn't know our final destination, but from time to time we stopped at a gas station and my mother and Cameron listened as a man with grease-covered forearms described and gesticulated. Then they leaped into the car, saying, 'OK, so we follow the highway to Exit 3 and then take a right (are you sure he said right?)'

We listened to the radio as we drove and a dozen times a day, from one radio station to the next, we sang 'Harper Valley PTA'. The warm-voiced DJs heralded each new city or state.

'Good morning, Baltimore. The weather is hot and sunny.'

'Hello, hello! This is Charleston and we're going to be "Killing You Softly with His Song" on this broiling-hot day in August. Man, is it warm today.'

'This is Savannah where we're in for a muggy day! Watch out for low-flying clouds.'

The harsh tones of the North-East were gradually replaced by the soft cadence of the South. We mouthed the new pronunciations, trying on the various accents.

'Ha, mah name is Ayshlay and ah am nan years owld.'

My mother and Yosy nattered in the front seat and from time to time Mummy called over her shoulder to us, 'How 'bout it, kids? Isn't this great?'

Our first stop each day was the International House of Pancakes where we got the children's 99-cent special: scrambled eggs, grits, two sausages and two buttermilk pancakes with a glass of milk. None of us liked grits, so Mummy just mashed together all of ours with butter and maple syrup for herself.

Dinner was at one of the wondrous fast-food joints next to the motel. As dark fell we kept our eyes peeled for whichever chain had a coupon for a free meal or a two for the price of one special: McDonald's, Kentucky Fried Chicken, Arby's Roast Beef Sandwiches, Dairy Queen. We had never eaten such glorious food: hamburgers on soft, squidgy white bread with delicious orangey sauce, chicken covered in thick crunchy breadcrumbs, soft ice cream dipped in a hard crust of chocolate. Perched on the piles on the back seat, belting out the new songs we were learning, and plumping up on good, old-fashioned, American fast food, we made our way to our new home.

'Welcome to the State of Florida,' we read on an immense sign.

'This is it!' we screamed. It was the last state on the map before we fell into the ocean, so even if Mummy hadn't told us, we would know that Florida was the place we were going to live. In any case, I should have realised she would head to the warmest state.

'No, not yet, kids, Florida is a big place, we have a ways to go.'

After a while, and certainly not as soon as we expected, we saw the beach and the water. Stacked in a layer of blue on white, just like a child's drawing, it looked totally different than the Caspian with its murky water and dark sand.

'Look at that, kids! That's what it's all about – that's why we came!'

Mummy swung Jessie into the parking lot and we raced down to the water's edge, leaping and prancing, kicking spray into each other's faces. She looked happy, her hair whipping in the breeze.

'Here, here! I want to live here!' I yelled near St Augustine on a desolate strip with enormous trees draped in Spanish moss like an enchanted forest.

'No, here, I want to live here!' cried Cameron when we passed Cape Canaveral with its NASA Space Center signs.

Rian jumped up and down on the back seat, crying, 'Me too! Me too!'

'So, kids, happy to be here? A little different from Iran, isn't it?' said my mother.

That reminded me. I hadn't considered our old life or even my father, despite the fact I had promised myself I would think about him every day. When we were in Connecticut, I had made myself cry each night by singing, 'My daddy lies over the ocean, my daddy lies over the sea,' to the tune of 'My Bonnie lies over the ocean'. I decided that for the whole rest of the drive I would do nothing but remember things about my father to make up for it.

17

Clack-Clack Boo-Hoo

'welcome to sunny
Florida, kids!'

Pulling up the blinds and gesturing out at the swimming-pool blue sky, the Crayola-yellow sun, the fluffy marshmallow clouds, the swaying green palms, my mother said, 'Well, kids, this is it! Isn't it beautiful? It's just like a postcard, isn't it?'

The Anchor Motel was paradise. We had a television and a pool and air-conditioning. Every morning my mother and Yosy checked in the newspaper for houses to rent and then we drove to look at them, circling neighbourhoods. Each day pot-bellied men with tattoos and skunk-haired women in house-dresses, in homes with the screen doors ripped off, where broken-down old cars were parked in front and dusty Coke bottles glinted in the sun-bleached grass, closed their doors firmly in our faces. Somehow two single women with three children, no jobs, no money and no credit history seemed a poor bet.

Finally, though, we were able to find a rental in the north-east section of Fort Lauderdale, just west of Dixie Highway and the railroad tracks. All night we could hear the clack-clack and boo-hoo of the freight trains as they hustled up and down the line that separated the fancy east side of the city bordering the beach from the west side. Rian and Mummy slept in one room in a big bed, Yosy and I were in another, and Cameron was on the porch. His room was called a Florida room, which meant that it had no heat, but my mother said that was why we had come to Florida, so that we didn't need heaters.

*

North Side Elementary School was one mile each way to our new house. We measured it on Jessie's odometer. The first day my mother walked with us so we would know the way. Every time she turned a corner, she would say, 'So you got that?'

I would turn to look at Cameron to make sure he knew because I was lost from the time we left the house.

'Wow, now that is cool. Class, check this out. So cool. Shake,' said Miss Hubeck as she flipped back a curtain of waist-length hair and offered me the tips of her long thin fingers. Her face was narrow and pale and she had brown eyes with very distinct lashes, like a fly's legs.

'Sit down over here, near Chip.' She waved airily, then read from the piece of paper that the principal's secretary had asked me to give her. 'So, it says here that you are from Iran and that you are nine years old. That must be a mistake.' She looked up at me. 'How old are you, Ashley?'

'I turned nine in June.'

I realised that somehow, between leaving Iran and going to Connecticut, another birthday had come and gone with none of us noticing it.

'Wow you're really tall. That's too bad; they brought you to the wrong class.'

She scribbled a note and handed it to me.

'Chip, can you take Ashley back to Mr Limmee's office and tell them she needs to go into fourth, not fifth grade.'

I trailed behind Chip as we walked down the long open hall on the second floor. North Side was built like a Spanish hacienda with open corridors around a big central court. Chip was big, his solid bum wedged tightly into grey trousers, his hair a short, old-fashioned buzz cut and he wore thick, black-framed glasses. I immediately developed a giant, clanging crush on him.

'Now you tell Miss Hubeck that Ashley is too in the fifth grade,' said the secretary to Chip, her voice indignant. 'Mr Limmee ascertained she is very advanced, so we are skippin' the fourth grade. Didn't your mama tell you, honey?' She turned to me with this question.

I shook my head.

So back up we went and Miss Hubeck plonked me on to a table with Chip and Burt and Mark. After a year and a half I was finally in school.

*

The sun slanted behind the buildings on Fourth Avenue, as cars slipped out of the parking spaces behind the stores, accountant offices and car dealerships that lined our walk home from school. Now that we had been in Fort Lauderdale a few months, the heat was abating and late afternoons were cooler. Our dusty bare feet slapped against the littered sidewalk. I hated the feeling of the dirt on my feet and often we cut ourselves, but Mummy didn't want us to wear out our shoes, so we put them on only in school.

Cameron and I scanned the ground, looking for empty soda bottles. Dragging our rusty red wagon, we inspected the weeds on the side of the road, dug in garbage cans and climbed into dumpsters. We probed every pay phone and the ground around parking meters for dropped change. Finally, we came to our most regular pay-off – the milk machine in the parking lot of the liquor store, where workworn men opened their beer cans on the way to their cars. I loved the sound of the pop and fizz as they peeled back the tops. The palm trees rustled above us and a few red berries dropped with delicate plops on to the sidewalk. A thin line of dust was visible on Cameron's teeth where his lips parted.

I guarded the wagon while he stuck his hand into the coin receptacle of the milk machine, contorting himself to get really far down. I eyed the men in their cars to ensure no one was watching. We stopped by the parking lot on the way to school, after school and some evenings Mummy drove us over in Jessie just before we went to bed. Cameron fingered the money. The shiny silver quarters and dimes, the slightly duller nickels and the copper pennies still seemed beautiful and foreign to us.

'How much?' I asked.

'Five quarters!'

A good day.

The wagon was heavy. Cameron pulled more than I did. Although he was small and skinny, he was strong. We were on our way to the Minit Market, which was further away than the 7-Eleven, because the day before the lady at the 7-Eleven had yelled at us, 'Don't bring me these damn bottles you collect off the street. They's dirty and I have to wash them before the Coke guy come take 'em.'

Behind the counter at the Minit Market, the pimply teen-ager took our bottles.

'One, two, three . . . seventeen bottles. You kids did good.' He counted out our money.

We hurried home to make dinner before our mother arrived from picking up Rian from day care. She had taken pork chops out of the fridge and I had to jumble them in Shake 'n Bake and put them in the oven at 350 degrees. I put the peas in a pot and opened some apple sauce, sneaking in a couple of bites. It was pink and smooth and yummy. Some things in Florida were definitely good: being in school, even if I felt the odd one out, the library and living with Yosy. But I was surprised how much we all had to work – even little Rian – to have enough money for food and rent.

'OK, kids, table set? Good job on the leaves, Cam. Just pick up those last few by the tree roots. Rian, help Cameron while I get things organised.'

'Mummy we made eighty-five cents bottle collecting and a dollar twenty-five from the milk machine,' I told her as she took the pork chops out of the oven.

'Great,' she said, pointing to her waitress's apron jingling with tips. 'Count that and see how much we've got.'

'I can't believe I've got a degree in English Literature from Barnard and the only job I can get is as a nurse's aide,' moaned Yosy over dinner before leaving for the nightshift.

She was applying for jobs as a reporter but the work situation in south Florida the autumn of 1968 was dire. Yosy explained to my mother about unemployment and inflation. There were no teaching jobs. In fact, my mother was lucky she had a job at the coffee shop in Sears Town. She wore a white uniform, a scalloped black apron and clumpy white shoes with ridges on the soles that she had to buy at a special shop. She didn't mind waitressing because she liked the customers, the other waitresses and the fat Greek man who owned the coffee shop. Sometimes, though, I could see the veins in her legs jump and throb. If it had been a slow day and she hadn't made enough money even to pay for Rian's nursery, she sat at the table, staring at a piece of paper on which she had written lots of numbers, smoking one cigarette after another.

*

Mummy dropped us off in front of Jordan Marsh, the fancy department store. Christmas carols blared. In front of the store, Salvation Army Officers clanged brass bells and collected pennies in their red pots.

'Enjoy yourselves, kids! This is what it's all about!'

She gestured out the window to the blue sky, the waving palm trees and the bright winter sun. My mother loved Florida. She absolutely adored it. She said all the time, 'Moving here was the best decision I ever made in my life.'

In the store, we gazed at the clothes and toys as if they were items on display in a museum. We found 'Santa's Grotto' and lined up with the other children. Finally, the three of us were pushed forward by one of the elves and Santa lifted Rian on to one big, plush knee.

'Well, whadda ya'll want for Christmas?' he asked.

We hesitated. He suddenly remembered to add a loud 'ho-ho-ho' and I jumped, startling him. He seemed surprised by our silence.

'Come on, guys, you know the drill,' he said and began throwing out suggestions. 'A bike? A Barbie? A hula hoop? A slinky? Some Hot Wheels?' His eyes flicked from me to Cameron, then to Rian and then back again. 'C'mon, kids.'

It had been so long since we had received a present, a proper present wrapped in shiny paper, that we didn't know what to wish. I looked at Cameron and we shrugged at each other.

'Ri, you choose,' I urged.

'Yeah, do you want some Hot Wheels? Some klackers?' Cameron cajoled him.

Rian whispered into the shiny white nylon beard and Santa said, 'That's great, kid. Guys, look up now for the camera and smile.'

We looked up, blinded by the flash, and moved forward, collecting a present from his helper, a bouncy teenager in an elf hat. When I unwrapped it, I found a small striped candy cane and an advertisement: 'Family portraits in a variety of backgrounds for only $5.99.'

We wandered around, staring at all the Christmas displays and presents before heading to the front of the store. Our mother had said not to be late so she wouldn't have to run around the store looking for us.

'She'll definitely be here by the time a hundred cars pass.'

'She'll be here when thirty-five white vans pass.'

'She'll be here in two hundred red lights.'

We waited, rooted to the spot she had pointed out, shifting from leg to leg, jumping around doing the pee-pee dance, squabbling with each other, questioning whether we were in fact in the right place, wondering the time, asking passers-by the time, sitting on the kerb, singing, humming, playing I Spy and Twenty Questions, counting cars and traffic-light changes, until finally we gave up and just waited, staring at the sidewalk.

Since we had arrived in Florida, we had spent hours and hours waiting: not a few minutes or even half an hour or an hour, but great swathes of hungry, bladder-busting, itching-from-sitting-on-crab-grass, eyes-burning, book-long-finished time. Even though I knew my mother was always late, I still worried: maybe she'd had an accident, maybe she had been run over, maybe she'd been murdered . . . Maybe she'd gone back to Switzerland to meet her friend Nounou.

I was jerked out of my thoughts by a very tall man.

'Hugh Howard Hoffman Junior! Pleased to meet you!' he boomed, holding out a hand the size of a dinner plate.

The three of us flinched against one another, backs pressed together, facing out. Mummy had warned us about strangers. *Why wasn't Mummy ever on time?* Now this weird giant was bothering us. Even squatting down, which he was now, he was taller than I. His coffee breath gusted over us as he howled, literally howled, with laughter.

'Well, mah, mah, isn't this something!' He leaned towards us, smiling broadly.

We backed away in a surreptitious crab scuttle.

'Ah'm here to pick you kids up.'

I eyed the people passing, wondering whether anyone would help us.

My mother hadn't gone out, except for work, since we'd arrived. Other than Yosy and our neighbours, I hadn't seen her speak with anyone. She had warned us about people like this, told stories about people kidnapping Cameron enough times that I was not about to let this strange man anywhere close.

I knew that Cameron was first kidnapped when he was born, when a nurse had switched him for another baby. My mother had jumped out of bed, blood streaming down her legs, and torn up the maternity ward, looking for him. She finally found him on another floor in a broom cupboard, swaddled in a chador ready to be smuggled out. Then, when we were toddlers, we were playing at the feet of our servant in the street outside our house. 'Where's the baby?' asked my mother when she came out to check on us. In the distance, she saw a woman break into an awkward run. My mother chased after her, knocked her to the ground and grabbed Cameron from underneath her chador. A passing woman had simply picked him up, put him under her chador and took off.

I pushed Cameron and Rian further behind me towards the store entrance and stared beseechingly toward the Salvation Army men. Cameron thrust out his jaw and cocked a fist.

'Ha ha ha! Boy, are you kids cute,' said the big man. 'I've got Rosemary Jones over there in the car. Rosemary, give the kids a wave.' He yelled across the parking lot to a Cadillac so large it looked like one of the yachts that ploughed through the Intracoastal Waterway.

Yosy waved from behind the windshield.

I crossed over, holding Rian's hand, and Yosy introduced us. 'Ashley, Cameron, Rian, please say hello to Mr Hoffman.'

We shook hands and crawled into the back seat of the car, glancing at each other and smiling 'Boy, these adults

are weird' smiles at each other. As we drove, Mr Hoffman
told us jokes.

'Hey, what do they call a man with no arms and no legs
in a pool?'

'Don't know.'

'Bob.'

'No arms and no legs in a pile of leaves?'

'Don't know.'

'Russell.'

'On a wall?'

'Art!' we yelled.

'On the floor?'

'Mat!'

By the time we arrived at the house, he had done black and
white and red all over, elephant in the fridge and chicken
crossed the road. Mummy was picking leaves up off the front
lawn, a cigarette in one hand. She was obsessed with taking
care of our front lawn. It was vitally important to her that all
our neighbours, who also seemed obsessed by their lawns,
didn't think we were the kind of people who would neglect
our own.

'Hello, Mr Hoffman,' she said, shaking his hand when Yosy
introduced them.

Yosy sat with her tanned legs hanging out the side of the
car.

'I met Hugh at my singles' night,' she explained.

She wore a beige-and-white sleeveless dress and her
glasses, shaped like cat's eyes, made her look very glamorous. Mummy was wearing the same striped green shirt and
pedal-pusher trousers she changed into every day after work.
Her hair was frizzy and pulled back from her face with an
elastic band.

'He was on crutches then – you had just come back from
skiing in Alaska, right, Hugh?' asked Yosy.

'Well, that's right. And I sure am happy we did meet, Rosemary. Mah, mah, you have got bee-u-t-ee-ful children, Patric. How'd you get a name like Patric?' He stood at the door of his Cadillac and watched while Mummy finished doing the lawn.

When she finished, he followed her into the house and, within a short time, he and Mummy were laying out a hand of gin rummy on the kitchen table. Yosy headed out to her job at the hospital.

'Toodle-oo!' she called.

She had chosen the night shift so she could go to interviews during the day, and get some peace and quiet while we were all in school.

We kids looked at the cards over their shoulders and learned in short order that Mr Hugh Howard Hoffman Junior was a tax accountant, a multimillionaire, a Methodist, a Republican, that he came from Ohio, had a wicked stepmother named Alice who was exactly his age, that he was born on Valentine's Day 1924, had never been married, lived two streets away, had never touched a drop of alcohol in his life, drank only coffee and Coke and *nothing* else, ever, smoked sixty cigarettes a day, ate every meal in a restaurant, swam exactly one mile each morning at the YMCA pool, had weighed 210 pounds (plus or minus one pound and only one pound) since he graduated from college, and had owned a Cadillac, which he traded in every other year, since he was twenty-five.

Most excitingly, when he last went to Moss Brothers, where he bought all his clothes, he had discovered a new fabric: polyester. He had bought two new suits, as he did every season, and each night he showered fully dressed, except for his shoes. He told us he soaped up, then stripped off and hung up his suit, his shirt, his underwear and socks to dry.

'It's dry by the next morning, can you believe it? Come over here and feel this material.'

He held out his arm. The jacket was a pink-and-green paisley, which he wore with green trousers and a pink shirt.

'Well, ain't that somethin', kids, ain't that somethin'?'

He stopped by every day to play cards. We started calling him 'Uncle Hugh' and my mother called him 'Hoffer'. Within a week we were all working for him: my mother picked us up after her shift at Sears Town and drove us to the concrete-block house that was also his office. A rusty 'Hugh Hoffman Tax Accountant' sign stood in the parched grass outside. His living room was full of people reading newspapers, flipping through documents or drinking the instant coffee we prepared for them. While my mother worked in the office, checking tax forms, typing letters and filing, Cameron and I cleaned the house, mowed the lawn, Turtle-Waxed the Cadillac, polished shoes and mended shirts. Answering the phone was my favourite job: 'Hugh Hoffman, Tax Accountant,' I said in a grown-up voice.

Cameron, Rian and I stuffed ourselves on the brownies wrapped in cellophane that were stacked in the fridge and drank a concoction we made of Cremora and sugar dissolved in water. I really wished I could show my father the amazing things they had in America, like cellophane and Cremora and flip-top cans.

Uncle Hugh didn't have a stove and only a tiny fridge. During the 'season', as he called the three months in which he worked twenty hours a day preparing tax returns, he didn't eat anything other than dozens of cups of coffee, a few brownies, or individual-sized apple pies, and handfuls of Librium tran-quillisers. He kept two extra-large jars of them right by the typewriter. One was filled with green and black pills that were ten milligrams each and the other with green and cream pills that were twenty-five milligrams. When I took him his coffee, he would shake a pile into his hand, throw them into his mouth and gulp them down.

My mother would say, 'Throw me a couple, too, Hoffer.' She kept spare ones in her change purse to take when she felt nervous, and sometimes if we were misbehaving she made Cameron and me take one, too.

When I asked Uncle Hugh how he knew how many to take, he said, 'You can never take enough of these things, can you, Patric?' and they both laughed.

When the last client left, Mummy and Hugh broke out the cards and began their penny-a-point gin rummy game.

'Ha! I've got you this time! Knock with three,' my mother crowed, throwing down her remaining cards.

A tap on the door one evening was followed by a half-hearted rendition of 'Dashing through the snow on a one-horse open sleigh'. The kids, standing on the front step in their shorts and T-shirts, were nothing like the image I had of old-fashioned Christmas carollers from our British School books. After the first verse, they trailed off, looking at us expectantly. Uncle Hugh's thunderous claps echoed and he yelled, 'Merry Christmas, kids. God bless. Here's a quarter for each of you.'

The quarters clinked into a jar.

'Thank you, Mr Hoffman! Merry Christmas!' they called as they walked towards the next house.

Cameron and I exchanged glances. Their jar held as many coins as our mother's apron when she came home from her job at Sears Town every day.

'Uncle Hugh, Uncle Hugh! Those kids just walk around singing carols and people give them money?' asked Cameron.

'Yeah, that's right. It sure is nice to hear Christmas carols. Gets you in the holiday mood. God bless 'em,' he replied, concentrating on his cards.

We bundled up the envelopes we had been stuffing – at a penny each.

'Cam, do you remember any Christmas carols from school?'

'"Jingle Bells", the first verse at least, and "God Bless Ye Merry Gentlemen".'

'We only need to know the first verse.'

'Bye, Mummy. Bye, Uncle Hugh!'

We grabbed Styrofoam coffee cups from Uncle Hugh's kitchen and dragged Rian towards the back door.

We came back after a couple of hours with $15.

'Well, would you look at that, you are some smart kids,' marvelled Uncle Hugh, who had made every single one of his millions of dollars all by himself.

We crowded around Uncle Hugh. 'Do you think you could drive us?' we asked, 'Because the thing is, we just can't walk far enough and we only have another ten days until Christmas.'

Uncle Hugh pondered and my mother chastised. 'Don't take advantage,' she said. 'Hugh's busy with the tax season.'

'Tell you what, kids,' he said, 'I'll drive you every night between now and Christmas, except Wednesday night because that's my singles night. All I want from you is that you go to church with me on Sunday.'

*

Uncle Hugh drove slowly down the street as we went from house to house, singing, 'Give us some figgy pudding, and give it *right now*!' We were dressed in red shirts and the boys were wearing blue trousers. We loved ringing the door bell and crying, 'Merry Christmas!' Everyone was happy and friendly and, after hearing us sing, inevitably offered us a cookie or gave us a few coins.

One night as were driving down Federal Highway, Uncle Hugh yelled, 'Merry Christmas!' out the car window at the top of his lungs. I found it surprising that an adult man acted the way he did, especially someone who was a millionaire. A group of tipsy revellers emerging from a bar stumbled around, searching for the source of the greeting. Uncle Hugh gave a series of cheerful honks and they waved.

'Don't you think it would be good to carol in bars where people are feeling sad because they're all alone and drinking at

Christmas?' asked Cameron. 'Plus if they're drunk, they'll probably give us more!'

'Genius! You're a genius. Your mom been feedin' you fish heads, boy? Whoo hoo!' yelled Uncle Hugh.

With a sweeping U-turn, horn blaring, we pulled into the parking lot of the bar. Uncle Hugh waited outside because he was a Methodist and didn't believe in drinking alcohol. It was dark and smoky and smelled of beer. I could feel the music crawling up my legs like pins and needles. We began to sing. The music stopped abruptly.

'No kids allowed in here.'

We hesitated, took a breath and continued, 'God bless ye merry gentlemen, let nothing ye dismay . . .'

The bartender looked at us, her hands on her hips.

'Come yere. Come yere, kids,' drawled a man sitting in a booth by himself, his legs sprawled wide.

We walked over, clumped together, a six-legged organism.

He handed Rian a dollar (a dollar!). 'Come on, Sally, have a heart. Give the kids a break,' he called blearily to the bartender.

We sang as each customer fumbled for their money. When we finished, Sally handed us a dollar and kneeled down to Rian. 'Can I just have one little hug from you, angel face?'

Rian smiled, his arms stiff by his sides, as she wrapped her arms around him.

When we returned to the car, Rian held open the bag to show Uncle Hugh all the dollar bills.

'Holy moly! We've hit on a gold mine, kids. You're true Christians helping these people out. Me too, boy! I'll tell you, before I met you and your mama, I dreaded the Christmas season. It's a lonely time for a single man.'

*

Our mother bought a tree, silver and glistening, at one of the second-hand stores. We made paper chains and hung up old Christmas cards that she had collected. She posed us with the tree, taking pictures of us in our pyjamas, pretending that it was Christmas morning.

'Smile,' she said, 'do it as if you mean it!'

She saved money, and bought a big canned ham. She was going to stick pineapple and maraschino cherries on to it with cloves.

'Kids,' she said, 'you're going to have a wonderful surprise for Christmas.'

We went to Jefferson's department store and bought each of our teachers a tiny bottle of Fabergé Wood Hue toilet water, which my mother paid for with the nickels and dimes she collected in tips. I sneaked back afterwards and bought her a bottle, too, with the money that Cameron, Rian and I had made. We bought gifts for Uncle Hugh, Yosy and our grandparents, who had just arrived to spend the winter with us. We wandered around Jefferson's for hours, weighing up the options. We paid for the presents, but other than that, our mother was adamant, no matter how strapped she was, or how much we begged her, she would never take our money.

'I picked hundreds of gallons of blueberries when I was a kid and babysat all my life, and every penny went to Lilly and Willy. I'm not doing that to you kids,' she said.

On Christmas morning we awakened when it was still dark. Rian was almost frantic with excitement. He was four years old and this was his first proper Christmas. Cameron and I, at least, remembered Christmas in Iran when Daddy came home from the job the day before, and Father Christmas filled our green stockings with oranges, matchbox cars and small packs of Tutti Nashan chewing gum. Presents wrapped in coloured paper lay under our silver tree: a Hot Wheels car for Cameron and a tiny doll with lavender hair in a perfume bottle for me. For Rian there was a slinky. Uncle Hugh had given Mummy $5 for each of us and she had bought presents for him as well.

Yosy gave us each a book. Her sister Virginia had sent me a bracelet with tiny seahorses embedded in plastic.

After we unwrapped the presents, we ate pancakes and went with Uncle Hugh to church. When we came home, the whole house was full of the burny-sweet smell of the ham. We crowded around our little table in the back yard as Uncle Hugh, Yosy and Mummy all smoked and talked about how amazing it was to be sitting outside with an orange tree shading you on Christmas Day. My mother forced Grandpa to actually sit down and have his lunch, but he soon stood up, too nervous to relax after all these years of eating at the kitchen counter.

We didn't hear from my father that Christmas and I wondered whether he was celebrating or whether he and Araboochie, driving from one job site to the next, even knew what day it was.

18

The Squeaky Wheel

*in our
back yard*

After Christmas, the playing cards were put away and we all worked to get out my mother's resumé. Uncle Hugh and my mother had decided that, since there was a waiting list of hundreds at the central Broward County teacher employment office, they would bypass it. On the first day back after the holiday, each principal would find on their desk a letter from Joan Patricia Dartnell, elementary school teacher extraordinaire. Uncle Hugh typed, my mother corrected and signed, and I addressed envelopes and stuffed the letters. Cameron and Rian licked, cutting their tongues and groaning about the taste of the glue. As I folded, I caught glimpses: 'First-rate teacher, studied at Gesell Institute of Human Development at Yale University.'

'Mummy, is that where you learned about reverse psychology?' I asked.

I was often stumped by my mother, not knowing whether she was using reverse psychology or reverse reverse psychology.

'Uh-huh,' she said, preoccupied.

I turned back to the letter. 'Speaks three languages fluently, expert in early childhood development and learning.'

I remembered my father saying she should be teaching us when he didn't have enough money for our school fees and now I understood why.

'You don't have to take no for an answer, Patric,' said Hugh. 'It's the squeaky wheel that gets the oil.'

My mother laughed ruefully before putting on her waitress uniform and clumsy shoes for her shift at the coffee shop.

*

'Kids, I got it! I got it! The principal was very impressed that I applied to him directly – ha!'

My mother was jumping around on the front lawn.

'Bring in the bags,' she called over her shoulder. 'I'm going to call Hugh.'

We peeked in the brown Food Fair bags and saw a celebration feast of steak and ice cream and frozen raspberries.

'Hugh! Hoffer! I got it! Deerfield Elementary, yes, I know it's an hour drive, but what can I do? Hayward Benson is the principal and he's just received federal funding for this new Migrant Education Program. Yes, yes, for the children of the people who come to pick beans and tomatoes and oranges. They want to get the kids into school before they're four years old and we'll have them from eight in the morning, so their mothers can work, and we'll feed them healthy food and give 'em vitamins. It's all about enrichment. I don't care if it's some lefty Johnson holdover, it's a job. Yes, I think that the car can make it. I'll just keep an extra can of oil in the back. Five thousand buckeroodies a year, summers off, ten sick days, ten personal days. Thank you, Hoffer! Thank you.'

*

'Cam, my leg won't move.'

I dragged it each step, pulling it with my hands. My thigh was huge and burning. The mile walk to school seemed to take for ever. In class, I watched the flies buzz in the window frame, unable to concentrate. During PE, I hobbled around. That evening the tight skin of my leg ripped like a piece of paper and hot yellow liquid spilled out, trickling into my panties and on to the chair.

'Jesus H. Christ, we've got to get the pus out of that boil.' My mother bent over, sniffing my leg. 'We'll get the head out and you'll be fine,' she said as her hands grasped my thigh. I fell back against the chair. 'Cam, run and get a rag. Jesus Christ, what a mess.' She mopped up the thick yellow pus.

'Mummy, stop, please stop.'

'What is it with you kids and boils?' she asked. 'I'll just get the head out.'

As she pressed her thumbs together, pus poured out. It felt as though she was drilling into my leg with fire. 'Mummy, please, please stop, please.'

No matter how hard she squeezed, though, no matter how much of the disgusting porridgy pus came out, the elusive 'head' never appeared. She was convinced that it was the source of the infection, so every day after school she squeezed, forcing the pus that had built up overnight to boil out over my leg.

'Take her to the doctor,' begged Yosy. 'She's sick. She's got blood poisoning. There are red streaks going up her leg.'

'What's a doctor going to do that I can't? It's a boil. What we need is the Ichthyol ointment Martin gave us for Rian when we were in Khomsar.'

That summer of 1967 in the dank concrete hut by the tunnel, an enormous boil had erupted on the back of Rian's head, forcing him to sleep on his stomach for months and leaving him with a shiny bald patch. She had cured it by smearing the foul-smelling Ichthyol ointment on it. My mother thought that we Dartnells were different from other people, though – stronger – that we didn't need to bother with anything as self-indulgent as a doctor.

'The school nurse says I have to go to the doctor, Mummy. I have a fever,' I told her one day.

'I've had boils all my life. We just have to get the head out.' She grasped my leg and squeezed.

'Patric, it's beyond that now,' said Yosy, looking angry.

'But how do I find a doctor and how much will it cost?' asked my mother, pressing harder. 'You know I don't buy all that bullshit, Rosemary.'

*

Slumped against the smooth cool wall, with the air-conditioning whooshing the antiseptic, icy air of the doctor's office around my feverish leg, I dozed. She had given me a ten-milligram Librium when we were in the car, so I barely noticed when the doctor examined me. Yosy had brought me, finally, ignoring my mother's protests that I didn't need a doctor.

'Why haven't you been to a doctor?' Dr Dobbs looked like the Wizard of Oz.

'It's just a boil,' I whispered.

'Just a boil? You have a severe infection. You need penicillin.'

'My mother doesn't believe in doctors.'

'Well, she's a fool!' He turned to his supply table. 'Are you allergic to penicillin? I'll give you a dose straight into the leg to clear it up.'

He primed what looked like a veterinarian-sized needle, a thin stream of liquid spraying from the menacing tip.

'*Noooo!*' I screamed.

I remember my only previous experience of a doctor had been when I was five or six. Despite my mother's disdain for doctors, on this occassion she knew I needed treatment. I was playing on the wooden jungle gym at the American Club when I banged my chin on one of the struts. Suddenly one of the children started screaming and pointing at me. The entire front of my shirt was soaked with blood.

My mother talked her way in past the guards at the gates of Armish MAAG, the American military hospital, but then the receptionist barred the way. My mother assured her we were American and would pay, but the lady said that wasn't the point. 'Just anyone couldn't expect to get the same treatment as a member of the American Armed Forces.'

When a doctor my parents knew walked past, my mother begged him to help me, but he said, 'No, I'm sorry but the rules are the rules. If we took care of your child, I would have to do the same for every sick and hurt child on the streets of Tehran.'

At the Russian hospital they laid me on a table in a dark room. A female doctor came in – tall and heavy with grey hair in a bun, a thick tweedy skirt and a man's shirt. She raised my chin with one finger and squinted at it. Then she took a curved silver needle with a long thread in it and pushed it through the skin of my chin.

I screamed. I hit. I kicked. I bit.

The doctor shoved me back down, told my mother to hold me, then tried to ram the needle through again. I had all the strength in the world. I kicked away my mother's hands and pushed away the doctor's fingers. She glared at me and went out, leaving the needle and thread dangling from my chin. She returned with two men, each of whom took an arm and a leg. I bucked and screamed while she sewed five stitches into my chin. When she left the room, she told my mother in Farsi that I was a bad child and would never amount to anything.

The penicillin in my thigh worked. Within a few days, the centre of the crater imploded and filled with a white nugget.

My mother was distraught about the scar – much more so than about the boil that caused it.

'I made you perfect and now you're marked,' she cried. 'I forced the Pasteur Institute to give you your smallpox vaccine on the sole of your foot so your arm wouldn't be scarred and now look at you.'

She was convinced that no man would marry me now that I had a scar on my thigh.

19

Two Nickels

*North Side
Elementary School,
school picture*

My mother loved her job at Migrant Ed. She loved her boss, Mr Hayward Benson. She loved her assistant, Mrs Elizabeth Gregory. She loved the other teachers: Miss Liz Allen and Mr Robert Miller and Mrs Paula Shields. She loved all the leftovers that the kids couldn't eat, that she and the assistants split – the half-filled cartons of milk, the cookies, the sandwiches, and the hot dogs and beans, which she brought home for dinner.

Most of all, though, she loved the kids. Every day she tried to make their lives better. They baked, they sewed, they read poetry, they listened to classical music, they looked at photographs and art books, they cut pictures out of magazines, they closed their eyes and guessed what something was just by touching it. She collected things with texture, with smell, that made sounds when rubbed together. At the Salvation Army thrift store, she hunted for beautiful bottles, old records, *National Geographic* magazines, dried sea horses, flapper dresses and top hats . . .

She also loved her salary but she hated, hated, hated wasting it paying rent. She scribbled on the backs of envelopes, consulted her bank manager, spoke with Uncle Hugh about tax credits and the Florida homesteading laws. Then Mr Cippolone, our landlord, needed his house back and gave us just a month to find a new home.

'Ya gotta buy a place, Patric. You'll be poor all your life if you don't,' Uncle Hugh urged her.

'But, Hugh, I don't have two nickels to rub together.'

She called Lilly and Willy in Connecticut and they agreed if she paid them a higher interest rate than they were getting at the bank, and they could come down every winter they would lend her the money. Uncle Hugh drew up a payment schedule for $14,000. The day she signed the agreement to buy 715 NE 14 Place was one of the happiest in her life. She had left Iran just over a year ago and her children were well fed and in school and she had a job, a house and a car. Cameron and Rian shared one bedroom, while my mother and I had the other. When my grandparents came down for the winter and took over our room, we moved onto the sleeper couch in the living room.

Yosy could afford a studio apartment around the corner because she had finally found a job as a reporter at the Broward Times. She would take me to concerts, art exhibits and ballets, and then write reviews for the paper. Sometimes she would include funny things I said, such as, 'My young companion questioned whether the prima ballerina wasn't too large to be leaping into the arms of her diminutive male lead.'

*

We lined up on the lawn for our picture on the first day of school. Ready for sixth grade, I wore a white hair band and a purple-and-white dress with a wide skirt.

'Smile. I'll send this picture to your father,' said my mother.

As we walked to school, I thought about him. I couldn't believe we hadn't seen him in so long. Soon it would be a new decade: 1970. America had a new president, we were all going into new grades, and my father had never even been to Florida.

In his letters, he asked me to describe my life, to tell him how I spent my days, to let him know how my mother and the boys were. He said he needed me to be the letter writer for the whole family. When he wrote to me, though, he didn't tell me anything about himself or his life – he just filled his letters with lots of questions, so I knew he didn't know what to say to me, any more than I knew what to say to him.

As I climbed the stairs to my new classroom, I found it hard to believe that I had ever lived in Iran or had a father at all. On the other hand, I definitely didn't belong in Florida.

*

'It's a fight, a fight between a nigger and a white!' the boys and girls in my class chanted as they pushed into a crowded circle on the playground.

'What's going on?' I stood towards the back.

'Janie and Meg Waters are fighting!'

I stared over the heads of my classmates. Janie's cheeks shone like polished cherrywood in the sun. Meg glared at her with bloodshot eyes. It was an unfair fight and I didn't understand why nobody was stopping it. Although Janie was bigger, loose-limbed and powerful, she was dim, with big blank eyes and a braying laugh. Meg didn't do well at school, but it wasn't because she was stupid – far from it: she was as wily and as sly as the ferret she resembled. She was a bad kid. All the Waters kids were. They were all slices of the same greasy pie: slick and pimply on the outside and watery evil on the inside. From the day I had arrived, she had picked on me, so I tried to avoid her.

They faced each other. Janie, towering over Meg, was staring dreamily beyond the softball diamond. Jerome, the only black boy in our class, gave a signal, and suddenly I heard Janie howl, a giant cry of indignation. Like a brown jacket unzipped to reveal soft rosy velour beneath, a long pink line extended the length of Janie's arm. Meg had scratched her with something sharp and the blood welled up almost instantly. The mood changed from hot fizzy excitement to hot heavy distress. Janie was hurt and none of us wanted Janie hurt. We didn't want the long cut, the milky tears, the wide, calling mouth.

Jerome put his arm around her. 'You awright, Janie?'

Mr Edwards, our gym teacher, polyester shorts hugging his big butt, huffed over.

'What is going on?'

He grasped Janie's arm at the elbow, his fingers below the wound.

'Y'all should be ashamed of yo'self, pickin' on a girl like Janie.'

Mr Edwards was the sole black teacher in the school. He had been extra-nice to me, helping me with the rules of some of the games, and showing me what a sit-up was.

We dispersed sullenly. Nobody had ever told me what was wrong with Janie, but it wasn't hard to tell that there was something. She was eleven years old and she didn't know how to read or write. She just sat in class, chuckling to herself and slowly turning the pages in her picture books.

'What was the fight about?' I asked Jerome, for I liked Janie and I didn't like Meg at all.

'It about you.'

'*Me?*'

'You know how Meg think you stupid and she allays say bad things 'bout you? Well, Janie, she say you OK, just too baby, and leave you be, and Meg say you wanna fight and Janie she say yeah.'

I was horrified that even Janie thought I needed protection, although I understood why: all my dresses were big puffy ones with smocking from the Salvation Army. I wore my hair in ponytails, I ate everything on my lunch tray and I didn't know anything about what was on TV. Perhaps worst of all, I loved school and happily did all the work.

'But why? Why would Janie fight for me?'

'Because when you read with us.'

Our teacher had set up a reading group where a few of us would read with the kids who couldn't read well.

'But all I do is read with you.'

'But you don't ack like we're dumb.'

I knew that a lot of the white kids didn't like the black kids. They thought it wasn't right that black kids came to the same school. There was a rigid pecking order in the classroom: white kids on top, then the two Puerto Rican kids, and last of all the three black kids. Even the mean white kids like Meg ranked higher than the black kids. I was white, but I was foreign, I had a weird accent, I read too many books. It was clear that all my efforts to wedge a place for myself in the social structure of our classroom hadn't worked if Janie had to defend me.

*

I really wanted to love Florida the way my mother did, but for some reason, and I knew it wasn't fair, I hated everything about being here. I didn't have a father? My mother worked eighteen hours a day and barely slept? We regularly checked the dumpster behind Food Fair for out-of-date food? It was all because we had left Iran and my father and come to Florida. My mother's constant chorus of 'Kids, isn't it gorgeous here?' didn't help. So what if there was a beach and palm trees and it was sunny all the time? We didn't enjoy them because we were too busy working.

20

I Won

*Uncle Hugh's
birthday*

A man leaped in just as I pushed the button to go up to Yosy's office at the *Broward Times*. I could see him reflected in the mirror in the elevator. He had stiff steel-grey hair, silver-wire frame glasses and wore a tie.

'My name is Tom Glenn.' He laughed awkwardly. 'What's your name?'

I looked at Yosy and she gave me an impatient nod.

'Oh, that's a very impressive name. Anybody ever call you Lee?'

'No, why would they?' I asked. I had never imagined that Lee was a nickname for Ashley, nor that my name was 'impressive'.

'You sure you don't have a nickname?' he persisted. 'Something your friends and family call you?'

'Yes, but that is what my friends and family call me.'

I thought I said it in a well-mannered way, but as soon as I said it, I could see that both he and Yosy thought I had a smart mouth.

'Oh well,' he said, 'you'll have to meet my daughters; they're your age.'

I smiled politely as we walked towards Yosy's desk.

'See ya soon, Ash-*lee*,' he said, giving me a wink. 'Get it?'

I nodded.

At Yosy's desk, I asked her why 'that weird guy' had talked to me.

'Oh, don't be so rude! He only asked your name, for Gawd's sake,' said Yosy, her fingers rapidly tapping the keys of her typewriter.

Yosy was writing an article about an artist who lived in Davy. He had done a pastel drawing of me that morning as she interviewed him.

'Sorry, Yosy. I'm sorry.'

I didn't want to annoy her. Yosy was my only friend. Some weekends when she went to Delray to visit her sister, she would take me and sometimes I would help her clean her flat and make jello for her.

'He sells advertising,' Yosy said, 'and he has two beautiful girls your age.' She said this as if the two were linked.

*

Tom was holding a bottle in a brown paper bag, which he handed to my mother as soon as he got in the front door. Yosy had decided that the whole family should meet the Glenns that Friday night. My mother had made chicken curry and rice, bought beer and put a glass in the freezer. We were amazed by this because she had never tasted alcohol and in Iran she had once even turned down a dare of $10,000 just to have a sip of champagne.

Tom acted as if he and I were old friends. Yosy introduced my mother and the boys and we all shook hands. His daughters Dana and Jacqueline both had wide faces with freckles and lots of blonde hair. Tom figured out while we were all still standing around that Dana was seven months older than I and that Jacqueline was the same age as Cameron. It was as if someone had pushed a button on my mother's back. She laughed, talked and poured beer into the frosty glass for Tom. She was so friendly to Dana and Jacqueline that I was sure they would realise she was just putting on an act.

We finished off the chicken curry even though she had used two whole chickens. I listened to everything: that the Glenns were from New Jersey; that they had been in Florida for about the same time as we had; that they lived in south-east Fort Lauderdale; that their grandmother lived near by; that Tom had sold advertising for a newspaper in New Jersey before he came to Florida. There were things I didn't learn, though, things like: did Tom have a wife and Dana and Jacqueline a mother? And, if so, why wasn't she here and what exactly was Tom doing over at our house, eating our food and putting his big feet on the coffee table that none of us was allowed to put our feet on, not even wearing socks, never mind big, clunky, brown street shoes?

As they were leaving late that night, long after Yosy had gone, saying, 'It's past my bedtime,' after we five kids had cleaned up the kitchen, run around outside and played Monopoly for hours, Mummy kissed Tom on both cheeks and said, 'Thank you, good sir,' and then she kissed Dana and Jacqueline goodnight. I felt absolutely sick to my stomach.

'*Thank you, good sir?*'

'So, next Friday night then.' Tom waved as he led the sleepy girls to the car.

*

I had a long list of things to do: peel and fry the onions, cook the hamburger meat, make the salad, get out the cans of vegetables, set the table, clean the bathroom, make the beds, and wash the kitchen floor. Cameron was busy outside, picking leaves off the lawn, cutting the grass and washing the windows.

As soon as my mother got home with Rian, the two of them got started Turtle-Waxing Jessie.

This had become the pattern since the Glenns started coming over every Friday night. When they arrived, I went outside and helped as well. Tom filled a glass I had chilled, rolled up his sleeves, took off his tie and then he and Mummy sat and smoked in the chairs on the front balcony as we washed Jessie and Tom's Pontiac.

When we were done, they came over to inspect the cars and make us do the bits that were still streaked. It felt as if we did each whole car over and over, and I mumbled under my breath to Dana that it would probably just rain anyway. 'What?! What was that?' My mother leaped towards me, angrily, her hand raised.

My mother and Tom both agreed that we had to learn how to 'do a job *properly*'. They agreed on lots of things about how to raise children: children should be seen and not heard; spare the rod, spoil the child; early to bed, early to rise; if you give an inch they'll take a mile; and children should eat what is on their plates.

The worst was the eating what was on your plate. Cameron hated sweet potatoes. Since it was the single thing he didn't like, I suggested to my mother that she just not serve them. She thought it was an important lesson for Cameron to eat them, though, so we had them almost every Friday night. She was adamant: he had to learn to eat sweet potatoes. Tom agreed.

When Cameron came into the kitchen and saw me opening the cans of sweet potato, his eyes filled with tears but his fists clenched at the same time.

'Eat the goddam potatoes!' Tom straddled Cameron who was on the ground next to the table. 'Eat 'em.' He pushed the sweet potatoes into Cameron's mouth and Cameron struggled, spitting them out and biting Tom's fingers.

Whap. Tom slapped Cameron across the face.

Cameron spat out again.

Whap. Tom hit Cameron across the other side of the face.

Rian, Jacqueline, Dana and I watched while my mother sat smoking at the table. 'Easy does it, Tom.'

Whap.

Cameron's face was red and his hair was soaked.

Whap.

Sweet potato was all over his face, inside his nostrils, in his mouth.

'Tom, be careful of the carpet. Don't stain it,' said my mother.

Rian was crying.

'Eat it!'

'No!'

Tom raised a fist. I caught my breath. 'Stop! Make him stop!' I screamed, my voice wrenching out of me. 'Make him stop!'

My mother stood and said, 'OK. That's enough. Cameron, you're not leaving the table until you eat it.'

As she turned away, Tom punched Cameron. She scraped sweet potato off the table and put it in a bowl. 'Don't get up until you eat that.'

Cameron sat at the table all evening. We kept going back to check on him. They could kill him and he would not eat the sweet potato. That was what I was afraid would happen. Even long after Tom and the girls had left, and Rian and I were asleep, he sat there. He told me the next day that he never cried and he never ate the sweet potato.

'So, I won.'

21

I've Got Something to Tell You

*Fort Lauderdale
beach*

'Get off the bedspread, Asho!'
I was lying on the pink, prickly bedspread that we had
bought from the previous owners, along with the beds, when
we acquired the house. My mother was obsessed with the
bedspreads. I couldn't see the point of a bedspread if you didn't
use it to keep warm or to keep the sheets clean when you lay
on the bed. We did not use these cotton candy-pink bedspreads
for either of those purposes. Rather, we folded them back
carefully at night as if they were an altar cloth or the American
flag. And we never, ever sat on them.

'Mummy? You know Robert, the guy who's doing the newspaper with me?' Robert and I had been working together most
of seventh grade on the school newspaper – I was the editor

and Robert did the production. 'Well, he works in the guidance office at lunch. Because he knows how to type and
everything, you know?'

'Ashley, what?' She was moving around the room, putting
things away, brushing her hair, opening drawers, closing them.

'Well, you know, because he works in guidance, he can look
in everybody's file.'

'Stop saying, "you know".'

'Well, anyway. He looked in this special file at the results of
the test that everybody in the school had to take and he said
that I have the highest IQ in the whole school.'

I had a hard time keeping a giant smile from bubbling out of
me. I had the highest IQ in the school! I had sung these words
to myself all the way home from school.

'What is it?'

I told her.

'No!'

'Why? What's wrong?' I could tell she wasn't happy.

'Nothing, I just would have expected it to be much higher.
Mine is *much* higher. They tested it when I was at Gesell. I
would have thought yours would be higher. Your father is . . .'
She trailed off.

I knew what she was thinking. Despite his many flaws, she
couldn't fault my father on his intelligence, his education, his
looks, his height, his athleticism. All the reasons she had
married him. Somehow, though, these attributes had all been
diluted when they passed on to me. Disappointingly, I was
nothing like her.

'Anyway, it's fine. I just would have expected it to be
higher.'

She looked at me in a way that suggested this information
explained a great deal.

'But, Mummy, Robert said that it is the highest in the whole
school, that in the whole of America I am one of the smartest

people.' I was gutted. 'Anyway, if you're so smart, what's yours?' I asked.

'He shouldn't have told you. Knowing your IQ changes everything. Forget it and don't ever tell anyone, especially the boys. And I will *never* tell you my IQ, ever.'

'Oh.'

'Now go and clean the bathroom. Really scrub the ring in the bathtub and the corners of the floor by the wall.'

I folded down the corner of my book and got the cleaning supplies. I scrubbed the greasy ring around the bath, dusting the bottom of the tub with Ajax, which turned blue as it touched the water and left a harsh grit in the tub if I didn't rinse well. When I finished the bath, I started on the floor.

*

'Willy, these kids are driving me crazy!'

It felt as if my grandmother had been screaming every minute since my mother had picked her up at the airport. This was the third winter they had come down and we were all pretty tired of it.

'My sugar is going up! I can feel it! Get me my testing kit! I need my pills! Get my insulin! These goddam kids! *Willy!*'

She spoke in millions of shrill exclamation points.

Willy shambled over and, using all his strength, hefted her out of the chair.

'Willy! Stop shaking! You're driving me crazy with all your shaking! Shake shake shake. All night and all day. First your hands and then your head and now your voice! Stop shaking, you stupid old man!' She hobbled out. 'Asshole.'

Once again, my grandparents had moved into my mother's and my bedroom, and we had moved into the living room and on to the Castro Convertible. When the Glenns came on Friday nights, Dana slept on the sofa bed with me and Jacqueline on the cushions on the floor. When Tom left at one or two in the morning, he hauled them out of their sleep and into the car, pushing them in front of him. Then my mother climbed in and smoked, falling asleep before Willy stumbled out at about 3 a.m. He sat in the big wicker chair at the foot of the sleeper couch, his knees bumping the end of the bed. Pretty soon, he would start snoring. Not delicate, grandfatherly snores, but huge, Paul Bunyan and Babe the Blue Ox snores.

'Grandpa!' I would shake him. 'You're snoring.' A few minutes later, I would awaken with a start and we repeated the whole process.

The next day my grandmother would scream at my mother that I had kept Willy awake all night. My mother could sleep through anything, so she missed the whole thing – the snoring, the waking, the snoring, the waking.

*

Cameron and I looked at each other and shrugged. Not again.

Every day by the time my mother got home from school, Lilly had a long list of things to tell her that we had done wrong. This time it was a fight for the television. Before they came, we didn't own a television but, this winter, my mother worked even longer hours at Uncle Hugh's office after school so she could buy them one at the Salvation Army. Most days we watched *The Friendly Giant* and *Mr Roger's Neighbourhood* from 5 to 5.30. Then we would have dinner and my grandparents would watch the local news, while Huntley and Brinkley went on about Nixon and inflation and the POWs. Recently there had been an oil spill off the coast of Florida from an oil tanker leak.

I went into the kitchen to look at the clock on the wall over the stove. I opened the cans and dumped peas and corn into the bumpy old pots. I counted out hot dogs – ten – and put them in a saucepan. I boiled water for my mother's tea. It was almost 6 pm. Where was Mummy?

'See? See what you kids have done to me! My urine is red!' My grandmother had just peed into a cup to check her sugar levels.

'Granny, it's not us. You ate a huge Hershey bar!' said Cameron.

I heard them squabbling from the kitchen. I looked out the back window and plotted about more ways we could get back at her. We did all we could. Cameron played his electric guitar as if he were auditioning to be in a rock band; when I hung her laundry to dry, I didn't hang the undies in the special way she had taught me so that the crotch was bleached by the sun; we put burrs in her clothes and bedsheets; and we hectored her constantly: 'I don't think you should eat that chocolate, that Danish, that roll, that piece of toast,' whatever it was that she was gobbling, 'because it will raise your blood sugar, Granny.'

'Little bastard!' she screamed at Cameron.

I glanced at the clock. 6.10 p.m. Where *was* my mother?

I set the table, putting Granny at the head, as far away from me as possible, for she was a rapacious thief, her fork darting out to grab a tasty piece of pork chop, a soft white Holsum roll. Grandpa, who ate a packet of hot dogs, a can of beans and a dozen sugar doughnuts each day, would stand hunched over the kitchen counter, wolfing his food down and choking.

6.15 p.m.

Granny nagged Grandpa relentlessly. 'Stop eating that garbage, you'll get boils!' And he did get boils, as if she had cursed him, all over his speckled bald head.

6.30 p.m. She was almost two hours late. Yosy walked through the front door as I put out the food.

'Kids, I have something to tell you,' she said. Turning to Granny, she snapped, 'Lilly, turn off the TV!' Then she continued, 'Your mother's in the hospital. Eat your dinner, brush your teeth and go to bed. I'll come over tomorrow afternoon to see if you need anything. Ashley, can you get everybody off to school tomorrow?'

Granny started screaming, 'That little bitch won't listen to me, Yosy! I told her not to put the vegetables into the pots so early. In this heat, putting food out!'

I looked at Granny. Hadn't she heard Yosy say that Mummy was in the hospital?

'Yosy,' I interrupted, 'what's wrong with Mummy?'

'See what I mean, she never listens to me! Rosemary, make her listen!' Granny's voice was a high-pitched whine.

'Yosy? Is Mummy all right?' I asked.

Granny grappled her way out of the chair and stumbled towards me. I flinched, sure she was going to hit me.

'You little bitch,' she rasped.

Something uncorked in me. I felt a wave of hot molten anger flow out of the depths of my guts, an anger that had been building for days or maybe even longer – months or years. I heard myself screaming, a plate clutched in my hands, 'Just shut up shut up shut up! Mummy's in the hospital and we don't even know why. *Shut up!*' I lifted the plate.

'Rosemary, make her stop! She can't talk to me like that!' Granny lurched forwards, her hand raised.

I felt Yosy gently pull me back. She took the plate and drew me into the kitchen.

'Ashley, it's a *woman's* problem,' she whispered, expecting me to understand. She finished setting the table and sat down in Mummy's place. 'Hot dawgs, ugh! Do you guys live on hot dawgs? You're going to turn into hot dawgs.'

Rian laughed until he cried, sobs bursting out of him like great big hiccups. Tears streaked his cheeks. He looked at us, trying to figure out how upset he should be. He was only six years old. My grandmother hobbled to the table, her eyes darting around, investigating our plates. I didn't understand how she wasn't concerned about Mom, who was her daughter, after all. Seeing I wasn't eating, she snatched my plate and began devouring what was on it. I was eleven and, unlike Rian, I knew how upset I should be. I could see that Cameron had a scared look in his eyes.

After dinner, Yosy helped me clean up and while we washed the dishes, she explained that my mother had been teaching when she had suddenly collapsed. 'She's been sick a long time, you know, bleeding . . .'

I rinsed the plates automatically. Bleeding? I hadn't seen any blood. Where was she bleeding? She was never sick. She saved up her sick days so she could go to the thrift shops during the week, before other customers had a chance to take the best things.

'Can we go visit her?' Cameron had come in and was emptying the garbage.

'We'll see how long she's in and how she's doing. She doesn't want to see anyone right now. She's not too well,' replied Yosy, wiping her hands. 'Tomorrow pack some clean nightgowns for your mother,' she yelled as she was leaving, 'the hospital ones are too skimpy.'

'Close the door before all the mosquitoes get in!' Granny screamed at Yosy.

Cameron, Rian and I brushed our teeth and went to bed silently. Without Mummy reminding us, we all took our fluoride pills.

*

When I opened the dresser drawer for the nightgowns the next afternoon, I realised that I had never looked in there before. Since I cleaned and scrubbed every single inch of our house, I thought I knew every corner.

Nightgowns and pyjamas were folded neatly and scented from the empty perfume bottles nestled between them. Hm, I hadn't realised she had brought the sea-foam nightgown from Iran, the one she had worn with Martin. Beneath it was a gold-flocked box, the kind you get in fancy dress shops. It wasn't filled with some antique lacy thing she had bought at a thrift shop: whatever it contained slid heavily backwards and forwards. Inside I found a pile of envelopes. There were white ones with stamps and also pale-blue airmail ones with stripes of red and blue around the edges. They were type-written, not addressed in my father's elegant angular handwriting.

I opened the first letter. Page after page of single-spaced, typewritten words. My eyes raced back and forth. Words and phrases leaped out at me. Things like 'I love you, I want to marry you, I want children with you, you are the most beauti-ful woman, you are gorgeous, glorious, glamorous.' The words crowded the pages. Handwritten notes jammed the edges.

I turned to the last page: 'love, Martin'. My hands shook.

In one letter he told her he had been thrown into jail because my father owed him money and he hadn't been able to pay his own debts as a result. The police had arrested him while he was at the dentist, having two root canals filled. In jail, he had been in so much pain, he had battered his head against the wall attempting to knock himself unconscious. He wrote that he wanted to kill my father, that he had led the police to where he was hiding. I tried to find the dates on the letters. Were these recent? Was my father endangered still? Was Martin's arrival imminent?

A shadow fell over me and I realised I was in Fort Lauderdale, at 715 NE 14 Place, sitting on the scratchy pink bedspread that I was strictly forbidden to sit on, and that I was supposed to be getting out my mother's nightgowns, not reading love letters from Martin to my mother.

'You know that's none of your business.'

Yosy pulled the box from my hands, stacked the envelopes inside and put it back under the nightclothes. I knew from the letters that Yosy had known all along that my mother had planned to divorce my father and marry Martin. I wondered why, if she had known that, she had introduced my mother to

Uncle Hugh and then to Tom. Not that my mother had been interested in Uncle Hugh that way at all.

Once when I asked my mother directly, she just shook her head and said, 'Me with Hoffer? No way!'

I helped Yosy get the things together and put them in a little bag. When she left, I sank down on the bed, staring at the drawer with the letters in it. I was tempted to finish reading them, but I was scared. Not of Yosy catching me: I knew she was on her way to the hospital. I was scared about what else I might find out.

My mother had always said that our father was going to come to Florida to live with us. That as soon as he had enough money he would come and build a duplex apartment in the backyard behind our house, and that he and my mother would rent out the apartments and make enough money to live. Now I knew that she and Martin had planned to meet here, after he divorced Brigitte. I felt like a bird that had flown into a window; my path had looked clear but I was lying on the ground, knocked out. I didn't know what the situation was now, though. Whether Martin was still coming. What was going on with my father.

What about Tom? The one time I had gathered the courage to ask my mother whether they were boyfriend and girlfriend, she had acted as if I were a complete idiot.

'I'm a married woman, you know,' she had said, with her usual hauteur.

Now she was sick; I worried she would die. All those millions of cigarettes she smoked had finally given her cancer. If only I could just visit her, I thought, and see her and make sure she was all right.

Then I remembered another hospital scene. It was one of my earliest memories: 20 January 1964. I was four and a half and Cameron three. My father was taking us to visit my mother in the hospital to see the new baby, a boy – the boy that grew up to be Rian. After a long drive through Tehran, we reached a big hospital that looked as if it had been crying: tears of rust streaked down from the bars that protected each window. Inside, the hospital was just as sad as it was outside. We trudged up staircase after staircase, my father taking the steps two at a time, a posy of pink carnations held behind his back. Cameron and I scampered to keep up. We tiptoed down a freezing hallway that stank of smoking kerosene and boiled rice.

My father said, 'Quiet! No children allowed!'

Cameron and I laughed; it was funny – a hospital where babies were born and there were no children allowed.

'*Mobarak, Khanoom eh* Dartnell,' said my father as he peeked around the corner of the door, his flowers thrust forward. He smiled his special foxy smile that he used with my mother, with the corners of his mouth closed.

We thought this was funny, too. He was saying congratulations to her in Farsi and calling her Mrs Dartnell.

'Get the hell out of here, Malin!' she screamed. The sound tore through the corridor. We stopped laughing and peered around to see if anyone had heard.

'I've just been ripped in two giving birth to your goddam baby and you bring me a lousy bunch of carnations and think everything is rosy. Get the hell out of here! I don't want to see you, mister!'

'Genie, I've got the children.'

'Take them away! I don't want to see them! My insides have been torn out, I'm bleeding to death, and you show up with a bunch of cheap flowers. Get the hell out, you bastard!'

Actually, I realised, thinking about her reaction all those years ago, it was probably better not to visit my mother in the hospital. But in any case, she never asked for me. Some days later, Tom brought her home. She leaned on him as he helped her up the path. She had lost weight. She settled into her favourite chair, asked for a cup of tea and began calling her friends. I garnered what I could as she regaled them with the drama of her illness.

'I bled like a stuck pig. I collapsed from losing so much blood.' Sitting with her feet up and smoking, filling her ashtray with butts, she said, 'The tumour was the size of a grapefruit. The doctor had never seen another like it! Hold on a minute.' She paused to call out to me, 'Bring me some more tea, Ashley,' then continued, 'It weighed five pounds! The biggest they've ever seen. The doctor says I have to quit smoking, go to a smoker's clinic at Holy Cross.'

It was clear that my mother had narrowly missed dying. The words 'tumour' and 'cancer' were practically synonymous to me. I watched her like a hawk over the subsequent months, beginning a campaign of hiding her cigarettes and telling her that the lady at the gas station wouldn't sell cigarettes to underage kids any more.

*

'Allo, allo! Thees ees a telephone call from Iran. Plees hold on.' The line sounded as if it were raining all the way from Fort Lauderdale to Iran.

'Hi, Daddy!' I called down the line, my shrieks probably audible to him without the aid of the phone cable under the Atlantic. We had been in America for three years and our only contact with my father had been a letter every month or so and a few phone conversations.

My mother grabbed the telephone, her lips tight and her pupils dilated. 'When are you going to send us money? Have you got your passport yet?' She held the receiver against her shoulder while she lit a cigarette and I could see her fingers tremble. 'You and your goddam promises. Did you know I almost died? That I've been in the hospital? You don't even know your children – Ashley is five feet nine and weighs a hundred and thirty pounds. Yeah, well, that's what twelve-year-old girls look like, buster.'

Subsequently, three sets of gold Cross pens arrived in the post. We were thrilled, but my mother was cynical.

'What the hell are you kids going to do with gold pens?'

Then one day as we ate dinner, our mother said, 'We're going to Iran this summer to visit your father.' She pronounced the word 'father' as if it were an epithet.

The boys and I raced around the house dancing and screaming, 'We're going to see Daddy! We're going to Iran!'

My mother sat at the table, smoking, and looked at me speculatively. 'So you really care about him?' she asked.

'No!' I said immediately. Then I hesitated. 'I guess, I guess so, he's my father.'

Iran, Summer 1971

my father on the job site

22

Like Family

the Reza family garden

I wanted to hate him, but as soon as he sauntered into the waiting area of Mehrabad Airport, his big loose-limbed walk instantly recognisable, his wolfish grin exactly the same, I stopped trying. He was so easy and fun. He teased us and held us, wiggling, as he poked and tickled; he clasped hands when we walked, blew his Nescafé breath in our faces, and whiskered us with his beard stubble. He told us funny stories about when we were little. He made up poems about us: 'Twinkle, twinkle, little Cameron, way up high, up in heav'n,' and 'Rian was a lion brave and bold, walked through the forest hot and cold.' With 'Ashley' he had more difficulty. 'Let me think a bit,' he said.

He acted as if he had seen us, if not yesterday, then just a short time before. He had rented a house in Tehran from an American family who had gone away for the summer. We each had a bedroom, there was a servant to take care of us, a pool, and shelves and shelves of Agatha Christie and Ngaio Marsh books.

We went up to our beloved Caspian to yet another job that he was doing up there. On the drive up, my brothers and I yelled, 'Do you remember that?' as we passed a landmark or went around a bend. We ate kebabs in little *chelow kebabis*, went to the sturgeon fisheries and lolled on the fine grey sand by the sea.

One day I showed my father the scar from my boil: 'Look, it's in the same place as your scar where your brother shot you with your air rifle.' In Florida I had clung to the idea that our twin scars were a special sign, a special bond between us.

'When did that happen?' asked my father, surprised.

Then he told me how at the same time I was suffering from my boil, a truck had hit him and knocked him out as he was crossing the road. The old lead pellet, which had floated in the flesh of his leg for thirty-five years, had penetrated his thigh bone. Within days, his leg had become hot and swollen. He squeezed it to get out the infection. It exuded thick yellow pus. Red lines shot out from the wound like the tentacles of a poisonous anemone. He squeezed and limped, limped and squeezed, travelling from one job to the next, sleeping in his car. Finally, he collapsed and found himself in a hospital in southern Tehran. His fever raged and he fluttered in and out of consciousness. He surfaced, finally, in a dark ward with people moaning, pervaded by the stench of vomit and faeces. 'I thought I was in hell, Asho.'

'*Agha*,' a nurse was shaking him, '*Agha*, we need to prepare you for the amputation. The operation is scheduled for seven in the morning.'

As soon as she left, he crept out of bed, limping from doorway to doorway, from one pool of darkness to another.

'I was wearing a hospital gown. My bum was flapping in the wind,' he said.

He hailed a taxi, found his car and drove for twenty hours to his job. Maybe they had given him penicillin, maybe it really wasn't gangrenous, but when my father told me this story, it seemed symbolic: that our matching scars united us. That somehow the link between us transcended the distance and the absence.

*

I bumped into Cameron and Rian as we all emerged into the hallway and ran towards the living room, drawn by my mother's screams. She was clutching her stomach and tears poured down her cheeks. She retched and vomited, then sank to the floor.

'What's wrong? Mummy, what's wrong?' cried Rian.

My father stood by the bookcases. In response to my questioning glance, he shrugged his shoulders.

'What's going on?' I asked, hesitant because I knew she was capable of great drama, although I also remembered all too clearly the time she had been in the hospital and I still didn't know whether she had cancer. I suspected she had agreed to come to visit my father because she knew she was very ill. She was grey in the face and heaving, catching the vomit-spit in clumps of tissue clenched in her hand.

'*Two thousand dollars.* Ashley, two thousand dollars!' she screamed, saliva flying out of her mouth. 'Asho,' my mother scuttled towards me on the ground and clutched me, pulling me awkwardly down to the floor beside her, 'Asho, he gave Sammii two thousand dollars for his daughter's wedding!'

'What?' I turned to my father. '*Two thousand dollars?* You gave Sammii *two thousand dollars* for his daughter's wedding?'

Sammii was my father's foreman. I felt sick.

'Ashley, you have to understand, Sammii's been with me for years,' my father explained. 'He's like family. His daughter needed a dowry and couldn't get married without one. It's common practice for the employer to pay the dowry. She had to buy a new stove and refrigerator, pay for the wedding – get set up for life.'

I turned my back on him. Sammii was *like family*, I thought. Sammii was like family and we were – what?

*

We had to put it aside for the moment – Sammii and the wedding money – because we were all going to visit my mother's friend, Theresa. It was a return to the days of concealing our dirty laundry and once again I found myself keeping quiet about all the things that weren't right.

The Rezas lived in the north of Tehran, in the foothills of the Alborz Mountains, above Tajrish Bazaar, in an area where marble-clad houses overlooked turquoise pools in gardens filled with roses and honeysuckle. We all made our usual efforts to pretend that we too were living perfect lives. My mother drank tea with Theresa, and my father and Parviz talked business, while we kids played in their huge garden, swimming for hours in their pool. We scrambled up the stairs as a dodge ball was hurled at us to tear off a chunk of bread and stuff it with goat's cheese before taking it down to the garden where we picked handfuls of *sabzee* – mint, basil, tarragon and chives – to put on top. Late in the evening, when she got around to it, Theresa conjured up a big vat of *khoresht eh bademjoon* and we all shovelled it in, before running off to climb the mulberry tree and crack *gerdoo* from the walnut tree to eat the soft white nutmeat.

It was a blissful existence and I didn't entirely believe it was real. I quizzed the three biggest kids about their chores, any jobs they had, whether they had to wash the floors or do the laundry, but they looked at me mystified. From the outside, their lives consisted of playing in the pool in the summer and boarding school in the winter, broken up by ski holidays.

Parviz, who was still not forty, was the head of the family. He ran a large and successful construction company. All his brothers worked for him, and his sisters and even his mother relied upon him completely, yet he seemed to take it in his stride, a chubby jokester with a jack-o'-lantern smile. We kids loved it when he cannon-balled into the pool and grabbed whoever was closest, throwing us in the air, tickling us, dunking us.

Late that night, we tried to extricate our mother.

'Come on, Genie, let's go!' said my father, gruffly. She was laughing, chatting and *tarofing* with Parviz. My mother loved the Persian custom of *tarof*. Parviz and my mother had a whole dialogue: '*joon eh man*' (my dearest one); '*tokhmeh haveej*.' (my little carrot seed); '*nazee nazee gol-eh piazee*' (my dearest, my little onion flower). It was past midnight. I watched my mother as her behaviour became even more grandiloquent and her flattery ever richer.

'Come on, Genie!'

My father tried to pull her away. For all of us, my mother's roller-coaster behaviour was wearing. Only a few hours ago she was retching.

'*Al hamdo lellah az eltefat e shoma* (praise be to God for your kindness).'

Tarof was perfect, I thought, for someone like her who hid so much. It seemed everyone here hid behind *tarof*. I found it shocking that having been gone for three years, no one the entire summer had said: 'How are you – *really?* What have you been doing – *really?* How in the world have you managed to support yourself and your three children – *really?*' No one asked and my mother just pretended everything was fine.

'*Enshallah ghorban* we'll see you soon,' she continued before finally being dragged away by my father. But we wouldn't and she knew it. We had already packed to return to Florida.

Despite her *tarof* with Parviz, she definitely didn't hold back when we got into the car.

'Look at their life! What does Theresa have that I don't?

Just because I married a lousy good-for-nothing and she married a prince,' she said.

I knew my mother loved Theresa. It wasn't that she resented what she had, but that she was disappointed and ashamed of her own situation.

'Why if Parviz is an engineer and you're an engineer, why does he make so much more money than you?' I asked my father.

Over the course of the summer, I had become increasingly disillusioned with him. Bond or no bond, scar or no scar. The incident about Samii's daughter had only aggravated my disenchantment.

'Ah well, Parviz is very intelligent.'

My father didn't yet catch on that I was angry.

'So the reason he's more successful than you is that he's smarter?'

'Well, it's not exactly that, Asho. Parviz is clever and he does an excellent job. But he's been lucky and I've been unlucky, and he's Iranian and I'll never be accepted the way he is.'

'Why don't you move to England or America? To a place you fit in? You will never be "lucky" here. You will never be Iranian!' I said. 'Don't you understand how staying here has hurt us?'

My father tried to interrupt me.

'No, let me finish!' I exclaimed. 'Look at the way other people live. Do you know how we live in Florida? When we're not in school, we're working. I'm twelve years old and I work as much as an adult. So does Cameron. Even Rian collects bottles. I should just work for Parviz; he'd probably pay me better.'

My voice was high and shaky, my face flushed.

'That's not true, Asho, darling; Mummy tells me you have a wonderful life in Florida. That you attend excellent schools and have lots of friends and live in a lovely house.'

'Don't "Asho darling" me!' I was incensed. 'Oh my God, I can't believe you told him that.' I said to my mother, furious. 'Mom, you didn't really tell him that, did you? That's crazy!'

I turned back to my father.

'Dad, just so you don't fool yourself completely, our schools are ranked the worst in America, I have no friends, we barely have enough money to eat. Do you realise that we get food out of garbage dumps? That we have never owned a *single* new toy or item of clothing? That Mummy and I sleep in the living room on a couch?'

My mother's hand snaked back over the seat and grabbed a chunk of my thigh, twisting it viciously in a 'horse bite'. I wrenched away, trying to escape.

Cameron glared at me, his eyes flashing, as if to say: why do you always have to cause so much trouble? He still thought the way I used to: that if we behaved, if we were really good, really clever, really athletic and really tough, my father would love us enough to take us back. Well, I saw now that wasn't how it worked. Other kids didn't have to win their dads over to get food and housing.

'Well, Asho, darling, I'm trying my hardest to earn enough money to buy a big house and get Mummy a nice Mercedes and some jewellery. If you don't like Iran, maybe we can move to South Africa, and I can get a plane and fly from job to job, and you and the boys can go to good schools, and Mummy can be a big *Memsaab* and play rummy all day at the club.'

He trotted out this dream, just as he had reeled out a version of it when I was eight years old, living in the Amir Abad flat, when I must have asked a similar question.

'In any case, Ashley,' he continued, 'I couldn't work in Florida, doing *small jobs*, building *small* houses on *small* plots of land. I like big, earth-moving projects.'

'What is wrong with you?' I groaned. 'Why don't you grow

up? There's a big gap between getting your food out of a dumpster and flying around in your own plane in South Africa.'

I threw myself back in the seat. All I wanted was a father who could afford to buy us a new pair of school shoes and drive an intact car with enough gas so that we didn't run out in the middle of nowhere. I didn't care about fancy jewellery or safaris. What I dreamed about was a set of matching towels from the Sears catalogue.

I vowed that I would never ruin my life with dreams. So what if he only liked to work on big construction projects and that he would be unhappy working in Florida, building concrete-block housing? Sometimes you had to do what you didn't like so that your wife and children didn't suffer. Wasn't that what being an adult was all about?

*

We were on the plane back to Florida after our summer in Iran. Tears ran down my face as I stared out the aeroplane window at the dusty bowl of Tehran.

'Asho, what's wrong?' my mother asked.

I tried to explain. 'It's just that when we came, I had hoped that it would be different.'

When he had said goodbye to us at Mehrabad Airport, my father had kissed each of us and then waved jauntily through the plate glass as we walked towards the plane. There was no mention of our visiting or his coming to Florida. It was as if well-liked acquaintances were leaving.

'Oh, Ashley, when will you learn? It's not you kids, or even me. The man just can't love anyone. I've told you about his mother telling me that he loved me as much as he was *capable* of loving anyone.' She looked sad as she said this. 'He does love you. It is just a very strange kind of love.'

'But why? Every other father in the world seems to love his family. I'm not even talking about rich people like the ones here in Iran. Look at Tony Terrano's dad or the Deckys'.

They're just normal people and their fathers don't abandon them. What if something happened to you, would he just let us die?'

'No, no, he would never do that.'

'How do you know?'

'I don't, Asho, but what can I do? I'm doing the best I can.'

I thought about that jaunty wave.

'Did he say anything about us coming back?'

'No. I'm not sure I would anyway. I don't think I could live with that man ever again.'

Florida, 1971–1973

my mother teaching

23

Never

becoming a teenager

After coming back from Iran, I had gone back to Sunrise Junior High School and eighth grade.

Our grandparents came down again that winter and this time it was to stay for good. They sent down fifty cartons containing antique silver spoons and dozens of plastic margarine tubs. Boxes lined every wall, towering over the convertible sofa where my mother and I slept in the living room. Sometimes when I awakened, I started because in the dark the stacks looked like people crowding around the bed. It reminded me of my grandparents' house at Halls Hill Road with all the cartons jammed into it. As time passed, the resemblance grew stronger, for my grandmother began pulling open the cartons and stacking her possessions on top.

After the summer in Iran, life in Florida seemed grimmer still. Whereas previously I had been able to fantasise about returning to Iran, now there was no prospect of that and, even if we were to return, the situation there wasn't great. I realised that Florida was no longer just a stopping-off place; it was where we lived and I was miserable.

*

'Ashley, set the table.'

'Put the forks on the left.'

'Not those salt and pepper shakers.'

'Tom's wine glass needs to be chilled.'

'Why haven't you put the dishes away?'

'Stop crashing them! You'll chip one.'

'Remember to chop the onions finely – not in great big clumps.'

'Did you put the garbage out?'

'I don't care what you're doing. Go put the garbage out.'

'What's wrong with you?'

My mother faced me, hands on her hips, face dripping with perspiration.

'Do something about that hair. Get it out of your face.'

'I'm sick of your nagging,' I muttered. My mother's fury was unrelenting. She had always been volatile, but since returning from Iran she seemed permanently enraged, and Cameron and I bore the brunt.

'What? What was that?' She leaped towards me.

'Nothing.' Sullenly.

'Don't answer me back!'

'You're never satisfied.' My eyes were slitted in hate.

'Don't look at me like that!' She slapped me on the arm and I fell back clumsily against the kitchen counter. 'God dammit, I hurt myself. Son of a bitch!'

She hopped around the kitchen holding her hand, furious that she had hurt herself hitting me.

'Why do you always hit us?' I hurled back, my arm stinging.

'How dare you?' Grabbing a wooden spoon, she ran after me. 'Don't you dare talk back to me,' she screamed.

We heard a knock at the front door.

'Hi, Auntie Patric!'

Dana, Jacqueline and Tom popped their heads in the front door. I didn't understand how my mother could simply return from a summer in Iran with my father and slot straight back in with Tom.

My mother greeted them, all smiles.

'Jacqueline, you look so pretty in that outfit, sweetheart,' she said as she hugged and kissed her. Once again, the sugary sweetness she showered on everyone else.

'I got these boots, Auntie Patric.' She raised her leg to show off shiny white-vinyl boots, with heels.

'Me too!' Dana did a twirl to show off her new boots and miniskirt.

I looked up from the kitchen counter where I was chopping onions. Recently Tom had received a raise, so he had bought the girls new outfits at Richardson's department store. I was jealous, longing to have at least one piece of clothing that wasn't second-hand. No, that wasn't fair, I thought. There was my new bathing suit.

On the first day of swimming at school, I discovered that I could no longer get the straps of my old bathing suit over my shoulders. After my mother had unsuccessfully searched all her thrift shops, we went to Penny's. It was bright inside the store and the lights made a hissing sound. There were racks and racks of clothes, hung neatly, and as I walked past, my fingers lingered over them.

'Get some suits and start trying them on,' said my mother.

From the teenage racks, I picked out a few colourful scuba-style suits, similar to the ones the other girls in my class wore.

'No, don't be ridiculous.'

I put them back and grabbed a few of the size 14 children's suits. As I tried them on, my mother sat in the dressing room, smoking and dropping her ash into the special little ashtray she made by taking the cellophane off her cigarette packet. As I tried on a suit, she lifted my arm and sniffed.

'You stink! Jesus Christ, you stink. You need deodorant.' She gagged dramatically.

Hyperaware of my increasingly animal body odour, I had tried to keep it under control – sometimes even going into the restroom at school and scrubbing with a paper towel and pink liquid soap. Dana had been using deodorant for ages now and had been urging me to ask my mother to buy me some. Stubbornly I refused.

I pulled a suit on over my baggy white underwear.

'Disgusting. Try another.'

'Another.'

So it went.

'Are there any more?'

'No.'

She stalked out and confronted the saleslady. 'I need a suit for a twelve-year-old *child*.' She emphasised the word 'child'.

I'm almost thirteen, I fumed to myself.

'Well, ma'am, I think you'll find that the ones we have are the ones she's trying.'

She strode back. 'Well, you can't wear any of these. When did you get so fat?'

I cringed against the wall of the dressing room, my arms crossed against my chest. It was true. All of a sudden, I was fat. A couple of days ago I had been normal. I couldn't even remember what I had looked like. I had been purely functional, whereas now I had dimples on my thighs and a blubbery stomach. Also there was my face. It hurt where it was spattered with pimples. And my hair. Always just straight and brown, now it hung in lank, greasy strands.

The saleslady handed in a suit.

'This is the last one, honey.'

She gave me a wink and I shrank even further into the dressing room.

'Now Mom,' she said, addressing my mother, 'all girls go through this. She's going through puberty. It's just puppy fat.' Turning back to me, she said, 'Don't worry, honey, as soon as you've had your growth spurt, you'll slim down and be gorgeous again.'

My mother ignored her pointedly and handed me the suit. 'I can't understand it. I'm perfectly proportioned. Your father is fine. Turn around.' She scrutinised me from the back. 'No, I really can't understand where you came from.'

I pulled on the suit, hunching over.

'Stand up.'

I stood, my shoulders sloping forwards and my head hanging.

Barely looking, she said, 'It's fine. How much?'

'Six dollars.' I twisted to look at the price ticket under my arm.

'Six dollars for a bathing suit! Jesus Christ, I can't believe I'm paying six dollars for a suit that doesn't even look nice.'

On the way home, I leaned my forehead against the window, staring at the face reflected there. She was right: I was ugly and fat and pimply and smelly. What did she want me to do? Cut off my head? Cut off my body? I couldn't snap my fingers and make my eyes blue or my hair golden and curly. I couldn't make myself 'perfectly proportioned'.

So yes, I did have an item of new clothing: my J.C. Penny, size 14, polyester bathing suit, green on the bottom, lavender on top, with a pink tie in front.

'I like your boots,' I said to Dana, the tears pouring as I finished the onions.

'You can borrow 'em,' she said.

We wore the same size shoes and clothes, and she always let me wear hers if I wanted – even the new ones.

She was the best friend I had ever had. I told her everything. I knew her favourite colour was purple. I knew her number-one food was spaghetti and meatballs. I knew she hated the space between her front teeth and the fact that she had such pale blonde skin. I knew she used a pink plastic razor to shave the fine hair on her legs, and I knew that every day she came home from school and cleaned the house and cooked dinner for Jacqueline and Tom. I knew that for Christmas he had given her a set of saucepans. I knew what subjects she took in school and her grades in each.

Sometimes when we had finished our chores, after asking permission, we called each other on the phone and talked about homework and what boy we had a crush on and the newest Glen Campbell song.

From the time I had met Dana and Jacqueline, I had known that their mother was in New Jersey. I hadn't questioned it – after all, my father was in Iran. What the circumstances were, why they were in Florida and their mother a thousand miles away, why she never called or wrote, why there were no pictures of her in their house, why she never sent presents – I didn't think to ask.

That was until the day I overheard Yosy tell my mother, 'What finally got the state to commit her was that she tried to kill Dana – and she got pretty close, too.'

After dinner, Dana and I walked around the neighbourhood after dinner. It was still light and we waved at our neighbours as we circled the blocks.

Almost immediately, I asked, 'Is your mother crazy? Is that why she doesn't live with you, because she's in a mental institution in New Jersey?'

'Who told you?' she asked.

'But how do they know she's crazy?'

'She's not crazy.'

'So then why is she in a mental hospital?'

'That's pretty obvious, she's *mentally ill.*'

'Oh.' Silence for a few seconds and then, 'But how can they tell?'

'She's schizophrenic.'

'How do they know?'

'Oh God. They just do.'

'How?'

'Well, she tried to kill me, that's one way.'

'Really? How?'

'Strangled me with my jump rope.'

'Why did she choose you, not Jacqueline?'

'I don't know! Can we talk about something else?'

'But I can see why she went crazy, being married to your father and with a brat like Jacqueline. You're the only normal one.' I said this sympathetically.

'I know.' She shook her head glumly.

It had grown dark, so I couldn't see her face. We walked around and around the block, the streetlight illuminating us for five steps as we walked towards it and then for five steps as we walked back into darkness.

'How come she didn't do it?' I asked.

She knew exactly what I was talking about. 'I fought her off.'

'Wow. How could you?' I thought of my strapping mother. I would never be able to fight her off.

'I didn't want to die.'

*

My mother's face reddened as the sun beat down and Tom hammered on. I barely paid attention. Tom was always angry about something.

We ran around the park and threw pebbles into the lake. Dana and I settled on a log and meandered over all the familiar subjects: what colour looked best on us, whether I would ever be allowed to use deodorant or shave, whether Dana should risk getting sunburned in order to some day maybe get a tan. During the conversation, I circled back to a subject Cameron and I had been worried about.

'So do you think they'll get married?' I didn't look at her. She sat on the log, picking out splinters of wood with her nails.

'Who?' she asked, her eyes large behind her blue-rimmed glasses.

'My mother! Your father! Who do you think, you idiot?' Sometimes Dana could be so dense.

'I hope so! I love Auntie Patric.' She grinned foolishly at the thought.

'Well, I hope they don't!'

I stared sullenly down at the ground, at the bits of ancient shell and coral. I really didn't know with my mother. She had never mentioned Martin. Since coming back from Iran, she had barely acknowledged the existence of my father and we were spending even more time with the Glenns.

After a few seconds I said, 'If they try to get married, Cameron and I are going to stand up when the reverend gets to the part about "Does anyone have any objections?" and say we do because he's an alcoholic and he's already driven one wife crazy.'

'Oh God, can you just shut up!' Dana's mouth was twisted and her shoulders hunched up. 'You are *so* stupid! My dad can't get married even if he wanted. It's illegal to divorce a "crazy" person in the state of New Jersey. You have to wait like five years or something.'

'Are you sure?'

'Yes. Pretty much.'

I danced around in the sand. 'They can't get married! Woohoo!'

Dana's big eyes watered. 'You know what that means? I'll never have a mother and my father's . . .' She struggled. 'Well, you know what he is.'

I didn't even retort, 'Well, I don't have a father,' because she clearly had the worse side of the bargain.

No matter how harsh Mom was, no matter how unpredictable her anger, no matter how many hours she left us by the side of the road waiting, we knew she loved us and would do anything for us.

As soon as I could find Cameron, I whispered the good news to him. It was the only time that day he smiled. Finally, the sun plummeted behind the Loblolly Pines, mosquitoes began zinging and gnats stung our ankles.

'We're starving,' we whined.

'Tom, let's go,' my mother said, gathering up her cigarette butts.

A while later we were still waiting, still sitting on logs, still throwing shells and pebbles into the lake. Racoons eyed us as they came out for their dusk foraging. Delicately they balanced scraps in their paws. The picnickers were long gone – home preparing dinner, loading briefcases and school bags for the next day. Another empty beer can clanked against the pile.

'Tom, let's go!'

Mummy stood up and strode to the car. Tom continued to sit there, legs splayed, and popped open another beer, the pfft sound loud in the silent evening. He drained it and threw the can somewhere close to the pile. He staggered up stiffly, falling to one knee in the uneven sand. As he approached the car, he banged into a tap jutting a few feet out of the ground. He looked down, baffled, and clutched at his trouser leg, finally pulling it up to reveal thick red blood pooling on his white shin. He shook his head and lunged towards the car.

'Let me drive. You're too drunk!' said my mother, grabbing for the keys in his hand.

'I'm not drunk! You think I'm too drunk to drive? You

can stay here, you bitch! Dana, Jacqueline! Get into the car.'

'Tom, you're too drunk to drive,' said my mother, kindly, to mollify him.

'I'm not! How would you know anyway? You've never had a drink in your life.' He said this as if it were a terrible thing. He folded himself laboriously into the driver's seat and dropped the keys, picked them up, dropped them again and cursed. Finally he started the car, which lurched forward with a screech.

'Get the hell into the car!' he yelled at Dana and Jacqueline.

They slid in and he hit the accelerator, flying into the empty parking lot where he slammed into a big yellow barrier on the way out. I could see Dana's white face in the back window.

'Be careful of the girls!' my mother screamed. 'Tom!'

There was silence. The car had disappeared through the trees.

'God damn him.'

We stared out at the empty parking lot. We were all probably doing the same calculation: it was at least four or five miles from John D. Easterlin Park to 715 NE 14 Place. It was quiet around us. We waited.

Suddenly we heard the roar of a car engine and saw the fishtailing rear lights of the Pontiac reversing back down the road. We ran, scattering like pigeons, to avoid being hit.

My mother walked slowly across the parking lot and leaned in the window: 'You'd better drive carefully, Thomas, with my kids in the car.' Her voice was tough.

We got in, subdued. All of us had been in car accidents with Tom when he was drunk. I had been in two.

'You scared? You think I'm drunk!'

He raced out of the parking lot, scattering gravel, but

missing the yellow barrier. He slammed his foot from the accelerator to the brake and in the back seat we five kids tumbled together, knocking elbows and knees.

'You think I'm drunk?'

He speeded up again and we entered highway traffic at terrifying speed.

'You think I'm drunk?'

Cars swerved, honking and yelling. We hurtled down the road, red traffic lights flashing in front of us for a second before we raced through them. A wave of honks followed us.

Tom laughed bitterly. 'You think I'm drunk! You think I can't drive! Let's see who can drive!'

We held on to the armrests and the backs of the seats. My mother propped herself against the dashboard. We laughed nervously.

'Tom, if the coppers get you, you'll lose your licence!' She tried to speak calmly as we roared down the busy highway.

'Lose my licence, lose my job, why should you care!' He jerked the car across the lanes and we bumped against the central barrier.

'Tom, stop! You're going to kill us!' my mother screamed.

He laughed and speeded up. I held my hands over my eyes as he slammed through traffic, car after car swerving to avoid him. We lurched to a stop, back wheels skidding all over the road. Then before we could right ourselves, Tom wrestled the car back into the traffic, racing, as if in some death-defying arcade game. We suddenly slowed down again, the car side-winding and sliding. My mother reached over to take the wheel. Tom slumped over, then suddenly came alive with a snarl, grabbed the wheel and revved back up to lunatic speed. It felt as if we were on some terrible theme-park ride where the only outcome was an enormous metallic crash. My mother's warm hand reached back from the front seat and rested on my leg for a moment.

Once off the highway, I felt safer. Surely he would have to slow down on these small streets, streets where kids we knew rode bikes, threw baseballs and ran around in the circles of light beneath the street lamps. Tom didn't slow down, though; he ripped around corners, his tyres squealing and the car tipping madly. Our screams filled the car. When he tore up in front of our house, swerving off the road and on to the gravel in front at the last minute, stones flew up around the car and pinged against the undercarriage.

After we had all jumped out, my mother leaned in the window and said in a deadly calm voice, a voice that I could tell she was having trouble controlling, 'Dana, please tell your father not to come here again. I never want to see him – ever. He won't remember this tomorrow, but you will. Tell him.'

Cameron, Rian and I stood staring. Never. Dana and Jacqueline looked at her, their huge eyes even larger than usual. Never.

'Girls, this has nothing to do with you. I love you both; you are like my own kids. I wish I could keep you, but he won't let me.'

'Damn right!'

Tom suddenly accelerated and she was thrown away from the car.

*

How did they get back together and when? One minute she was saying, 'I'll never see him again in my life,' and then the next, 'Set the table for seven tonight, honey. Uncle Tom and the girls are coming over for dinner.'

For a brief pause, the house had been calmer: my grandparents had packed their cartons and moved back to Connecticut and a retirement community – driven out by the fighting, the stress and our grandmother's ill health. Now here we were again, putting the six-pack in the fridge and the tall glasses in the freezer, to get nice and frosty, just the way Tom liked them.

'Mummy, why don't you just stop buying beer and wine?' I asked.

She gave me a hard look and said, 'Don't be ridiculous.'

As we ate, Mummy quizzed Tom on his week and regaled us with stories about her job at Migrant Ed. I sat watching, my insides frozen, as she performed for Tom and the girls. I couldn't believe she was trying to win him over. How dare she? How dare he? They never mentioned the incident in the car. I was furious at her, at him, at the world. He had come close to killing us and nobody even brought it up.

'OK, who can guess how many of the kids in my class have never been to the beach?' my mother asked, her voice vivacious. 'Remember, these are kids who live less than two miles from the ocean,' she primed us.

'Well, we live less than two miles from the beach and we barely ever go,' I said, 'unless Yosy takes us.' I was reckless now, challenging her.

'That's not true! How can you say that! We go all the time.' She kept a smile fixed on her face and looked around the table, waiting for an answer.

Cameron and Rian, Dana and Jacqueline, sat quietly, unwilling to jump into the fray, anxious about my belligerent tone.

'When was the last time we went?' I challenged my mother.

Oh God, why couldn't I just keep my trap shut?

'None of them has *ever* been to the beach,' she said, glaring at me. 'You wouldn't believe how many of these kids have never tasted a fresh vegetable or had a piece of fruit. Their parents travel around the country, picking oranges and peaches, lettuce and tomatoes, and they eat hot dogs, TV dinners, macaroni cheese. When we feed them fresh food, they don't even recognise it.'

'We rarely eat fresh vegetables.' I interrupted her. 'You always say cans are cheaper.'

Shut up, Ashley, I told myself. Just keep your mouth closed. Why couldn't I just let her yap on and on? Why did it matter to me that she always had to show off for Tom?

'What the hell is going on here? Are you going to answer back every time I say something? Are you trying to make a liar out of me in front of the Glenns?' she yelled, her face red and furious.

Tom sat back in his chair, drinking his wine, smiling smugly. He was enjoying the tension between my mother and me.

'No, I just think you're being hypocritical.'

Hypocritical was my favourite word. I had a very sensitive nose for hypocrisy and anything she did seemed hypocritical to me.

'It's your usual "Do as I say, not as I do",' I said, 'just like your smoking. And his drinking.'

I turned cold. I had gone too far.

She jumped out of her chair and grabbed me, dragging me from the room. 'Stay out until you know how to behave! We're just trying to have a nice dinner and you have to give me a big mouth. Always a big mouth with you.' She pushed me into our bedroom and slammed the door.

I lay on my bed feeling sorry for myself. I could hear her ranting to Tom and the kids about how her one child who had never given her any trouble had suddenly become such a little bitch, answering back all the time.

'I can't take this any more,' I heard her crying. 'I work so hard for these bloody kids and for what? I get no thanks.'

Oh God, I thought, it was always she who was right, always me who was wrong.

Someone knocked.

'What?'

'Can you come out so I can talk with you?'

'Go 'way.'

'Please, just come out.'

I wiped my eyes on my shirtsleeve as I followed Tom on to the balcony at the front of the house.

'Do you mind if I talk to you? Give you my opinion about what I think's going on?'

I was surprised. I'd never had a one-to-one conversation with Tom and I was not used to such a respectful tone.

'OK.' I sniffled, still reluctant.

'Well, let's start with what you think.'

I hesitated.

'Come on,' he said, 'take a guess.'

'Well, she hates me,' I said, 'I can't do anything right.' My throat was clogged up and I was in danger of tears overflowing. 'I'm not smart enough, I'm not pretty enough; I'm not anything enough for her . . . She's never satisfied with anything I do. She's a complete hypocrite.'

'Well, I thought you were smarter than that. What do you *really* think is going on?'

I paused. I was nervous of a trap. I knew that whatever was happening would end up my fault.

'Don't know.'

'Come on, Ashley! How old is your mother?'

Again, I faltered. She was so secretive about her age. I looked at Tom suspiciously: was he just trying to find out Mom's age?

He laughed. I could see that he had already had a lot to drink and for the first time I realised that maybe he actually started drinking before he even got to our house.

He said, 'She's almost forty. And that's a very hard age for a woman, particularly for a woman like your mother who has always cared so much about her looks.'

He looked at me expectantly, as if I should jump up and down and say, 'Wow, that's amazing, I understand perfectly. Tom, you're such a genius!'

'So?' I said.

'So? Here you are nipping at her heels, reminding her of everything she was and never will be again.'

'So?' I repeated.

'You can't see how jealous your mother is of you?'

I gasped. 'You think Mom is jealous of *me*? No way.'

I thought about how much smarter and prettier, more athletic and better at everything she was than I.

'You really aren't as clever as I thought, are you? You know what she hates?'

I shook my head hopelessly. It was pretty clear that Tom was completely drunk.

'She hates this.' He ran his finger down my left breast, flicking the nipple with his nail, almost as if he were playing marbles in the playground.

I flinched back. 'What?'

He laughed again and I could see his small white teeth gleaming in the dark. He ran his finger down my breast and flicked the nipple again. 'This.'

'What?' I crossed my arms across my chest.

'Oh yes, you know. Don't play games with me, Ashley. You know *exactly* what I'm talking about.'

He pulled my arms away and stared at the front of my shirt. 'You must see what it is that she's upset about.'

He kept flicking my left breast.

'She's ageing and you're blossoming into a beautiful young woman. She loves you, but she can't stand what you are becoming.'

Flick.

Flick.

Each time he touched my breast, I stepped back. With each

painful flick of his big broad-nailed thumb, I stepped back until my butt was pressed against the ageing, rusted, white, curly-flowered, wrought-iron fence my mother spent so many hours sanding and repainting.

'She doesn't like it when she sees men looking at you and not her.'

'What?' I was shocked. No man had ever looked at flat-chested, pimple-faced me. 'That's crazy!'

He pressed against me, his whole body, and I could smell the sour vomit smell of white wine mixed with cigarettes. He pushed harder, trapping me against the fence. I leaned back as far as I could, but I was afraid I was going to topple over with him on top. I was worried our neighbours would see us.

Ever since we had moved to Florida, my mother had been concerned about the neighbours:

'Pick every leaf off the lawn.'

'Don't wear those shorts.'

'Don't fight, don't yell, don't scream – in front of the neighbours.'

She was obsessed.

'Uncle Tom, I'm going to fall, you're too heavy.' I pushed him awkwardly, already off balance from his weight.

He lurched backwards heavily, catching himself on the hurricane shutter. 'Dammit!' He shook his arm in pain.

I slid around him and into the small box of light in front of the open door. Rian and Cameron were watching *Hawaii Five-O* a few feet away in the living room. From the table, my mother yelled at Dana and me to do the dishes.

'Coming, Mom!' I was never so happy to do the dishes.

'So now you understand what's happening?' Tom followed me, a self-satisfied grin on his face, as he continued to rub his arm. Throughout he had held a wine glass in his hand. He drained it now.

'Yes, thank you, Uncle Tom.'

Just as I turned to go inside, he grabbed me and pulled me to him. My nose bumped into him and I smelled an acrid metallic odour mixed with his deodorant. I was surprised. My mother loathed people who smelled. I stood absolutely still and stiff. He hugged me tightly and then, getting no response, released me. I stumbled through the screen door, blinking in the bright lights of the house. He came in behind me and I noticed he was swaggering. God, he believes he's solved everything, I thought. Surreptitiously, I rubbed my tender left breast. He handed me his wine glass before rejoining my mother.

'What's wrong?' asked Dana with her big eyes and toothy grin, standing tall in her new high-heeled boots.

'Nothing.' I felt numb. 'He wants some more wine.'

Dana took a fresh chilled glass and filled it. I turned to wash the used one. My mother had bought the thin, fluted antique crystal wine glasses at one of her second-hand stores as he preferred his wine in fine stemware. My hands were shaking and I fumbled, dropping the goblet in the sink where it shattered.

'Oh God!' I cried.

Dana pushed me aside. 'Hurry. Get a paper bag,' she ordered.

I ran to the utility area and groped for a bag. She quickly picked up the big pieces of glass and dropped them in, cleaning up the shards with a used napkin, which she stuffed into the bag as well. When the Glenns came over, we used linen napkins. Dana buried the paper bag under the garbage in the can.

'Go put it out back in the trash, underneath some stuff so nobody sees it. They'll never know.'

I marvelled at her bravery.

The next Friday, when we were preparing for the Glenns,

my mother counted out napkins for me to iron. She asked me, 'We're missing a napkin and a wine glass. Have you seen them?'

'No, not recently,' I said, and I turned back to my iron.

24

Some Good Men

*my mother
with Yosy*

'Cam,' I said, 'he's never going to send for us.'

I dipped my brush into the thick white paint and began dabbing it carefully in the corner where the wall met the ground.

'I know,' agreed Cameron.

We were painting a duplex just around the corner from Uncle Hugh's.

'Boy, you kids know how to work,' one of his neighbours had said one day as she passed. When she found out that he paid us 50 cents an hour she said, 'Come over and do some painting for me and I'll pay ya eight bucks a day – each.'

'Stop talking. Get back to work,' said the woman.

We continued painting, grimly acknowledging to each other that we had badly underestimated how hard this job was. Still, $16 per day was a lot of money.

It was weird, I thought, as I painted: we had gone to Iran last summer, and here we were, another summer upon us. Nothing had changed. We still rarely heard from our father and our initial enthusiasm about writing him had worn off within a letter or two. For him, too, judging from the number of letters we were receiving.

I brushed paint up and down the side of the house, marking my trail like a giant snail, with a clean line of white against the mildewed old paint. Cameron was on the ladder further along, doing the hurricane shutters. It was getting really hot – so hot it felt as if I were covered in a thick oily layer from head to toe. It made me move slowly, think slowly and even feel slowly – a slow-motion person.

We had been in America practically four years – four long years. We had known the Glenns for three. I was thirteen and Cameron was almost twelve. Another school year was coming to an end. This year I would be moving to the high school, which was across the street from Uncle Hugh's.

I could hear deep teenage voices yelling in the sports field next to the high school and I wondered dully how they could be so energetic. The woman brought us each a glass of Kool Aid. It was sweet, tart and metallic. She worked alongside us and even she was finding it hard and hot. Now she wanted to talk.

'So what's this I hear about you movin' back with your dad?' she asked, sitting on a stool and painting the bottom section of the wall.

'We're not, ma'am,' I answered.

'Well, now that I've found you guys, I don't want to lose you,' she said.

'No, ma'am,' I said. Whatever she said, I mumbled, 'Yes, ma'am' or 'No, ma'am.'

It took weeks for us to finish the outside of the units. As soon as we were done, she wanted to get started on the inside.

'Damn right she does,' said Mom, 'she's never going to get anyone else who works that hard for that price.'

We couldn't do it in any case because now things had changed. We were going back to Iran. The decision seemed to be made instantly. My father called, told my mother how much he missed and loved us, murmured '*Ap saay pi hai*' and we were off.

The catalyst for this was Cameron. First of all, he was turning twelve in September, which meant that his airline ticket would then be full price. Second, but more importantly, he was close to becoming a teenager and, my mother was terrified she couldn't control him once he was bigger than she was. She was at her wit's end as it was: she was undergoing painful dental work, the car was on its last legs, Tom's drinking had accelerated and under the Republican administration the Migrant Program was being cut. There was no way my mother wanted to teach in the regular school system that we three kids attended.

'Jesus Christ, it would kill me,' she said.

It was all decided. The boys would move back to Iran before Cameron's birthday and live with our father, while my mother and I stayed in Florida to clean and paint the house and get it ready to sell or rent before we joined them.

*

We hadn't heard from the boys for three days and my mother was hysterical. I thought they had probably just forgotten to call. She was so upset, though, that the thought trickled into my mind like a poison gas: maybe some evil person had kidnapped them as they went through the airport in London. It was possible that Cameron and Rian had asked someone directions and then that person realising they were alone . . . They could be in Nigeria right now or Norway.

'Goddam son of a bitch. How could he do this to me? Where are my boys?' my mother ranted. 'Call Hugh for me!' she ordered.

She had taken to asking me to dial her calls for her. She grabbed the phone once I had him on the line.

'Hugh, can you find out how I can get Interpol to locate them?'

Interpol sounded like something from a James Bond novel and I thought she sounded so worldly, bandying about words like that.

'No, how can I call him?' she continued. 'I don't have a number. He doesn't live any place. He doesn't have a phone.'

I could hear Uncle Hugh's voice bellowing down the line. I missed Uncle Hugh. We hadn't seen as much of him now my mother was back with Tom.

'I know the boys have to live some place, Hugh! God dammit, I don't know where he lives or his phone number. Get off my back! All I have is his PO Box.' My mother was screaming at him. 'No, I don't have any friends' numbers. Find out about Interpol.'

She slammed the phone down.

She paced around the house smoking. I walked behind her, emptying the ashtrays into the rubbish.

'Stop following me around, you're driving me crazy!'

'Stop smoking so much! How many packs a day are you up to? Four? Five?'

I was terrified she was going to die of lung cancer. In health class they had shown us pictures of the lungs of a cigarette smoker and I had done the calculations: she had started stealing cigarette butts from ashtrays when she was nine and was smoking full-time by nineteen. She had been smoking four packs a day for over twenty years. She could die at any time.

'Patric, I found out about that Interpol group you asked me about!'

Uncle Hugh blasted into the living room, his voice booming and his head almost touching the ceiling.

'Well, honey, I don't want to upset you, and you know how

much I love those boys, but it isn't going to work. It would cost ten thousand dollars, as well as expenses.'

He sat down in the wicker chair, his big bloodhound face settling miserably into its jowls.

'They said they would have to send someone to Iran and you would have to pay the plane fare and hotel.'

'Bullshit! That's bullshit! They always have Interpol people working in Iran,' ranted my mother. 'Hugh, do something! Negotiate with them. Tell them to get one of their men in Iran to find Dartnell. They all know him.'

I was impressed by how much my mother seemed to know. Also how important my father must be if an entire international organisation knew of him.

'Well, honey, let's just think this through. How long have the boys been gone now?' He counted off four days on his big fingers. 'Well, if we don't hear anything by the end of a week, I'll pay for you to go to Iran to find them.'

'Me? How the hell would *I* do that?' she snapped.

'Let's just take this one step at a time, honey. If there were something wrong, you'd have heard about it. The State Department said if there's a problem they most likely would have been notified.'

'The State Department! They're useless! Two children kidnapped, missing . . . you think they would know anything? How? Just tell me how, Hoffer!' My mother was stampeding back and forth across our small living room.

After a few minutes, Uncle Hugh persuaded her to have a cup of tea and play some gin rummy. She kept muttering, 'Goddam son of a bitch, how can he keep doing this to me?' about my father.

Finally, later in the day, the phone rang and she leaped to grab the receiver. I searched her face to see whether the news was good or bad. She turned away, frowning deeply.

'Stuck in Amman? What? That bastard! Put him on.'

I circled the room, trying to hear.

She screamed, 'What! You goddam bastard. I kill myself raising these children and then you abandon them in some godforsaken country! God dammit, Dartnell . . .'

I laughed aloud and danced around the room, yelling, 'Yippee dippee doo!' and jumped to tap the door frame the way I had seen high-school boys jump to touch the rim of the basketball hoop. It was my father! He had the boys!

When my mother got off the phone, she told me that Rian and Cameron had spent three days in a hotel in Amman. My father had bought and sent the tickets, knowing that they would have this layover. She told me, 'The bastard said the tickets were cheaper. The airline paid for the hotel.'

By now I had learned, at least a little. 'Mom, didn't you look at the tickets before they left?'

I knew that the tickets would have indicated each leg of the journey, as well as the departure and arrival times. I couldn't believe that, after being caught out in London on the way to America, she wouldn't have checked. I berated myself: why hadn't I inspected them, knowing my father, knowing my mother?

'It didn't say,' she responded, snootily, hurt that I was questioning her.

In a few weeks, we received air letters from the boys, telling us that they had stopped on the way from the airport and had their hair cut. My mother had let it grow, knowing it would distress my father to have long-haired sons.

We continued to get scrawled letters from time to time that my mother wouldn't show anyone for she was ashamed of the boys' spelling mistakes and poor writing. They told tales of racing through the desert late at night, trapping jerboas; days on the job; weekends pig shooting in the hills. We heard very little of school or regular meals or dental flossing or taking vitamins. When friends asked my mother, though, everything was wonderful.

'Oh yes, the boys are fine, attending a lovely little British School in Esfahan. Out on the job with their father. Just what boys need, you know, a father.'

During the months the boys were gone, the house had never been more empty. After they had left, Tom had stormed in, yelling, 'What the hell are you playing at, woman?'

She screamed that she wouldn't be going back if he were more of a man. Glasses were broken. Doors slammed. I was sent to bed, while Dana and Jacqueline sat in the car. Midnight came and went. After many hours, Dana and Jacqueline came back to the house to ask for a drink and to find out when they would be going home.

'Get the hell back in the car!' Tom yelled. 'And don't come out again.'

The next thing I heard was a piercing shriek. I leaped out of bed and ran to the window. Tom and my mother dashed out to the car. He wrenched the door open and grabbed Jacqueline, who was clutching her hand, screaming. Without hesitating, he reached in and dragged Dana out, hoisting her into the air. Stepping back, he lifted her and threw her against the car. Her head hit the corner of the open door and she fell awkwardly on to the gravel, limp as a Raggedy Ann doll. My mother, who had been comforting Jacqueline and examining the finger she had caught in the door, quickly ran to Dana, whose head was bleeding.

'Tom, she needs to go to the hospital,' she said. He pushed the girls into the car and took off.

After that, my mother handed in her notice and stopped working. Precipitously she pulled me out of ninth grade, telling me one Friday to inform the school I was leaving. I went from teacher to teacher, showing them a note she had written and shaking their hands.

She needed my help to paint the house while she stocked up. Each day she planned her round of thrift stores. She knew when each shop put out new goods and she planned her journey to maximise the number with fresh supplies. Before she left, she would dictate the list of things I had to do before she returned. Soon she had filled the boys' bedroom with suitcases and each day she came home with piles of clothing: silk Emilio Pucci blouses, swirling Vera dresses, long Halston jerseys. She was spending all the money she was saving from not having the boys.

'Mom, why do you need all these fancy clothes?' I asked as she had me try on one formal dress after another for her.

'You'll see, Asho, life in Iran isn't like here – there are parties, there are bridge evenings, there are clubs. Our life's going to be different – your father has promised. We'll need lots of beautiful clothes.'

My memories of Iran didn't encompass parties or fancy clothes. I remembered fishermen at the Caspian, dragging a long armour-plated sturgeon from the sea; '*Barfieh, barfieh,*' the call of the men who shovelled snow as they tromped through a suddenly silent and briefly beautiful Tehran; squatting in the dust and eating a red ripe watermelon that one of the workers had split by dropping it on the ground. It was always quite shocking how different the Iran I loved was from the one my mother remembered.

There was no mention of Tom during this period. One day when she was out, I called Dana who told me that after he had thrown her against the car, she had needed stitches and had a black eye for days. She hung up quickly, though, because Jacqueline was under orders to tell on her if she spoke to me – and the threatened punishment was worse than just a black eye.

*

One night I heard the sound of a police radio sputtering and crackling. A woman's voice droned. The noise wound its way in and out of my dreams, meandering around in a way that felt eerily real yet utterly dreamlike. I sat up. My mother's bed lay empty, the sheets grey and abandoned in the dim light. The bedroom door was ajar and the cold blue flashing lights of a police car illuminated the living room in bursts.

'Mom, what's going on?' I asked from the doorway. She was kneeling on the floor, peeking out the front window.

'Sh! Get down! I don't want them to see us!'

I could see the whites of her eyes as she looked up from where she was crouched.

I stooped and scooted to the window. Two policemen leaned against a police car, their massive thighs bulging in their uniform trousers as menacing as the rolling muscles under a Doberman's thin skin. Tom's Pontiac, parked askew, was out front. It had been weeks since I had seen his drunken, bloated face and heard his hectoring voice. I could tell from their postures that the policemen and Tom were having a serious, manly conversation, standing with their legs spread and their hands clenched behind their backs.

'What's going on?' I whispered to Mom.

'Sh!'

Her breathing was heavy. In the light from the police car, I could see the fine lines in her forehead and the nimbus of curls springing out around her head.

We watched and waited. The conversation between these three big men, who looked as if they had played football for a university like Notre Dame twenty years ago and had put on some weight subsequently, suddenly ceased. The policemen shook Tom's hand and one of them clasped his shoulder. The police turned to get into their car.

'Jesus Christ, this can't be happening!'

My mother leaped up and was out the front door in a flash. For someone who never ran because of the cigarettes, she certainly moved.

'Officers, officers!' Her voice quavered.

The three men looked back, suspended in mid-step like characters in a film. They hadn't realised that Tom was driving to our house specifically. They must have thought he had simply skidded to his crazy stop randomly, in front of any old house.

'Officers! How can you let him go! He's drunk! He won't leave me alone; he follows me, he calls me all night. I'm terrified!'

The policemen walked back, reluctantly, to the pool of light around the street lamp. Tom followed and I saw the flare of his lighter as he lit a cigarette.

'Now, ma'am, let's get this straight. What exactly is your problem?'

I felt like yelling, 'It's not her problem, it's that jerk you're talking to!'

My mother hadn't told me about Tom harassing her but I should have known. Every night she locked all the doors and drew all the curtains. In the morning when I awakened, the phone was off the hook and buried under a pillow.

'Do you know this man?' they asked my mother.

'I just want him to leave me alone!'

'Do you want to file a police report?'

'Officer, just tell him to leave me alone!'

Even I could tell she sounded like a petulant two-year-old.

Tom broke in, 'You're going to ruin me, woman. Don't do this, think of the girls.' He grabbed her by the arm.

She shook off his hand.

'Officers, please, how can a poor woman, raising her children, making a living, defend herself against, against . . . this!'

She threw up her hands to point to Tom, who was leaning against the car, smoking the cigarette he had just lit.

Hunkered down behind the window, I saw Tom as the officers did and I didn't think she would convince them. He looked perfectly respectable in his work clothes, a short-sleeved shirt with grey polyester trousers. His hair was short and his silver-framed glasses glinted in the moonlight. She, on the other hand, looked dishevelled. Her hair was sticking out all over and her old flannel pyjamas flapped around her legs. Her face looked haggard and frantic in the shadows. If she didn't swing the policeman over to her side, she would have Tom to deal with, and he would be mad. Mad with a capital M. I didn't know if she could make it back to the house if the police left.

'Please come this way, ma'am,' said one of the policemen.

My mother began to sob as he led her towards the squad car, where they sat talking together. Tom and the other policeman waited quietly. Finally, they got out and the policeman had a word with Tom before he walked very carefully to his Pontiac and drove slowly away. A policeman accompanied my mother back to the front door and told her that her only alternative was a restraining order.

She said, 'But, officer, I don't want to ruin his life.'

'Well, ma'am, if it's a choice of his life being ruined or yours, I know what I'd do. Goodnight, ma'am.'

When she came back in, she lit a cigarette and said, 'Get back to bed, Ashley! I didn't want you to see that. You're not getting a very good impression of men, are you, my daughter? There are some good men in the world. I've even been with some good men.'

She laughed sadly.

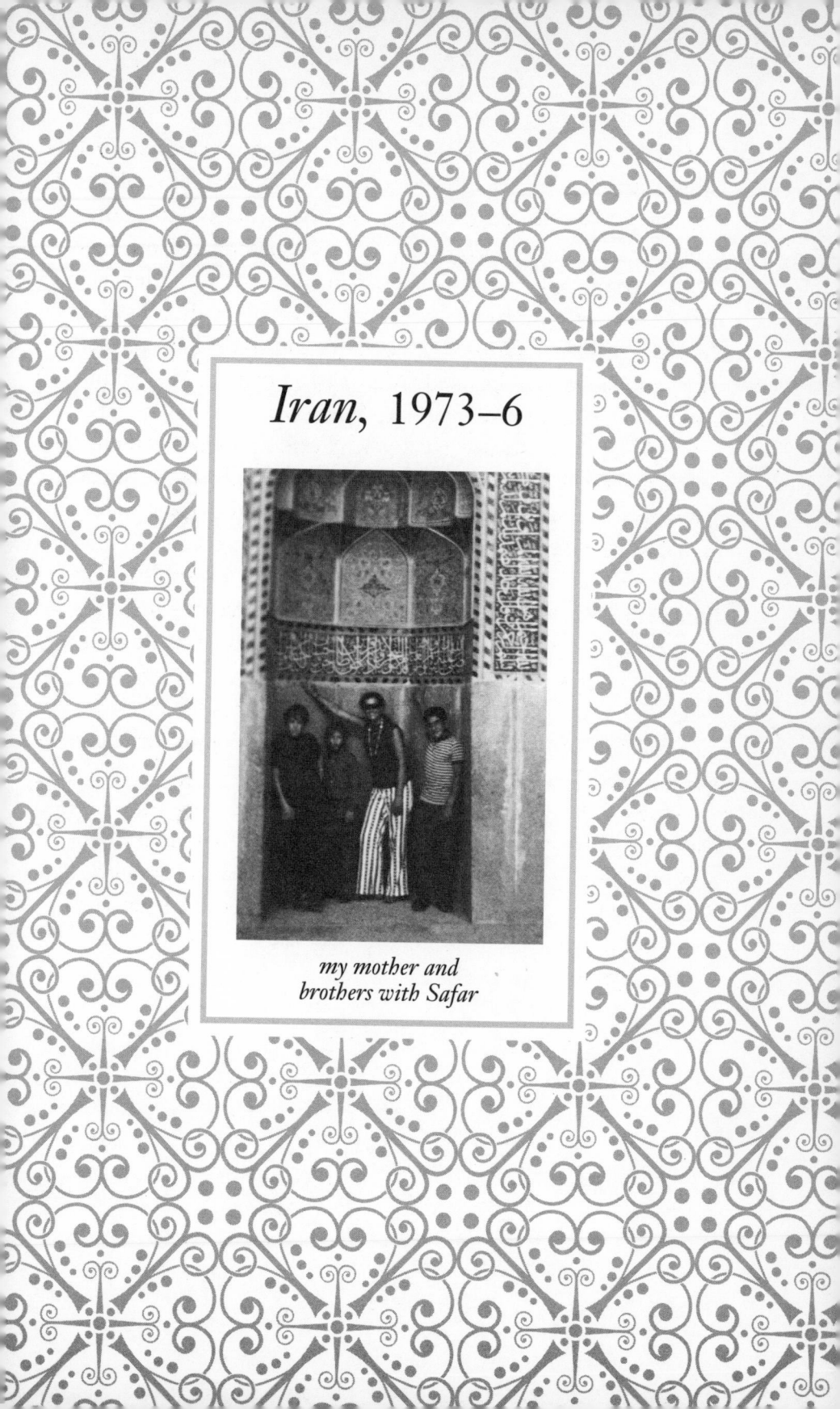

Iran, 1973–6

*my mother and
brothers with Safar*

25

This Isn't Sunny Florida, Missy

the local village store

One hundred and fifty-eight million seconds; 2.6 million minutes; 43,800 hours; 1,825 days; 260 weeks. Five years. Five years that had seemed a million.

Almost to the day that we arrived in America five years earlier, we left. Instead of carrying two suitcases filled with ragged clothing, we sent sixty suitcases crammed with glamorous gowns and cocktail dresses, carefully selected from thrift shops all over Fort Lauderdale. Instead of arguing about the $28 fare with a grumpy coach driver, Uncle Hugh chauffeured us to Miami Airport in a purring Cadillac. My mother carried a small red bankbook that showed she had a couple of thousand hard-earned dollars in a savings account. She still owned her little house on 14th Street fair and square, having decided to rent it to Yosy. She had arrived in the US homeless, penniless and jobless and through sheer determination, *she had survived.*

Now she was ready for a break.

*

The plane surged into the sky and the coastline of Florida receded behind us. Typical of many women faced with a life event, my mother and I were dressed for show and not for comfort: in dresses, pantyhose, high heels.

'Mom, what do you think it will be like in Iran?' I asked once again.

In all our preparations, she had avoided talking about the specifics of the move. Now that she was belted into the seat next to me, I wasn't going to let it rest.

'Where are we going to live? Where are we going to school? Is Dad going to be on the job all the time?'

There was a long silence. My mother's head rested on the back of the seat and she tapped her cigarette on the little table before she lit it. She flared her nostrils, always a sign of anger or annoyance.

'Mom?' I insisted.

She ignored me.

'Mom?' My voice went up a notch in intensity.

She snorted, spurting cigarette smoke. 'Who the hell knows with your father!'

'No, seriously, Mom. Where are we going to live?'

'*I* don't know.'

'But where will we go to school? In Cameron's letter he said he's the oldest in the school and that they don't even really have a teacher for him.'

'Your father will have to figure it out.'

'So you don't know whether we're going to live in Esfahan or Tehran or where I'll go to school?'

'No.'

I stared out the window. I couldn't believe it. All those

phone conversations. All those months off work to prepare for the move. All that time spent buying stupid dresses. I turned back to my mother.

'Mom, do you know *anything* about when we get to Iran? You realise I've already missed a semester of school?'

'Ashley, I don't know the answers. I've done it all for five years, now it's your father's turn.'

My anxiety, which had gathered into a tight hot grenade in my chest, threatened to detonate. I gritted my teeth. So that was how it was going to be. I squeezed my eyes shut. After a few minutes, I pulled out my book and began reading, avoiding looking at my mother. I didn't need to worry, though; she was not in the least concerned about our conversation or me. She was smiling and gesturing to a well-dressed Asian man sitting a few seats ahead.

'Say hello, Ashley.' She nudged me. 'He thinks I was married to a Chinese man,' she whispered, 'because, you know, you look half Chinese with your slitty little eyes.'

A man was standing by his seat, bobbing up and down in a series of half-bows to my mother.

'Mom,' I wailed, 'we're on the plane going back to Dad and you're still flirting with other men!'

'I am *not*!' she said and twisted away from me.

After a few minutes she turned to me and said, vehemently, 'I want better for you, Asho! A man who loves you, cherishes you. Beautiful food in lovely restaurants, nice clothes . . .' She hesitated. 'Don't marry the wrong man, as I did. Marry someone who is going to treasure you, treat you well. You deserve it.'

'So do you,' I replied, resigned. I had heard all this before.

'Well, it's too late for me now, isn't it? I've made my bed and now I have to lie in it.'

'But maybe Dad's changed; maybe he'll be different. He was better that summer, wasn't he?'

'Huh! He'll never change.'

'Well, why are we going back then?'

'I'm tired, Asho, bloody tired. I can't do this any more. There was a reason that God designed human beings to have two parents. It's damn hard to do it by yourself if you're the woman and you're stuck with the kids.'

'So do you wish you had never had kids?'

I asked her this because it was a refrain she returned to like the chorus in a song: 'if you're stuck with the kids, if you're stuck with the kids'.

'No, I just wish I had married a different man.'

*

An hour or so before landing, when suddenly the entire planeload of passengers stands up and stretches, my mother too got up and made her way to the bathroom. Weathering the storm of knocks from irate passengers, she took her time and finally emerged, hair brushed, lipstick applied and sweetly perfumed.

'Brush your hair so you look nice for your father,' she ordered, handing me the brush.

I scowled. I was not pandering to some man just because he was my father. After what she had said earlier, why was she?

We walked across the runway to the low white building I remembered from my childhood. With my pantyhose laddered, my hair askew and my polyester dress twisted and itchy, I felt groggy and uncomfortable. It looked as if most of Tehran had gathered at the airport – most of the male population, at least. My mother and I towered over the majority of the glowering men in the terminal. I looked around, wondering whether all Iranian men had moustaches. Also, why were they all looking at me in that weird, appraising way?

'Do up your dress,' hissed my mother as we queued at passport control.

I glanced down. My dress was undone slightly at the neck. I did it up.

'*Salam, Agha*,' chirped my mother with a big smile.

'Why are you in Iran, Mrs Dartnell?' asked the immigration official in broken English.

'We lived here for many years and we are just back visiting friends.'

Oh God, I thought.

'How long will you be staying? Can I see your return ticket?'

'A few weeks. We have to pick up our return tickets at Iran Air in town.'

He flipped through every page of the passport. Mom's face was bright, blank and hopeful. He knew something was amiss.

'Who is meeting you here?' he asked.

'Our friends,' replied my mother.

He looked down at our passports, scrutinising them further.

'You were here two years ago?'

She nodded.

He called another official to look through the documents. They flipped through a large ledger filled with handwritten Farsi. A tiny, clear trickle of sweat worked its way through the ringlets at my mother's temple. She stood resolutely, her eyes fixed on the middle distance. The queue behind pressed against us. The other man ran his finger down the list of names. Finally, he closed the book and both men looked up, sceptically. I held my breath, my fingers crossed so tightly they throbbed.

I knew exactly what was going on: my father was still living in Iran illegally and we were entering on tourist visas. We had done the same two years earlier when we had visited, but then we had a return ticket and we really were just visiting.

227

My mother had said repeatedly she wouldn't return until my father got his affairs in order and we could live in Iran legally. That had been part of the delay in Florida before joining the boys.

'Thank you, Mrs Dartnell.'

I uncrossed my cramping fingers.

'Don't say a word, Ashley. In Iran, the walls have eyes and the floors have ears. There is no one and no place in this country that is safe – *remember that.*' Mom whispered this out of the side of her mouth as we walked to collect the suitcases.

As we approached customs, she said, 'Whatever they want, just let them take it.'

If I had felt groggy before, I was now as alert as a greyhound before a race, quivering and waiting for the gun to go off.

Our suitcases were hauled up on to a counter and the cranky zips and locks undone. A man in a uniform pawed through our clothes, lifting up a colourful dress here, a bra there. My face grew warm. Yuck. He jumbled all four suitcases, literally turning them over, and then at the end he simply turned on his heel and walked to the next passenger. We scrambled to repack the bags, kneeling on the floor in the middle of the baggage area.

'Bastard. Bastard. Your father will be waiting outside.'

The terminal was so crowded, we couldn't see Dad or the boys anywhere. I felt shaky. Our reception back to Iran had hardly been what I had expected. I stood on tiptoes to scan the crowd: no tall tanned man with black hair flopping over his forehead; no almost thirteen-year-old boy with big teeth and big eyes; no nine-year-old with a dimple in his cheek.

My mother lit a cigarette. 'They'll find us. They know our arrival time and your father knows the airport.'

Half an hour, forty-five minutes, and then an hour. Men in

tight trousers with mismatched jackets stared at us, bumped into us, clicked their fingers and whistled at us.

'Go look around and I'll stay here and watch the luggage,' ordered my mother, after glancing at her watch.

'No! I can't just barge into all these people.'

My dress, which in Florida had seemed strait-laced, now seemed revealing. Almost every man who passed looked at us and said something or made a 'kiss kiss' sound, as if calling a dog, and almost always accompanied by finger clicking.

'Stay here.' My mother broke into the crowd of men author-itatively, glaring at them as she passed.

After a while, she returned. My skin felt thin and my eyeballs ached.

'Mom,' I asked, carefully, 'does Dad know we're coming tonight?'

'Of course he goddam knows we're coming, he bought the goddam tickets.'

We sat waiting, slumped on the suitcases. After a while I asked, 'Can you call him?'

My mother's voice, when she finally answered, burned with fury. 'I don't have a phone number for him, and anyway, take a look around, Ashley, this isn't sunny Florida. Do you see any phone booths?'

I gazed around at the cracked marble walls, the flickering fluorescent lighting, the windows coated with dust. The airport seethed with people. Men spat sunflower-seed husks on to the floor, and along the walls people sat with large bundles tied in chadors. There wasn't a phone in sight.

'Well, go to the airport guards and tell them we need to borrow a phone. You speak Farsi.'

'Are you *crazy*? Are you absolutely *mad*? *Nuts*? *Insane*? Your father's not even legal in this country, we enter on tourist visas, and you say I should go ask the guards where he is.'

I pursed my lips and stayed silent. A long while later, we

were sitting on our suitcases outside the terminal. It was late at night. The airport building was empty.

'Mom, I think we should just take a taxi to a hotel.'

'A hotel? A hotel!'

It was as if I had suggested admitting ourselves to a mental hospital or a prison.

'A hotel?' Her voice was harsh.

'Yeah, a h-o-t-e-l.'

I spoke slowly and condescendingly. How had I let myself get into this position again, relying on my parents? I had thought I was being so clever, checking and double-checking the tickets. I had never imagined that he wouldn't pick us up.

'And how do you think they'll find us if we go to a hotel, Miss Know-it-all?'

'We can come back tomorrow and wait again.'

'You are crazy, you really are. Even if I knew a hotel to go to, how do you think I would pay for it and the taxi, and then how do you think we would get back? This is not Florida, missy, this is Iran, and it is not safe for two women to be wandering around Tehran in the middle of the night.'

Everything she said dripped with sarcasm.

'You didn't even bring money, did you?'

I shook my head and slumped on the suitcase. In the books I had read, when faced with hardship families came together and figured out ways of solving the problem. In our family, we were crippled by fighting with each other.

'I didn't bring money because I knew if I did, he would just take it. Do you think I want to be here? Do you think I want to be in this position?' My mother glared into the night, muttering. 'Goddam son of a bitch. I can't believe I came back. He'll never change. God damn him to hell.'

'Fine, Mom. Fine. We'll sit on the side of the road of this nice safe airport for the night. And then if they don't come tomorrow, we'll just sit here and then we'll starve and die and they can find our skeletons sitting on these suitcases here. At some point we are going to have to make a move. Plus, I need the bathroom.'

We sat and waited. And waited. And waited.

'What if he's died? What if they've had a car crash?' I fretted.

It was a dark night and the glow of the street lights was feeble.

'Don't worry, he hasn't died. I wouldn't be that lucky,' she said.

'*Khanoom? Khanoomeh* Dartnell?'

A fat man holding a cigarette ran towards us, jacket flying, face sweating, eyes shining with anxiety and joy.

'*Khanoomeh* Dartnell! *Bebakhsheed!* Escuze me, Meesus Dartnell!'

I recognised Sammii, the foreman, the one my father had given $2,000 for his daughter's wedding. Despite this, my mother fell on Sammii and they both wept in each other's arms.

'Where are *Mohandes* Dartnell and the boys?' my mother asked.

'A delay on the job,' Sammii explained in a rushed voice, the blood vessels in his bulging eyes so prominent I thought he would have a stroke right there in the airport parking lot.

'It's the usual thing, Sammii,' said my mother, 'you've known him almost as long as I have. Would you do this to your wife and daughter, Sammii? Will this man ever change?'

Sammii stopped dead in his tracks and looked up at my mother, who was almost a half-foot taller in her high heels.

'*Khanoomeh* Dartnell, *beh Khoda, fekr nemeekonam.*'

I translated haltingly in my head; I had forgotten much of my Farsi. 'For the love of God, I don't think so.'

My mother wanted to drive straight to Esfahan, but Sammii dissuaded her as there would be no benzene pumps open during the night, and the road was dangerous. We should get some sleep. Also, he needed to pick up some parts to take to the job tomorrow.

The hotel was in southern Tehran, on a big, noisy maydan. The room was tiny and threadbare, barely big enough for the two wooden beds with thin quilts thrown on top, stinking of an unimaginable combination of fly spray and filthy toilets. As we entered the dimly lit room, *soosks*, the scrappy Iranian version of a cockroach, raced down the walls and disappeared under the beds. We fell on to the covers and slept in our clothes, exhausted.

26

Home to Iran

at the Esfahan bazaar

I awakened to the sound of roosters crowing. I sat up.
'Mom, wake up! Listen!'

Outside, horns blared and donkeys brayed. I was hungry
and thirsty and I desperately needed to go to the bathroom,
but these sounds had taken me straight back to my childhood
and I was bubbling over with joy. I was home! Home to an
Iran as warm as a ripe cantaloupe in the hot sun, an Iran where
friendly people offered legendary hospitality, an Iran where
you wake up to the sound of sheep baaing and men hammer-
ing, an Iran where plates were filled with mounds of fluffy
white rice, slick with butter and redolent with the charbroiled
smell of kebab. Now, despite the long uncertain wait at the
airport, despite the grotty hotel, despite everything, these
sounds clicked into a place in my head, like a key that fit
perfectly into a lock, and welcomed me back to the land of my
birth. I was home to Iran.

'Bedbugs,' said my mother when I showed her my welts.

That was the only word she said to me that morning. Once again, she acted as if everything were my fault. We sat on the hard bed, the morning light streaming through the window revealing the chipped, mustard-coloured paint on the walls and the peeling floors. Sammii arrived and hustled us out. Proudly, he showed us his small white Paykan.

'*Aghayeh Mohandes* Dartnell bought this for me,' he said. '*No eh no.*' Brand-new.

My mother's lips tightened. We had all loved our car, Jessie, but Mom had literally held her together with chewing gum and Scotch tape.

*

Traffic surged around us despite the early hour. In the years since we had been gone, the roads of Tehran had become clogged with thousands and thousands of cars, all darting and honking chaotically. Already men were screaming at each other out of the windows and, judging by the number of crushed fenders and doors, bust-ups were common. There were few women about – none of them driving, and just a scattering, in their chadors, going to the bread shops or crouched in front of the *joob*, getting water for breakfast. We pulled over within a few minutes and Sammii waddled out to buy us each a small glass of hot sweet tea and *sangak* bread from a *cha-ee khooneh*. Of all the Iranian breads, *sangak* was my mother's favourite: thin and crusty, with big bubbles where the dough popped in the hot oven. Click click: I had the feeling of the key turning in the lock again and the deluge of familiar sensations.

'*Cigar meetooneen bekharie?*' asked my mother. She was stocking up on cigarettes. Sammii returned a few minutes later with a few packets of the Viceroys that she preferred.

I sat in the back seat, the neck of my dress pulled up over my nose to diffuse the smell emanating from Sammii. That was another thing I had forgotten – all the smells. People here didn't have access to the water and clean clothes that I had taken for granted in Florida. It was broiling hot already, yet most of the men were wearing long *shalvar* and shirts with a woollen vest or jacket. Despite the fact that the Shah's father had made the practice of wearing the chador illegal, most of the women on the street were covered from head to toe by the long veil.

On the side of the road, as we left the city, were the flocks of small goats with their downtrodden air I remembered from my childhood. I kept my face pressed to the glass so I wouldn't miss anything. Try as I might, though, I slept for the first part of the drive to Esfahan. My mother, tough as ever, shared cigarettes and nattered with Sammii, milking him for information about my father. My head rolled against the window as we bounced over the serrated roads and I awakened from time to time to overhear the conversation.

'Dear God, no! He has been faithful to you, utterly. He only works and sometimes he goes to his family,' said Sammii.

'His family?' asked my mother, instantly suspicious.

'Yes, *Khanoom*, you know, *Aghayeh* Fred and *Khanoomeh* Jill and *Khanoomeh* Susan and the boys.'

I recognised the names of Fred and Jill. Fred was my father's cousin who had moved to Iran in the mid 1960s with his wife Jill and three sons. He worked for one of the big pharmaceutical companies, selling baby formula. My mother loved Fred, who was a jolly, red-faced man with a passion for British folk songs. He was another one of the many men who, I had observed, were almost unable to look away when he was around her. Susan, I learned, was Jill's unmarried sister.

My mother's antennae were up. 'Did Mr Dartnell spend time with Susan?'

I wondered to myself why it was perfectly all right for her to 'spend time' with Tom but not for my father to see other women.

'*Nakher, Khanoomeh* Dartnell, don't say such things!' Sammii sounded shocked and upset.

Finally, we were on a long straight road passing through mile after mile of desert. My eyes grew weary of the tan terrain and I couldn't tell whether the dust eddies and swirls were real or just my eyes blurring. Sammii drove straight down the middle of the road, avoiding the rutted edges, swerving to avoid oncoming cars at the last minute. At one point, we passed a farm where watermelons lay green in the dirt, their vines withered and reptilian.

'Mom, look, see that?' I pointed to the fields filled with melons and the low, dirty, concrete buildings. 'It looks so familiar.'

I had that same feeling – an unlocking of a part of my brain or heart – that this was a place I had been before, a road I had travelled.

'Yes, you've been there,' she said casually, 'we knew the owners.'

I was dismayed that I barely remembered the farm; I was the one in the family with the supersonic memory. I was the repository of the family's recollections of Iran.

As we left behind the dusty watermelon farm, where the melons were ripening, sweetening and reddening in the hot sun, I worried about what I remembered. I tried consciously to imagine Dad and the boys in my head: Dad with his strong chin and his distinctive walk. His hands with their prominent veins and blunt fingernails. I had never seen his hands dirty, never seen his nails rimmed in black, despite the filthy conditions of his work. I couldn't re-create his voice or his accent, though. I tried to describe them to myself: his voice was high for a man's – not high like a woman's, but somehow light, not low and heavy. His accent was English, but soft, not clipped, and definitely not American. He had an awkward accent in Farsi, although he could read and write it, and recite Rumi's

poetry and the Koran. I could *describe* his voice and his accent.
But I couldn't actually hear them in my head.

I remembered Cameron better – or at least as of September,
when I had seen him last, but he must have changed. When he
left Florida he was small and skinny; I towered over him by at
least eight inches. He might have gone through puberty without my knowing or even thinking about it. And Rian? He had
been eight years old, a little boy with twinkling eyes. I wondered
whether we would still be such good friends, whether he and
Cameron still fought, whether they both still loved animals.

My thoughts spun around like the dust eddies in the desert
around us, while the car bumped along the potholed road for
450 long, hot, dusty kilometres.

*

Esfahan was picture-postcard beautiful with azure minarets
silhouetted in a transparent blue sky. Turquoise mosque
domes glowed in the afternoon sunlight. A wide river, the
Zayandeh, wound its way through the city with graceful
bridges arching over it every few miles. Broad avenues, lined
with immense trees, followed the path of the river. It felt as if
I was arriving in a city from the *Arabian Nights*.

Once off the capacious avenues, Sammii drove through back
streets so constricted I feared the walls of the houses would
scratch the sides of the car. As the streets narrowed, I became
more excited. For months I hadn't thought about how much I
had missed my two brothers or allowed myself to acknowledge
how alone I had felt without them. We had always been the
three musketeers – us against the world, fists up.

On the other hand, the thought of seeing my father raised
conflicting emotions. I wanted to see him and have our family
together, of course. But if it was going to be the way it had
been during the month we spent two summers ago, with all
the tension, all the fighting, the stinginess, the judgmental
views about how girls should behave, then no. My father had

missed the sixties, holed up here in Iran, and he still thought wives and children – especially girl children – should behave the way they did in some Victorian vision he had of the world.

I tried to imagine us as a family but my mental picture was always intruded upon by discord and fighting. We hadn't been a family in so long, maybe ever. Could we be one now?

'The Jolfa section, *Khanoom*. It is the old Armenian section, one of the most ancient neighbourhoods in Esfahan.' Sammii was explaining about where we would live.

'So it is a nice house then?' my mother asked. In Iran, the Armenians, like the Jews and the Baha'is, were often well educated and affluent.

'*Khanoomeh* Dartnell, I have known you for many years and you are very dear to me. I have seen your three children born and I have lived through some difficult times with *Aghayeh* Dartnell. I have to tell you honestly, although it pains me to do so, it is not a house. It is the office.'

My mother squinted out the window. 'So he hasn't found a house for us?'

Sammii hesitated a moment. 'Well, it was once a house, but now it is the office. In truth, I don't know where you will sleep, *Khanoomeh* Dartnell.'

Sammii spoke using lots of *tarof* – all flowery words and false politeness. If he weren't driving, he would have been wringing his hands.

He bustled us in through the glass doors on the balcony to a waiting room, where chunky bulldozer parts and air filters were stacked along the wall.

'Esmail, take the suitcases in,' he yelled. Workers sat drinking tea and smoking. 'Sit down, *Khanoom*, sit down.' Sammii shooed the workers off the sofa and dusted it off with a flourish. He was the foreman for a reason.

'Safar!' he screamed. 'Safar, *cha-ee beeyar*.'

A young man, wearing a shirt so small that it gaped open,

came in with a tray of tea. Workers squatted around us, their clothes dusty and torn. An older man, wearing a suit and thick glasses, was at a desk, working an old-fashioned adding machine. His fingers flew across the keys and then, zing, he pulled the lever and wrote down a number. Click click click click zing. When we arrived, he had stood and bowed deeply over our outstretched hands. Our dresses were dishevelled – the stripes on my dress that had been white were now tan. I squirmed and scratched, bloodying the bites on my arms and legs.

'Where is *Mohandes* Dartnell?' Sammii bustled around, shouting.

'*Khanoom*, can I get you another cup of tea?' asked Esmail, with a shy smile. His eyes were a light cat's-eye yellow.

Sammii peeled off a couple of thousand rials and gave them to Safar. He determined from the polite accountant that my father was en route from the job and picking the boys up from school on the way.

'So much for a warm welcome,' muttered my mother.

The sole acknowledgement that two boys lived here was a rickety metal table with a Scrabble set, some playing cards and schoolbooks stacked in a corner. Safar reappeared with pistachios and some *gaz*, the sickly-sweet white pistachio candy indigenous to Iran. He also carried a bag with two plastic plates and a couple of forks and knives that he had just bought. I realised that they didn't even have dishes for us. Boy, I thought, Dad really had done *nothing* to prepare for our arrival. We had been getting ready for months in Florida and he didn't even have a place for us to sleep.

I don't remember exactly the first thing my mother said to my father, but certainly it contained some of the following: goddam, bastard, abandoned at the airport, son of a bitch, repeat of the same thing, goddam, sitting on a suitcase freezing my ass off, middle of the night, unfit for a beggar, bastard, goddam, son of a bitch, live in this shit hole, who do you think you are? She did not kiss him hello. Her anger even distracted her from saying a proper hello to the boys and I could see the disappointment on their faces. When she finally turned to them, they leaped around, laughed and boasted about their exploits. Their hair was short and they had grown so much their trousers were up around their ankles. My father kissed me and gave me a quick huggle buggle, saying, 'How's my big girl?' but my mother's anger diverted us all.

The boys dragged me off to show me the office, the orchard next door and their pet jerboas, which were funny little kangaroo-rat-like gerbils they had caught in the desert. They then introduced me formally to Safar and Esmail.

Rian teased Safar: 'What kind of monkey do you think Safar looks like, Ashley?'

I had a hard time with the Farsi. After almost a year, the boys were fluent again and my mother seemed never to have forgotten it, chatting away with Sammii in the car. I understood most of what was said when I knew what they were talking about. When it came to figuring out specifically what kind of monkey the five-foot-tall and three-foot-wide houseboy looked like, I had no idea. The four of them burst out laughing.

'I am beeg noze monkey,' stumbled Safar in broken English, gleefully showing me a picture of a proboscis monkey in a nature book. The monkey had an enormous nose that dangled like a red banana. Cameron and Rian screamed with laughter and Safar showed his tiny white teeth in a bashful smile.

'Yes, I monkey this,' he said proudly, pointing at the picture.

I turned to Cameron and Rian. 'How can you be so mean?'

They screamed with laughter again.

'We're not making fun of him. He was looking at the book and he said he thought it looked like him!' said Cameron.

'When he eats, rice goes up his nose, it's so big!' Rian was practically shrieking with glee, while Safar laughed so hard that tears came to his eyes. 'He asked if he could have the book to show his family when he goes to his village,' Rian said.

The boys and I joined our mother in the office. We watched while my father finished talking with the workers who had been squatting around the perimeter of the room, conferring with the Armenian accountant to determine how much cash they needed from the bank and then going through a list of spare parts that Sammii needed to bring back from Tehran. Mummy sat on the sofa, smoking and glowering, while the boys told her about the wild pig hunt they had been on recently. Finally, my mother asked my father what we were having for dinner. She had not eaten all day and I had nibbled just a few pistachios and *gaz*.

'That's up to you, Mummy!' he replied with a sarcastic twinkle. 'This is your castle now and you are the queen of it. Safar and Esmail will buy whatever you need to cook. Just tell them.'

My mother looked as if he had walked over and slapped her across her face. She was taken aback for only a second or two, though; her ability to take stock rapidly and hit out hard was one of the things I really admired about her.

She jerked up and screamed, in front of the poor old Armenian accountant, 'If you think I left my life and my house in gorgeous Fort Lauderdale, Florida, to come over here and live in a goddam office and cook in some filthy kitchen, you got another thought coming, buster! You get someone to make us some dinner. Don't tell me you and the boys wouldn't have eaten tonight if we weren't here!'

My father smirked and said, 'So happy to see nothing's changed with you, Genie.' He turned and disappeared.

The boys and I glanced at each other. In a while, Safar carried in a tray with a big plate of eggs scrambled with tomatoes. The boys and I had bought warm *barbary* bread at the baker around the corner. It was the most delicious thing I had ever eaten – the bread warm and soft, smeared with butter, the eggs runny and pink with the cooked ripe tomatoes. For dessert, we had tea and more *barbary* with butter and honey.

After dinner, the boys took me to their room. We pulled the mattress off the top bunk and took it into our parents room next door. Mom would sleep on the bed and Dad on the floor. The boys moved upstairs on to the roof where they slept on quilts in the open air.

I lay awake in their room, my body clock off and my mind awash with thoughts about this next phase of my life. I hadn't allowed myself to anticipate anything, but I certainly wouldn't have predicted any of the past twenty-four hours. I had absolutely no idea what would happen next.

27

Mad Dogs and Englishmen

*the blind
school pool*

At dawn we piled into the car and glided through a ghostly Esfahan before travelling a teeth-bashing hour on rutted roads to the site. Once there, my mother and I sat in the car, parked next to the canal, which daily grew longer and penetrated further into the desert. The boys ran off: Rian to catch lizards and build rock forts, Cameron to leap on to the trucks and the bulldozers. There were no toilet facilities. The men normally squatted a few yards from where they worked and our presence meant that they had to search for places further afield, giving them the perfect opportunity to wander by and stare at the *Khanoom* and her daughter, broiling in the car.

I watched the men sweating over their pickaxes and shovels, the bulldozers smoothing the sides of the canal, the loaders depositing huge heaps of the desert sand into big Benz trucks. I had already finished the Louis L'Amour and Zane Grey novels my father had next to his bed. My mother sat and smoked, sometimes cutting her toenails or tweezing out the grey hairs just beginning to sprout in her reddish-blonde curls.

During these long periods that we baked in the car together, she was largely silent, but from time to time she would burst into a diatribe against my father.

'Can you believe that he would bring us to this shit hole? Asho, I've made a terrible mistake coming back. He hasn't changed. What else could I do, though? I tried so hard in Florida but I thought it was the best for you kids, especially Cameron, to come back here. The boys need a father. But how can I live with this man? After five years in charge of my own life, he won't let me make a single decision. Won't give me fifty rials. Won't even take us out for a bloody *chelow kebab*. Jesus, what have I done?'

Her monologue continued.

'Look at him – mad dogs and Englishmen out in the midday sun.'

My father jogged around the site, hatless.

She looked at the thermometer taped to the dashboard. It's a hundred and forty-five degrees in the goddam sun and he's running. The man is mad.'

Naturally, I agreed with her. Naturally, I thought it was ludicrous that he had brought us from Florida and dumped us in his office, all of us sleeping on makeshift beds, our clothes in piles on the floor. Naturally, I was distraught. But, it was *her* decision, *her* choice that had led to this situation and *she* needed to figure it out.

'Mom, we've got to sign up for school. Where are we going to live? What's the date?'

Questioning her was never a good idea, though. Cornered, she lashed out.

'There are more important things than your school!'

'Not to me!' I yelled as I tumbled out the door, slamming it so hard the dust rose around my face.

I was furious they had yanked me out of ninth grade a semester early to sit around Dad's job site. I strode around, kicking rocks, dodging the piles of human shit covered with flies that dotted the work site every few feet. There was no place to sit, no shade.

When we had begun visiting the site a few weeks previously, there was a village close by, so I would watch women washing clothes, pounding the laundry on rocks and then spilling a dribble of water from a *satl*, pounding again, dribbling, pounding, until they had washed out as much of the Tide and dirt as possible in that desert environment, where half a cup of water was enough to wash a pair of trousers.

Sometimes I watched a man separating wheat from its chaff. He threshed a huge pile of grain, flaying it again and again with a beater and then flinging it high into the hot wind to blow away the husks. A haze of dust and chaff hung in the air around him. Then he would crouch, sifting the wheat and picking out pebbles and insects. It was slow, hard work and he looked miserable doing it.

Near by women squatted, their chadors tied around them like giant romper suits as they pounded the grain with mortars. They stared up, unseeing, at the big equipment rumbling past. My father had pointed them out and said, 'This village will be transformed by the canal. For the first time ever, they will have water to grow crops, to drink, to wash. It will be a miracle for them.'

Now the job had moved past the village and there was nothing to watch beyond the monotonous back-breaking work of digging the canal. I found my father and followed him around, listening as he explained to his men the next step in building the canal. To me, the work they did each day looked exactly the same as the work they had done the day before, so it seemed ridiculous that my father had to be so closely involved in staring through the surveying equipment and leaping into the canal to check the depth and the tilt of the walls. He assured me, though, that a mistake of a few centimetres a day would result in the canal ending up in the middle of nowhere. He showed me the drawings, described how the height of the walls was determined, how rapidly the water would flow, how to judge the pressure of the water. When I asked if I could do anything, help in any way, he laughed.

All the while, the white-hot sun pounded down. My long-sleeved shirt and trousers chafed my chapped skin, my tongue was parched, the unrelenting heat made me feel faint. I could barely stand. I stumbled and hot flashes of colour rose in waves in front of me.

'Dad,' I gasped, 'how do the workers manage the heat in their thick clothes without hats, with no water?'

'You're not fit, Ashley!' my father remonstrated. 'The workers are strong. Every day you should do a trot down the canal for a couple of miles. Your mother didn't make you work or exercise in Florida. You're soft. Look at how much stronger the boys are.'

'I'm fit! All we did in Florida was work. It's boiling.'

'That's not what your mummy says. She says all you did in Florida was have fun.'

'What? She's lying.' I was not about to let either of them off that easily.

'Oh really?' He walked away, cutting me off before I could respond.

Despite the heat, I raced back to the car. 'Why did you tell Dad that we had such a good life in Florida?' I asked my mother.

Her cool grey eyes ignored mine and she smoked steadily in the front seat.

'Why?'

'Well, we did. Better than this.'

'I hated Florida!'

'Well, I hate this!'

I started to answer but then shrugged. Maybe Florida was better than this. At least after my chores, I could go to the library, read and go to school. We had food and a home. Here in Esfahan, day after day, we went to the job; night after night, we returned to the office, ate scrambled eggs, waited until the last worker left and rushed to take a bath before the hot water ran out. My mother disappeared immediately after dinner to her room. My father read the paper and worked. The boys and I played Scrabble or cards.

At bedtime that night, I lay awake, not tired because in the afternoon I had succumbed to a heavy, coma-like sleep in the stultifying car. I pitched and rolled for hours, worried about our situation, finally falling asleep in the early morning hours when the dogs had stopped baying but the cocks had not yet begun to crow.

*

The small lane, a calm passage between the cacophony of the main road, with its honking cars, and the still compound within, led to the blind school. We were here after days of begging and pleading from the boys that we leave the job early 'and show Ashley and Mummy the blind school'.

We laughed and chattered as we ran our hands down the dried-brick walls leading to the school, pulling out bits of straw and tickling each other's ears, pretending to be flies. The entrance door was wooden and unassuming. Painted decades ago, it had faded to a mottled aqua like weathered copper. We rang the bell repeatedly, its clang reverberating until its echo faded into the shadows. Finally we heard the flapping of the caretaker's slippers and the door opened to reveal a man, a felt hat atop his head, a long white shirt over his baggy *shalvar*.

'*Salam, salam alaykom*,' he greeted us, and led us into the serene world of the Church Missionary Society in Esfahan.

The tall trees whispered overhead and shaded the school, which was adjacent to the church of St Luke. We followed him silently to the pool. The water looked as thick as velvet: an impenetrable, opaque, agate green. A babble of voices preceded the entrance of a group of blind children, their blank eyes oozing, but with smiles on their vacant faces. They entered the pool tentatively, then pulled themselves around and around the edge. A bony-shouldered man with potato-coloured skin helped a teenage girl to swim. Her shrieks of fear and pleasure pierced the tranquillity of the churchyard.

'*Yavash*, careful, calm down,' the pasty man crooned, in his English-accented Farsi.

We sat by the pool, waiting for the blind kids to get out. Members of the church could swim here when the children weren't using it. Looking at them in the pool made me feel sick. As well as being blind, many of them were also alarmingly, painfully crippled, their teeth rotted, their hair chopped off in chunks. The missionaries picked these children up off the streets. Although it was a dying custom, there were still parents who maimed their babies so they could make a living as beggars. As they grew up, the children became less appealing, earned less money and ate more food, and then their parents abandoned them.

'Dad, why are these kids blind?' I whispered.

'Trachoma,' he explained. 'It's terrible – extremely painful. The eyelid turns in and scratches the cornea, which causes the blindness.'

'Ugh, it's gross. Can they treat it?' I grimaced.

'It's too late for these children and treatment is expensive, but I think that once they're here the missionaries teach them a trade so they don't have to beg.'

'How many are there?'

'Here, a couple of dozen. In Iran? In these poor countries? Multitudes.'

'Oh God, poor kids.' I buried my face in my hands. 'I'm not going in the pool. I'll catch it. I can't believe you let the boys swim in there.'

'Don't be silly. You're not going to get anything.' My father's response was clipped. He had no tolerance for 'girly' behaviour.

'You just told me it's *highly* contagious,' I yelped. 'There must be a million,' I changed my mind, 'ten million trachoma germs, floating around in that disgusting water, just waiting to latch on to my eyes.'

My mother chipped in from the sidelines, where she sat sunning herself in a bikini, for after weeks without lunch and nothing more than scrambled eggs for dinner, she had lost twenty pounds and felt thin enough to appear publicly in a bathing suit. 'Have some sympathy for these poor children, Ashley!'

'I do have sympathy for them, I just don't want to go blind!'

The pale missionary pulled himself out, water streaming off his scrawny chest. He walked around the pool, hauling children out by the arm, draping them with ragged towels and murmuring to them to go in and get dressed. They inched along the walls, much as they had crept around the edge of the pool, until they found the door and went out to find their rooms. He gently lifted one child into a rudimentary wheelchair.

'Ask him, then, if you don't believe me,' said my father.

I scowled at him.

'Hello,' said my father, walking over to the man. 'My, ah,

daughter is worried about swimming in the pool.' He stumbled on the word 'daughter'.

The young missionary looked over at me, shaking his long hair so that water sprayed in all directions. 'Uh no, swim here every day, never had a problem.'

'Do you worry about catching diseases?' asked my father in a way that indicated he couldn't believe how ridiculous I was being.

'Uh no, not really. Never thought about it.'

The man smoothly bumped the child down the steps out of the pool enclosure.

Course not, I thought. You believe God is going to protect you! Well, why should he protect you, you stupid twit, if he didn't protect these children from getting these diseases and from their own parents injuring them?

'See ya then.' He gave a cheerful wave to my brothers.

'Bye!' they yelled to his back. His swimming trunks hung off his hips and his ribs stood out all down his spine.

I sat near the edge, stubbornly refusing to go further. The pool became still for a moment, then the boys and my father cannon-balled in, shattering the silence. I marvelled that something that just a few seconds before had looked so impenetrable, when disturbed became clear and crystalline. The boys leaped around, flipping and splashing, jumping off my father's shoulders and pulling each other under. They were tanned and wiry.

'Come in, Ashley, you silly goose!' yelled my father. 'We've been swimming in the pool for months and none of us are blind.'

I reluctantly conceded this was true, and it *was* boiling, and dust from the job had coated my skin and collected in my hair and ears. I slipped into the green water. The cool slipperiness of it, soft and silky, caressed my arms and legs as if it were soft, heavy, emerald satin. The top layer of the water smelled dank, like disease. I imagined a thick layer of pus and infection floating on top of the pool like an invisible scum, but I squeezed my eyes shut and lost myself in the water.

*

Esfahan was tranquil early in the morning. The sound of traffic and street vendors calling out their wares only gradually replaced the sounds of birds in the *chenar* trees and the water rushing in the *joob*. I sat at the gate of the British Consulate, my elbows on my knees, reading my book while waiting for the library to open. Occasionally I looked up at a knock-kneed donkey, its panniers packed with bricks, being chivvied along by its master, or to see a joobhopper, loaded with wild-eyed sheep, drive past.

The slim Indian librarian emerged, as silently as a genie, glowing in the early-morning light. She was an apparition, materialising suddenly and soundlessly out of nowhere. The rooms, lined with books, were silent and dark, the sunlight diffuse, the dust motes hovering in the stillness. With its leather armchairs, the library was redolent of a more civilised era.

The librarian glided around, shelving books, her slender hands deferentially placing each volume. I chose one, two, four, or seven books, sank into the chair by the window and floated away. When it was lunchtime, the librarian drew me back into the real world. While I read, my spirit was far away, which made the return to reality abrupt and painful. It always took me a few minutes to get my bearings before I stumbled outside.

The business of a small regional consulate in a dusty oasis town continued around me, with people intermittently coming and going and phones occasionally breaking the silence. Infrequently, someone interrupted with a 'And what are you reading now?' Some days my parents gave me 50 rials to buy a packet of biscuits at the supermarket across the street. Most days, though, I sat outside, oblivious to the flies buzzing in my eyes, the sun beating on my head, the grass itching my legs, the rumble of my tummy and the dryness of my mouth, completely and totally absorbed in my book.

In the late afternoon, Rian or Cameron burst through the gates of the British Consulate, calling in a high piping voice, 'Ashley, come on, we're here.' Stiffly, I would unbend, fold over the corner of my page and leave the tree-shaded, bird-twittering haven.

Now on the days when I went out to the job, I armed myself with books. For the first time, I was reading 'real' books and my head was full not only of the characters and stories but also of the magic of the writing: Waugh, Maugham, Greene, Buck, Hemingway, Steinbeck. I loved the tangible heft of the books themselves, in hard covers, bound in cloth. I rubbed the cross-hatched texture with the plump ball of my thumb. But mostly, I loved the stories. Each time I opened a book, I offered up a brief prayer, silently communicating my intense thanks to the author: thank you for saving me from this day; thank you for taking me away; thank you for showing me another way to be.

Without my escape of books, my mother was finding the tedium of the job, day in and day out unbearable.

'Lin, let's do *something, anything,*' she pleaded.

The blind school pool every once in a while was not enough. My father and brothers suddenly remembered Team House, a small social club established by the US military where Americans gathered to see a new US film every Friday night. It became the highlight of my mother's week. Behind the locked metal gates, a movie screen was set up and chairs set in rows in a leafy garden. We never knew which film would arrive that week from a US army base somewhere in the world, but we could rely on the fact that it would be something exciting:

Charles Bronson, Clint Eastwood or Steve McQueen, fighting Indians or Germans or Russians.

My parents headed straight through to the smoke-filled bar, with its tart smell of fermented hops, where my mother drank tea and my father an American beer. A poster of a naked pregnant woman, her breasts resting on her out-thrust belly, presided over the counter, like a Madonna above an altar. Below her, a dark-skinned Sikh with a comical handlebar moustache sullenly dispensed drinks. The bluff, friendly voices of the Bell Helicopter and American military personnel rang out as they described the latest incomprehensible behaviour of their Iranian colleagues.

As dusk turned to night and bats began to flit through the trees, we sat on the folding chairs on the lawn to watch the movie. After each reel, there was a break during which the younger kids ran around playing chase. Occasionally the celluloid broke and we would rupture into yells, claps and whistles until someone came out to splice it together. When the film finally spluttered back to life, we would burst into applause.

My brothers zigzagged about, fireflies flashing around them, while I sat by myself, staring longingly at the small knot of teenagers, hoping that one would look towards me. There were several girls and one boy, Robert, whom I quickly became fixated on – learning all about him, his family and where he came from in America, eavesdropping on his conversations. I was not really interested in Robert. He was short and wore white trousers that stopped well above his ankles and a red shirt that matched his father's. However, he was the only boy.

I listened to the teens as they complained about missing their friends, their schools, their houses, their grandparents, the food, the movies, the fun, the freedom of America. They didn't understand why the Iranians hated them so much, spitting at and heckling them, and they felt hurt. After all, they hadn't asked to come here. The hostility they met made no sense to them. No one had ever behaved this way towards them before. They had never seen people going to the bathroom on the street, never seen crippled people or blind people, and they found it disturbing. Their parents lectured them about adapting to the culture and fitting in, but they didn't get what they were supposed to do or how they were supposed to do it. Just walking down the street had become a problem. They felt watched. There were no activities they could pursue, no foods they were familiar with, no shopping malls, no supermarkets, no restaurants, no play areas. They were isolated behind walls, often sick with 'Tehran tummy' because the food seemed to be contaminated with anti-American germs. All of them seemed to spend their time either vomiting or on the toilet.

For them, like my mother, this Friday night at the movies was the one time they were free to have fun. They could have a Coke, a candy bar and watch a movie. They laughed and gossiped and flirted.

I wanted more than anything to be included. There were so few of us: no more than fifty or sixty in total, and no more than five or six teenagers. They must have noticed me, and I tried desperately to look nice, spending hours in careful preparation. Despite the long conversations I had in my head, explaining that the Iranians they saw on the street were poor, had no running water to bathe in, owned nothing more than the clothes on their backs, were malnourished and lacked medical care, I was mute. I was only half a degree different; I had no room to lecture and I knew it.

*

Even as a teenager living in Esfahan with little contact with anyone, I was aware of an escalating resentment among Iranians. Billions of Iran's oil dollars were being spent on

American weaponry and to fund the Shah and his cronies' lifestyles. For more than four centuries, the expression *'Esfahan nesf-e-jahan'*, or Esfahan is half the world, had described this extraordinary city. Esfahan was as much a hub of foreign activity in the 1970s as it had been during the sixteenth-century reign of its founder, Shah Abbas. There were thousands of foreigners in Esfahan. A large Russian population was employed at the steelworks. There was also a sprinkling of missionaries who had been there for decades.

What was different during the summer of 1973 was the Americans. By some estimates there were 100,000 Americans in Iran by the mid 1970s and a fair number of those flowed through Esfahan. It was quite common to see American families wandering around in shorts and tank tops. In the intricately tiled Shah Abbas Hotel, right around the corner from the main mosques, American businessmen from various arms manufacturers, such as Bell Helicopter and Raytheon, mixed with uniformed military personnel and drank alcohol from a bar glittering with imported bottles.

There were two American colonels stationed in Esfahan – one Air Force and one Artillery – and on the Fourth of July they organised a big celebration. My parents had become friendly with a major at Team House and he invited us. After watching an ostentatious array of fireworks, my parents argued in the car on the way home: my father contemptuous and wary. 'Mark my words, these displays only antagonise. What right do you Americans have to come and blast your fireworks?'

My mother was defensive, taking my father's criticism personally. 'Why can't we celebrate? You think that when Iranians live in America they don't celebrate Norouz?'

My father was benefiting too from the increase in oil revenue expenditures for, despite the military build-up, despite the excesses, despite the corruption, there was more money being spent on roads, tunnels, bridges, irrigation canals and satellite systems. He finally had a profitable job – which was how he had been able to bring us back to live with him. Even so, my mother couldn't understand how she had been able to provide a higher standard of living on a teacher's salary in south Florida than my father as a foreign engineer in Iran. My father on the other hand, found it hard to fathom that she couldn't understand that he needed to plough back into the business the money he made. He didn't think it was a sacrifice living in the office and sweltering in a car on an arid job site for twelve hours a day. He genuinely thought she should enjoy it as he did.

Their antagonism went far beyond the financial, though. My mother felt that my father had 'gone native' and that all his empathy was with the Iranians, while my father thought that my mother's time in America had made her blindly patriotic. My mother was no longer interested in exoticism and adventure, preferring security and comfort. My father had never been interested in domesticity and responsibility, and after five years on his own, he was less enamoured of it than ever. The only reason for them to be together was to provide a home for us three children, but there was little they agreed upon about child rearing. My mother wanted my father to discipline us and rein us in, while my father wanted to have fun with us. He yearned for my mother to take some domestic responsibility and 'do something useful'. No one addressed what would happen in the autumn when school began.

28

Walls Have Mice and Mice Have Ears

*together
again*

The nights in Esfahan were hot, so we slept with the sliding glass doors open to catch the breeze. In the orchard next door, feral cats howled, their screams piercing our sleep. They scrambled over the wall to stalk our forecourt, prowling for food, knocking over the animal cages. One night they eviscerated the pregnant guinea pig, leaving a half-eaten carcass, the intestines unravelled like pink spaghetti. The stray dog we had rescued from the road, its fur filthy with faeces, scuttled around, whimpering and suffering its own private hell. The two houseboys, Esmail and Safar, squatted on the roof crooning Turkish songs; they came from a village in the north where there was a large ethnic Turkish population. Radios blared throughout the night. Early in the morning, roosters crowed, competing with each other for the longest, most raucous blast. Then the mullahs began their call to the faithful and the dawn resonated with their loudspeaker prayers.

Despite the normal high volume of noise, one night I awoke suddenly to an unfamiliar rhythm of sounds. My senses were acutely alert, my adrenalin surging, my ears almost thrumming as they attempted to identify the source. I listened. The sound was catlike and mewling, but it was so regular and persistent that it couldn't have been one of the cats next door. It was more insistent; a continuous, high-pitched whimpering like a baby. I waited for someone to pick up and comfort that sobbing baby, but it went on and on. I wanted to sleep, I badly wanted to sleep, but the sound was so close. *So close!*

I jerked up in bed. That couldn't be a neighbour's baby, it was right next door. I hesitated. My mother would hate it if I knew she was crying. Still, she sounded so strangled and tortured; she sounded as if she were in agony. I waited, fuming at my father for making her so miserable. It went on. And on. It was unbearable.

I crept out of my bed and around the balcony to my parents' room.

'Mom?'

I parted the curtains and peered in.

'Mom? Are you OK? Why are you crying?'

I whispered, trying not to awaken my father.

'Mom? Are you OK?'

My whisper was louder, more urgent.

In the dark, I saw movement. My mother was crouched over my father on his mattress, her nightgown hitched up around her waist. It took me a minute to understand what was happening.

I scurried back to my bed, covering my hot face with my hands. I couldn't believe it! All those rants. Forcing me to choose sides. What a betrayal.

The room next door was silent. I was angry one moment and embarrassed the next. I didn't know what to hope: that my interruption had stopped them or that they had continued.

I wanted my mother and father to get along. I couldn't bear the thought of packing up and going back to Florida. Unlike the American kids I eavesdropped on at the movies, my previous life held no allure. The life here in Esfahan was no better, though.

I lay in bed, wondering what would happen. Finally, in a night that now contained only the normal sounds of cats and dogs and scratching rodents, I drifted off.

*

The missionary threw down the gauntlet when he emerged from the pool, huffing and puffing. 'Well, I've done my hundred and fifty for the day.'

Cameron shot me a look that said: if that skinny, geeky, God-loving do-gooder did 150 laps . . .

We dove in and trawled through the green, the stench of the top layer of the water hitting us each time we surfaced. Back and forth, back and forth. Periodically Cameron emerged like an otter, his glossy head breaking the surface, to call to me: 'Seventy eight' or 'A hundred and three'. Then we plunged on, for we *had* to beat 150. Our arms ached, our legs turned rubbery, our breath grew ragged. On the first day we broke the 150-lap hurdle and then we began increasing the number of laps by big gulps of ten.

This was the first time in my life I had pushed myself physically in the pursuit of pleasure or sport. My arms ached from swimming, not from painting a house or washing a floor, and I gloried in the fact that, for the first time in five years, I had no responsibility. No washing or drying or ironing or weeding or cutting lawns, cleaning people's houses or babysitting. I loved the actual swimming, the rhythmic strokes, the silence when I submerged, the cool of the water. After four or five laps, the dust and grime of the job site were gone; after a few dozen more, the fight my brothers had in the car fragmented and disappeared; some time after one hundred, the image of my mother crouched on top of my father began to lose its power.

I could hear my parents, plonked at the side of the pool, chatting with the young missionaries. I caught snatches of the conversation each time I surfaced: my father asking about their universities and their degrees; my mother interrupting with probing questions about Reverend Gurney, who had run the blind school and was now the pastor of St Luke's next door. Reverend Gurney had been our minister in Tehran when we were growing up. He and Mrs Gurney were Jack Sprat and his wife. He was thin and bony, his collar gaping around a bobbing Adam's apple. She was a round, floury woman with a sweet manner and a stern tongue.

At church when we were young, Reverend Gurney would question my mother avidly, his eyes magnified behind his glasses. 'Does Mr Dartnell do much work for the royal family? Does he work for Princess Shams?'

My mother was always careful with her answers and instructed Cameron and me to avoid answering anything about 'our business'.

'I know that Reverend Gurney is a spy,' averred my mother to my father later when he returned from a job and she was sitting at the kitchen table with him, drinking tea. 'What better disguise than a priest?'

My father thought my mother was ridiculous, fantasising about the Reverend and his wife being spies.

'Come on, Lin, what do you think? Is he MI5? CIA? Savak?' my mother pushed.

'C of E, Genie, C of E.'

'What's C of E, Daddy?'

'Church of England.' My father chortled, before grabbing me and tickling me with his whiskery chin.

'Oh.'

I felt as disappointed as when my mother's friend Nounou had replied, 'A white horse fell in the mud,' when I asked about a dirty joke.

Here we were five years later in Esfahan and Reverend Gurney was at the blind school. I overheard my father telling my mother that the Gurneys had lived in Esfahan when they first came to Iran as young Australian missionaries.

'Did you know,' my father said, 'that one day the Gurneys found a little baby girl abandoned outside their door and they adopted her and raised her as their own?'

As we walked through the church courtyard, we ran into the Reverend and he clasped my mother's hand and smiled in a dazed way. 'Mrs Dartnell? Patric Dartnell? Yes, yes, of course . . .'

I was shocked at his wasted figure, in khakis and checked shirt, the uniform of the British expatriate. My mother took his appearance as clear proof that he had been a spy and that Savak had caught and tortured him.

'Just look at him, he's a broken man,' she said.

My father shook his head. 'He's just an old man, Genie.'

My mother shot him a sceptical look and retorted, 'Well, *you* would say that, wouldn't you?'

'Leave it, Genie, just leave off,' my father replied.

I knew what she was hinting. My mother had an abiding suspicion that my father was a spy, working on behalf of some government or other, which was why he managed to stay and work in Iran with no passport or work papers. He was the perfect Ian Fleming-style secret agent: he knew Farsi fluently; travelled the length and breadth of the country; disappeared for long stretches of time; and pursued an unrelenting exercise regime with jump ropes, bull workers and springs. Most importantly, it allowed her to think that there was some overriding reason he lived in such miserable circumstances and treated us as he did.

'Don't be ridiculous, Genie. If I were a spy for the British or the Americans, the Iranians would have taken care of me long ago, and if I were a spy for the Iranians, I wouldn't be in Iran, would I? I'd be in Russia or China or Europe. Don't be stupid, woman.' My father shook his head before adding, with disgust, *'And be careful what you say.'*

This refrain, 'and be careful what you say', was constant. My parents warned me about expressing any political beliefs or saying anything critical of Iran and the Shah.

'Every third person in this country is being paid. You say something and they run to the police. They get a thousand rials and your life is ruined,' said my father. 'Watch what you say. The Iranians have an expression, "Walls have mice and mice have ears." If someone approaches you, be polite, but don't tell them anything.'

They were worried that, in an unguarded moment, I would let slip my opinion that the Shah should divert the money he was spending on arms to helping his country or declare that it was shameful Iranians were so poor that they crippled their children or used the *joob* as both a toilet and source of drinking water. If I ever complained, or even observed that it didn't seem right that the rich should be so rich and the poor so poor, my parents immediately shushed me.

One night I was particularly irate about the Iranian habit of torturing dogs. My father explained, irritably, they considered dogs *najess* or unclean, that it was part of the culture.

'But Dad, did you see those men dragging the dog behind their car near Si-o-seh pol today?' asked Cameron.

Packs of dogs roamed Esfahan, scrounging bits of garbage and dropping litters of emaciated puppies under the bridges. For sport, men chased them down and tied them in a noose to the back fender of a car. Initially they drove slowly, watching and cheering out the back window as the dog trotted along, trying to keep up, but then they sped up until they strangled the dog or dragged it to its death. This was what had happened to our dog, Diggie, who had been left for dead by the side of the road.

'Don't say anything in front of Safar,' my mother hissed as he entered the room with a tray.

I looked at her. 'Mom, he'd never seen an indoor toilet before he started working for Dad; it's hardly likely he knows English! Anyway, Mom, this isn't political!'

It was difficult not to absorb their paranoia as we *were* always watched. Everywhere, people stared at us openly and sometimes angrily. A day rarely passed when we were not approached and asked where we were from and what we were doing in Esfahan. We might be asked for money, or to help them go to university in Amreeka or Englestan. Would I marry them, could we take their picture, did we have any Khooroos Neshan (the local chewing gum), or cigarettes, did we want to buy a lottery ticket, a broom, a pair of plastic sandals?

When those asking were poor, my mother's natural kindness emerged. No beggar ever left her without a few coins; no child approached that she did not photograph and give a packet of gum or Smarties; no stranger asked to touch her fair curly hair whom she denied.

Every lottery ticket salesman in Esfahan knew her. A ticket cost a toman and each week she ended up with dozens. On the day they announced the winners, my father would read the numbers out of the newspaper while she ripped up her losing tickets. Once in a while she won a few thousand rials and her tradition, when that happened, was to give the person who sold her the tickets a small cut. My mother always tried to annotate the lottery tickets and remember who had sold her which batch.

'I think it was the old man by the bridge, wasn't it, Lin?'

We detoured in the car on the way home and handed him his 50 rials. My father, taking the view that the whole thing was silly, thought she should do something useful like cook for the family.

From time to time, however, the person approaching us seemed more menacing, less random. He might stop us as we walked around the bazaar and ask questions that were more specific about my father or his work. He might know our name and where we lived. Then we took off as rapidly as possible, but the encounters always left me feeling scared and sick.

Sometimes my father would say, 'Be careful what you write in your letters to Rosemary and Hugh, I think they may be opening them.'

Often we received letters that had been unsealed and scotch-taped shut again. That is, if we were lucky. Regularly we got mail from Yosy, saying that we hadn't answered her, and we realised our post had simply disappeared.

*

'Dad, why do you live here?' I asked. 'Why do you love it so much if you have to worry even about the people closest to you – Sammii, Safar, Esmail?'

'Every place is the same, Asho. All governments are corrupt – the Shah's no different. Look at Nixon and Watergate.'

I argued with him, citing the Constitution and the Bill of Rights, and how the very fact that Nixon would have been impeached proved that all countries and all governments were not corrupt.

'Asho,' he said, 'I'm here, this is my place.'

I continued to argue: 'You're only forty-five. You can change. You can do new things.'

Suddenly my mother leaped up.

'Leave it! Leave it, God dammit! He loves this country. He loves these people. You will never convince him to leave until his dying day. Believe me, I've tried.'

Her voice was harsh and her face drawn in and bitter.

*

The Great Bazaar, located at the top of the Shah Abbas Square, was a labyrinth of alleys lined with dozens of tiny shops. Everywhere we wandered, men darted from their stores, calling, 'Madam, come here, buy from me.'

With not a little pressure from my mother ('Once in five years you should buy your daughter a present'), my father took me to the bazaar to buy me a fourteenth-birthday present. While my mother and the boys browsed, we went to an alley-way filled with gold workers, hunched over their green baize cloths, wearing thick magnifying glasses and twisting gold wire to make intricate jewellery. The trip was memorable for much more than just the beautiful gold and turquoise bracelet that he bought me. This was the only occasion I had spent time alone with my father since I was eight years old. He, too, must have been aware of this, because he asked me a most bizarre question.

'Do you like the name Benjamin, Ashley?'

'What?' I asked. 'I mean, I beg your pardon?'

He repeated the question.

I looked at him as if he had asked me whether I liked eating frozen dog turds or whether I had recently participated in a voodoo ritual.

'What? I don't understand . . . Benjamin?'

'Yes, I was just wondering, you know, if you like the name,' he asked in the formal, almost stilted way he always spoke.

'OK. Benjamin.'

I looked over at him and thought to myself, boy, Dad was pretty weird. All these years of living in the *biaban*, in the wilds of Iran had really had an impact on his sanity if, the first time he was alone with me, this was the direction of the conversation.

'No, Dad, I don't like the name Benjamin. It's too biblical, too old-fashioned.' Then, typically of me, 'Is that all right? You're not insulted or hurt? It's not a name that's special to you, is it?'

He responded, 'No, no, not to me, but perhaps to your mummy. Has she ever mentioned the name to you?'

'No never,' I said.

The conversation moved on and we meandered past carpet sellers who pulled out dozens of rugs to spread before my father while in another shop, I tried on great fluffy embroidered sheepskin coats that made me look as if I lived on the Russian steppes and smelled like freshly killed mutton. Distracted, I forgot his question about Benjamin and soon we found my mother and the boys.

'Let me see, let me see.'

She asked about my new bracelet, but then decided my father should keep it in his pocket to avoid thieves catching sight of it.

Her eyes shone as she walked from one store to another, particularly the ones stocked with old Iranian crafts, or 'antiquities' as she called them. She had an eye for the exceptional piece. The bright-orangey glow and glitzy design of a modern copper *tongeh ab* diverted me while she delved inside the shop to unearth a carved silver dagger or painted wooden pencil case. While she rummaged among the piles, we bought tiny paper sacks filled with *pesteh* (pistachios), *toot* (dried mulberries), *keshmesh* (raisins) and *badam* (almonds) from a stall where huge tin bowls were filled with dried fruits, nuts and spices. Finally, after pawing and pondering, my mother made her decisions. She hated to *chooneh* or bargain, though, which was the standard practice in Iran. Shopkeepers quoted inflated prices, knowing buyers would bargain them down.

'Asho, Cam, Rhidi, go find your father. I need some money and I want him to come and get a good price for me.'

She never had any money. My father would not even give her enough to buy a packet of cigarettes. She had to ask him, just as we had for our dried fruits and nuts, and he doled cash out very sparingly.

We found him deep in the bazaar, caressing a silk carpet. He loved the Safavid carpet designs of Esfahan: ivory carpets with rose or light-blue central medallions, and he yearned to buy a pair.

'Some day, Asho, we'll have a beautiful pair of Esfahani carpets and we'll live like pashas, hey?' he said as he grabbed my hand and trotted through the bazaar; he would never walk when he could run.

We arrived huffing and puffing. My mother stood outside the shop, smoking. After conferring for a moment, Dad went in to bargain with the shopkeeper. He emerged, carrying two parcels. She quickly determined that he had not followed her instructions.

'What did you buy? How much did you pay?'

He finally admitted the figure.

'What! I could have done better myself. You're useless.'

'What do you want with this rubbish anyway?' he retorted, handing the items to her, and thrusting his hands in his pockets. 'If you don't like the way I do it, do it yourself.'

She shook her head and muttered, 'Goddam man will never learn.'

Finally, all done with her 'antiquing', we went to the shop that made desert boots. Hanging from the walls were hundreds of pairs of soles, cut from old tyres, and uppers in assorted colours, made of suede or leather. Cameron and Rian each tried various soles for size and then chose their uppers. We would come back later to pick them up, when the boy in the shop had sewn them together on his machine.

After we left the bazaar, we crossed the immense square, filled with fountains and flowers, and climbed the old stone steps of the Ali Qapu Palace. Vast and empty, the bare bones of the building looked as if they had been picked clean by vultures, but, like the Acropolis and the Colosseum, it was more beautiful in its bleached purity. At the top of a seemingly endless number of steps, we were standing high up in the palace, staring out at the Imam Mosque to the south and the Mosque of the Sheikh Lotf Allah in the east. The sun was setting and the turquoise domes of the mosques against the golden sky were as dazzling as the finely worked jewellery we had seen in the bazaar. Black swallows, their scimitar wings flashing, built their nests under the eaves.

'When Shah Abbas built this square three hundred years ago, they played polo here,' explained my father. He was always most comfortable when he recited facts. 'Iran was the centre of the world and Esfahan was at the hub. Half a million people lived here and there were traders from all over the world. They invented amazing things here like pigeon towers to produce fertiliser and *qanats* – water management systems to distribute water.'

We gazed at the square and the Zayandeh River beyond with its graceful arched bridges. This must be the loveliest spot in Iran, I thought, maybe the world. I imagined Esfahan when it was on the old caravan route linking Iran with the rest of the Middle East. Men on camels and horses, with dusty turbans draped to protect their faces from the wind-storms that swept the desert, followed the trade routes. I pictured them entering this beautiful oasis, seeing the green after weeks in the desert. I knew how important water was in this parched land. My father was building an irrigation system, after all, and had explained to us that only about twenty per cent of the total land mass of Iran was cultivated and most of that solely because it was irrigated.

He had told me that in the Dasht-e Kavir, or the great salt desert to the north, and the Dasht-e Lut, the great sand desert to the south, virtually no rain fell. Bakhtiaris, Baluchis and Qashgais, the nomads of the Middle East, had wandered these wastes for generations, herding their drought-resistant goats. As we drove back and forth to the job, we saw these wanderers, with their ragged black tents, by the thousand on their annual migration. Their children, with their sun-bleached hair and sunburned faces, dressed in colourful clothes, ran behind the mottled herds. My father knew the routes and the histories of all these tribes.

'These nomads don't follow the rules of any government. They are truly free,' he said wistfully. 'But they are a dying way of life.'

Like the nomads, Dad loved the great expanses, the restless moving around, the freedom from possessions and taxes. He had never owned a house, never settled down. I thought about how different my parents were: how the first thing my mother did in Florida was buy a house and furnish it. How she couldn't bear to sell it when we came back to Iran. Her fixation on her bedspreads and wrought iron fence, the state of her lawn. She daydreamed, sitting on a wall and staring inwards into this beautiful but bare palace, while my father looked out at the horizon, always admiring innovation and invention: roads, bridges, aqueducts, irrigation systems. He had never been interested in being tied down to possessions or friends or family.

I had taken to analysing my parents' behaviour, trying to make sense of why they acted as they did, attempting to find the underlying cause of their discord, perhaps trying to pre-empt and improve the situation. My father's odd question about the name Benjamin popped into my head and I tucked it away to ask my mother. Another example of how eccentric they both were, I thought to myself. They really were opposites. It seemed to me that my mother was obsessed with the past and my father was always looking forward; my mother focused on the detail and my father the big picture; she loved people and their behaviour, while he was interested in nature and how things worked.

The one area where they were perfectly aligned was that

neither was at all introspective or self-analytical, which I found frustrating, for I felt that if they didn't understand themselves, they would never change. I told my father my observations and he nodded, uninterested.

'What's your point, Asho?' he asked.

'Well, either it means you are perfectly suited or it means that you are completely unsuited.'

'Well, I know the answer to that one.'

He sniggered and turned to run down the stairs just as he had run up, not waiting for any of us.

*

We drove straight up the side of the mountain. It felt as if the car could tip off backwards and end up on its back like a turtle. New grass blew in the wind, grass that would be green for only a few weeks before it dried out in the heat. Herds of sheep and goats jumped nimbly from rock to rock, watched by a dusty boy. Iranian sheep and goats were not like the fluffy white sheep and silky-bearded goats of European fairy tales; they were small and piebald, the goats dragging long ears shredded by thorns and the sheep often with fat bobbing tails slapping their bums.

We climbed and climbed, the back of the car skidding around the tight turns in the road. My parents had called a temporary truce. Both loved these excursions out into the country and it seemed our family was never happier than when we were off to explore a sight to which few foreigners had access, living the pages of *National Geographic*.

'Look, there isn't a single telephone pole, or vapour trail, or anything that shows that humans even exist!' I cried excitedly. It went down like a lead balloon. None of them thought it was much of an observation.

'This tribe we're visiting,' my father explained, 'is a tribe of beekeepers that follows the flowers all over the country.' He continued, 'Some of my workers on the job are from this tribe. That's how we found them, isn't it, boys?'

'The honey is amazing, Mummy,' said Rian. 'You should taste it with butter on *barbary*.'

Rian had tried so hard to engage my mother all summer, trying to pull her out of her funk through sheer energy and charm.

'They camp in these mountains for as long as the grasses and the wild flowers bloom, and the bees can feed, then they move on,' explained Dad.

We came to the end of the road but, instead of stopping, my father just drove the car across the grass until it looked as if we were going to fly off the side of the mountain and soar across the blue cloudless sky. The car bumped and banged around and sometimes got stuck. At one point we all got out, reducing the weight, to dislodge the wheels.

Finally, we saw before us black tents with their sides billowing and flapping in the wind. Small children were squatting and playing in the waving grass, while a few women did chores in colourful skirts, wearing headscarves with tiny coins sewn along the edges. The nomads looked as they might have hundreds of years before, sitting on coarse carpets that they wove themselves in their winter camps. Their tents were made of rough, sturdy, black material. The sole indication that we were in the twentieth century were the ubiquitous dusty plastic sandals the children wore. Dad leaped out of the car, his shirt stuck to his back with sweat. We followed, Cameron, wiry and muscled in ill-fitting shorts, and Rian, brown-cheeked and getting taller and thinner – no longer a little boy. I wore a long colourful gypsy skirt with a peasant blouse, a style probably copied from these nomad tribes.

A dark-suited man with a short-cropped beard and close-fitting round cap greeted us with ritual politeness.

'*Salam, alaykom*. Come with me, come with me! We'll have some tea.'

I was always astounded by traditional Persian hospitality: a group of foreigners appear out of nowhere and are welcomed open-heartedly. This seemed to be disappearing in the city of Esfahan as more Americans descended on it. The man gestured and we followed him to an area tented with dirty white canvas and open on the sides. He called to one of the women as we went. '*Chay-ee beeyar.*'

Bees hummed around the heads of playing children, their eyes blackened around the rims to protect them against the sun.

The beekeeper described their travels since the last spring and the quality of the honey they had collected. I had a hard time following the conversation, despite the fact that my Farsi had improved, as his accent was different from any I had heard. We drank our tea and, while he talked, the man busily opened small clay bowls sealed with a layer of beeswax. Using tiny teaspoons, he offered us a taste of the honey from each region. It was like eating late spring distilled: green grass shifting in the wind, wild flowers spreading their scent through the air, birds chirping, bees buzzing, the warm lazy heat of the sun. The beekeeper laughed at our rapture.

'*Man goosht doost daram,*' he said to me when I told him I could live on hot *barbary* with butter and honey. I shook my head. I would take honey over meat any day.

After drinking her tea, my mother wandered around, looking at the tents, smiling and photographing the women and children. After a while, she returned to the car, stretched her feet out the open door, smoked and enjoyed the breeze.

Meanwhile, my father spoke with the beekeeper about the productivity this year versus previous years, the effect of rain-fall on the flowers and, most importantly, the weather the nomads predicted for the coming winter. My father had another year of work on the Esfahan canal and the weather conditions over the coldest months would determine how rapidly they progressed. He set great store by the predictions of the beekeepers.

'They know by the bees' behaviour what the weather will be,' he said. My mother, despite being so superstitious that she punctuated many of her sentences with, 'Knock on wood' and '*cheshm nazar*', the Iranian evil-eye protection, derided this, of course. But whatever the beekeeper said gave my father comfort.

Soon we were bumping back down the mountain. Five or six hours of driving, a few pots of honey, a weather prediction for the forthcoming winter: life in Esfahan, at times, did seem to be exactly like coming out of an arid desert to an oasis.

29

Cold Baths and Brussels Sprouts

Esmail and Safar on the job

'It's crazy,' I said, 'that I have to be so careful.'

'Well, you do.' My mother glared.

'But, Mom, it's ridiculous. The Bell Helicopter people wear shorts and sleeveless shirts!'

'I don't care if they go naked. It is inappropriate for a four-teen-year-old girl to wear a bathing suit or shorts in the middle of Esfahan. You are not on the beach in Florida, missy; this is a Muslim country.'

We were going inner tubing down the river and I had made the mistake of assuming I could wear a bathing suit with a T-shirt over it. My parents preferred that I stay in the car, though, or, if I insisted on inner tubing, that I wear jeans and a long-sleeved shirt.

We squeezed into a Land Rover, along with an enormous inner tube from one of Dad's big trucks, and followed along the dirt roads to the Zayandeh Rud. There, we leaped in, grabbing the sides of the inner tube, slipping and sliding off into the fast water as the current sped jostling through mini rapids and sweeping into small whirlpools. We laughed and screamed and hooted as we passed villagers washing their clothes and watering their animals on the banks. The carcass of a dead sheep floated by, bloated, and waterlogged, but for most of the route the river was clear and fast moving.

Once in a while one of us lost our grip and Dad then paddled frantically to grab us, for once we were unencumbered by the heavy tube, the current swept us rapidly down the river. As we approached Esfahan, watermelon rinds and bits of debris flowed past us. We all kicked and pulled, fighting the force of the river to get over to the bank. Once ashore, the boys lay gasping on the ground, drying off in the sun. My father quickly wrapped a big towel around me and shoved me into the car while I blustered. I had worn a big baggy T-shirt over a pair of cut-off shorts.

'God, what a pain, being a female in Iran!' I yelled.

*

One day, as I read on my bed, I heard a scuffle outside the sliding door.

'What are you doing?' my father yelled in Farsi.

'*Bebaksheed, Mohandes*. Excuse me,' I heard Esmail whine.

I jumped out of bed to see why my normally calm father was so agitated, only to see him slap Esmail across the face so hard that Esmail's eyes watered and his cheek burned crimson.

'*Borro*,' my father ordered. 'Go.'

'Dad, what are you doing?' I screamed.

'He knows what he did,' said my father and turned on his heel.

The rest of the day, Esmail slunk around with red eyes. My father refused to tell me what had happened. Neither of my brothers knew and both were as shocked as I that my father had hit Esmail. Dad had never spanked us. Moreover, although we had heard about other *mohandes* who hit their workers, my father never hit any of his. I soon found out about Esmail, though.

'What the hell is this?' asked my mother, standing on the opposite side of the room, as far away from me as possible, holding a pair of my underwear with the very tips of her fingers.

'Um, my underwear?' With my mother I felt guilty despite the fact I had done nothing – that I knew about, at least.

'Why did Esmail have them?'

I thought for a minute. 'Uh, sorry, Mom, don't know.'

'Don't know? *You don't know?* Did you or did you not give them to him to wash?'

'Oh, yes!' Relief washed over me. Maybe he had just dropped them or put them in my brothers' laundry pile.

'You can't give your *underwear* to Esmail to wash! He shouldn't be touching your *underwear*. You're a woman now, not a child. Your father found him hanging them on the line where all the workers could see them.' Her voice was scorching in its fury.

I looked at my white cotton bikini pants and suddenly saw them as sexualised – *nagess* and disgusting.

'Mom, is this why Dad hit Esmail? Because it wasn't his fault. I put them in the wash.'

'Your father and I have noticed Esmail and even Safar looking at you inappropriately.'

Instantly I reddened. 'Mom, I'm sorry. I thought I was supposed to give him my clothes to wash; the boys do. He was just doing his job.'

I babbled away, awkward at the dirty idea my mother had introduced, a filthy snake in the undergrowth that I hadn't noticed.

'Never, ever give anything of yours to them to wash – ever. Do you understand me? Why do you think anyone should wash your clothes, missy? At night when you bathe, rinse your underwear out and put them on a hanger in your room to dry.'

Her anger blasted across the room like a fireball.

'OK. OK. No problem.' But I knew it was lunacy, because if Esmail wanted my undies, he had ten hours a day to track them down when we were all on the job. 'Whatever you say, Mom.'

'Never, never, be alone with him. And don't be so familiar. Be a lady. Have some dignity. How dare you play with the boys and them?'

'I will, I will, I won't, I won't.'

Soaked with sweat and embarrassment, I was ashamed that I had behaved in an unladylike fashion, but I didn't know what I could have done differently. I always covered myself, I never touched them, and I only joked with them when they played with the boys. It wasn't my fault that Esmail and Safar looked at me in a weird way. If my parents were so concerned about the appropriateness of a teenage girl living with two young unmarried men, why was I living in the middle of an office, with thirty or forty men coming in and out at all hours of the day and night? When I awakened in the morning, there were men squatting in front of my bedroom curtain.

I stormed out, down the road, slamming my fists against my chest, against my hips, slapping my sandals in the dust.

*

'So how do you fancy a proper British public school to teach you some manners?' asked my father. 'Your mummy and I have decided that all of you need more discipline and more competition. A good dose of cold baths and Brussels sprouts in a strict boarding school will do you good.' He smiled craftily. 'Get rid of those spoiled American habits. Turn Ashley into a lady, and Cam and Rian into men.'

I examined his face closely: was he kidding? Had we come all the way back to Iran after five years, only to be packed off to boarding school? Why hadn't he just sent us straight from Florida and saved all the bother? And what was all this 'your mummy and I' business? They rarely spoke to each other. Also, the part about turning me into a lady: that really enraged me. They had probably decided finally to get a divorce and this was their solution to dealing with us.

'I think Gordonstoun looks best, Mummy,' he said, ignoring my disbelieving look.

He often referred to her in the third person or as 'Mummy' or 'your mummy'. I wondered why he had never been able just simply to call her by her name, why he had given her all those nicknames. He was sitting in his usual position on the filthy old couch, his legs crossed, a newspaper like a shield spread across his lap. If any of us approached him, he just lifted the paper and buried his nose in it.

'Only one wash a week – a cold one on a Saturday. None of this lying around for hours reading in the bath.' He eyed me significantly. 'Bracing walks and runs through the Scottish moors. No heat in the halls. They'll be better for it, won't they, Mummy?'

I walked over, grabbed the newspaper out of his hands and sat at the table, pretending to read it.

Both my parents thought I was soft – overly bookish, too tender-hearted, far too liberal. Not tough enough.

'Gordonstoun was started by Dr Kurt Hahn in 1933 when he left Germany because he perceived a "decay in contemporary society",' read my father, again looking at me significantly.

'What are you saying?' I asked. 'Let me tell you, I'm not going to some stupid boarding school where I'm freezing all the time. Forget it! If you think we're spoiled, you should see what other kids are like. In any case, where are you going to get the money to pay for it?' I paused. 'And the reason I spend hours reading in the bath is that there is no place for me to go in this office! If you see me near Safar or Esmail, I get in trouble, I can't be seen by the workers – so where should I *be*?'

'Well, you're not other children, are you? We have higher expectations of you,' interrupted my mother, pointedly using the word 'children'.

I shook my head. 'How can you have *any* expectations of us when you don't even send us to school?'

'Temper, temper, Asho!' my father teased me.

I left the room. I could overhear them as they went through the brochures. They had set ideas about the correct mix of athletics and academics. Most important was somewhere that would give us *backbone*. Somewhere that would make me less wimpy, less girly. Tougher – like Cameron. Despite the fact that Cameron often gave my parents a hard time, they both admired him tremendously: he was *so* tough. Gordonstoun also excited my mother because the Queen had sent Prince Charles there to stiffen him up and she had visions of us hobnobbing with the British aristocracy. I was incredulous to hear her ask my father, in all seriousness, how he would feel if Prince Charles wanted to marry me.

'Oh Mummy, Charles isn't good enough for our Asho,' he mocked.

The next day in the car, I was sullen. 'I'm not going, you know.'

'You'll do what we tell you,' snapped my mother.

At the British Council library, I sat in my chair, feeling as if I were locked in the hot car on the side of the canal with all the windows shut. After hours of churning, I came to the realisation that boarding school could actually be great: no more crazy anger from our mother, no more penny-pinching and neglect from our father. I would be in an environment where people actually valued reading and going to school, where women wouldn't be restricted . . . I would be free!

'OK, I'm happy to go,' I said later that afternoon. 'In fact, it will be a pleasure to get away from the lunacy of our so-called family.'

Of course now my attitude changed, so did theirs. Suddenly, after weeks of bloody battle with each other, as soon as I fought back, my parents united against me. More specifically, after years of my giving her my undying support, my mother had gone over to the enemy.

She stood abruptly and came at me, her hands windmilling. I dodged low, ducking my head while she slapped at my neck and back.

'Who do you think you are? How dare you say that? I slaved for five years to support you, to buy a house for you. Look at these veins!' Mom pointed to the spider's web of broken capillaries on her thigh. 'And ulcers. I'm a nervous wreck because of you kids and this is the thanks I get!'

When the tirade finally tailed off, I said, 'That's why I want to go to boarding school. Exactly. Thank you. I don't need to say anything else.'

I walked out, almost tripping over Diggie. I bent down to ruffle his soft fur, glossy now from his diet of scrambled eggs, and I realised I was the same as Diggie – always yearning for attention, eager for scraps of information, desperate for the least bit of affection. Well, I'd show them I wasn't a pathetic puppy at their beck and call. They would see I didn't need them.

When they dropped me at the library in the morning, I slammed the door without a backward glance, and when they picked me up I maintained my stony silence, even ignoring my brothers, my eyes fixed on the page of my book. I stayed in my room, sneaking just a few scraps of bread from the kitchen to eat on my mattress, my eyes still glued to my book.

After a few days, my father tapped on the door between our rooms and came in to sit on the bed.

'Asho, darling girl, why don't you come out and eat with us? It's really upsetting all of us too much that our darling girl is being so difficult.'

Each time he called me darling, he pronounced it 'duhling' in a simpering, kiss-up-to-me way.

'Please, Asho darling, come along, Asho, be a good girl . . .' He wheedled and smiled. Duhling. Duhling. Duhling.

I hated his soft, cocksure voice, his smugness, his unwilling-ness to take any responsibility for the situation.

'I'll only come on the condition that we fill out the applica-tions and I can leave this crazy family.'

'OK, darling girl, anything you want, anything for you. I promise, I promise.'

I looked at him sceptically.

When I entered the office, Cameron and Rian cheered and clapped. Just because of me, the already precarious equilib-rium of our family had tipped and emotions were sloshing around. We were used to our parents fighting, to the boys being at one another's throats. We were not used to Ashley rocking the boat.

Mom did not look up from her plate piled high with rice and *kubideh kebab*. It figured: when I'm not eating, they buy kebab, I thought. We ate scrambled eggs and *barbary* five nights out of seven, because my mother never entered the kitchen and my father never instructed Safar and Esmail to buy or cook any differently than they had in the months before our arrival. As far as my father was concerned, if he had his yogurt, his brew-er's yeast, his vegetable juices and a tin of Nescafé, he was happy. As far as my mother was concerned, if she had her ciga-rettes and her tea, she could survive. She had already lost thirty pounds and I had lost twenty. The boys and my father were already grasshopper thin.

My mother kept her face hard and her eyes averted. I knew that she would never, ever apologise, not even if her toenails were pulled out one by one.

'Why should I?' she'd say. 'I've never felt guilty about anything I've ever done and I never will. What's that Piaf song again? *Je ne regrette rien.*'

After dinner I got out the applications and began filling them in, using my father's fountain pen. Each time I asked a question, he looked up from the newspaper and answered tersely.

'What year would we be in the British system?'

'Just put your ages.'

'Dad, what degree did you get at Cambridge?'

'Mechanical Sciences Tripos.'

'How do you spell the psychology school Mom went to at Yale?'

'G-e-s-e-l-l.' The pen whispered on the thick paper.

After a few evenings of work, I handed the applications to my father. There was much information missing – school records, teacher and school head recommendations – but I had done the best I could and in my best handwriting.

My head was filled with thoughts of boarding school and, on the way out to the job, I slipped in questions about how it might work. Both my mother and I gradually forgot we were at war. A plan evolved: we kids would go to boarding school and my parents would travel from job to job. Apparently they wanted to stay together. My mother would buy a small flat in London and, during the school holidays, we would meet there. Since my father was still living illegally in Iran, he wouldn't join us, but eventually he'd get his papers in order.

'I promise, Genie, I promise.'

The foundation of my parents' boarding-school plan, beyond the notion that it would make us into 'men', was that they wouldn't have to rent a house in Tehran, so they could pay our school fees with the money saved. Despite the fact that I was looking forward to boarding school, I knew this plan upset both Cameron and Rian.

'How could he send us to boarding school?' asked Cameron, who had tried so hard to impress my father, learning how to drive the equipment, cutting his hair, doing the Royal Canadian Mounted Police exercises with him, studying the constellations. He thought he had covered all bases.

'Don't you *get* it? He doesn't care about any of us,' I said, with bravura.

Rian was even more upset because he had been hurt when my mother sent him to Iran and now they were bandying him about as if he were an unwanted pet.

Over the course of the summer, I asked my father repeatedly whether the letters from the boarding schools had arrived.

'Can Sammii go get them, Dad, *please*?' A maggot of hope gnawed through me: if only I could escape to boarding school.

My mother overheard him one day putting me off and she snarled, a frantic hardness making her voice brittle, 'Lin, tell her the truth! Stop lying for *once* in your life and tell her.'

'What? Dad, what's happened? Did we get turned down?'

'Nothing, nothing's happened, darling girl.' He buried himself in his newspaper.

'Lin, tell her. Be fair to the child,' said Mom, her nostrils flaring.

She had perfect nostrils, as she had pointed out to me on many occasions. They were perfectly oval and perfectly symmetrical. When she flared them, they became perfectly square, like little boxes, the rims whitening.

My father began edging towards the door. 'Come on,

Mummy, don't make trouble.' He glided out of the room, as slippery as axle grease.

Tears slid down my cheeks. Every day, every night, I had thought about boarding school, envisioning a new, uncomplicated life, an existence with schedules and rules and libraries and books.

'He never sent them, Ashley,' said my mother. 'When he realised how expensive the schools were – well, he would never pay that much, would he?'

'But why did I fill out the applications, waste so much time? He knew how much they cost from the day he got the brochures.' I tried to stifle my tears. 'Why dangle the possibility? Why did you let him? Why have you been lying to me all these weeks? All those stories about buying a flat in London and all that stuff?'

'He let you fill out the applications to avoid an argument. He thought you would just forget all about it. You never would have gotten in anyway.' My mother snapped a wavering flame on her lighter and lit her cigarette.

'How do you know?' Once again, it was my fault, my weakness.

She deflected me. 'Come on, Ashley, get real.'

'But that whole thing about not renting a house. And schools here costing money so it would all even out? Why didn't you tell me?' I wailed.

'Why should I? It was your father's responsibility. And where was I supposed to live? I'm not going to spend my life going from one construction site to the next.'

I shook my head, bewildered. 'I thought you wanted to. I thought you wanted to have a life of your own. All you do is complain about being trapped by us kids. You could leave Dad, go back to Florida, to Pakistan . . .'

'Why should I? What's wrong with me? Who died and left me the whipping boy?'

'What?'

'The whipping boy.'

'You think you've taken punishment on my behalf?' I gulped, almost unable to get enough oxygen to breathe. 'What have I done wrong? You think you're the one who's suffered? You're the grown-up – you've made your own life. We kids haven't asked to live in this chaotic way. Come on, Mom.'

'That's right, baby,' she said coolly, ignoring my questions. 'It's my turn now. You kids have had it too easy. No more Mr Nice Guy.'

30

In the Shadow of Damavand

Persepolis

'Pack up! We're going to Tehran tomorrow,' she said from the doorway. 'Take everything. We're not coming back.'

Suddenly, pre-emptively, with no discussion, visible planning or thought, we were on the move again. One of my father's workers drove us in a rattletrap car, playing chicken with the lorries coming in the opposite direction. He left us on the side of a road, handing my mother the car keys.

'Why does he need such a big flat? Do you think he has a girlfriend?' I whispered to my mother.

We were staying in an apartment that my father rented. Why hadn't we come here the first night at the airport? Why hadn't we stayed here all summer, as opposed to at the office? Why did my father even have it? These things were never discussed.

'Don't be ridiculous!'

She dismissed the notion that my father might have had women in his life. She seemed to think that he was so self-contained, so selfish, that he was incapable.

I wandered around. The flat was muted; all the blinds were down and desiccated leaves surrounded a lifeless plant. Leather sofas hulked like great dark walruses in the open-plan sitting room and squished down with a whoosh when we sat on them. The black coffee table, under its layer of dust, was mirrored, reflecting back the room's abandoned luxury. My mother prowled around, opening drawers, slamming them shut, pulling open cupboards, sniffing the cologne in the medicine cabinet. The boys had turned on the TV. Once I had seen this flat, my mother's views about my father seemed to me naive. If he could rent this flat, buy this furniture, he could certainly go out with women. I told her so.

'No!' she snapped, and thrust 500 rials at me. 'You three! Go buy some food.'

The boys and I ventured down in the ponderous lift.

'Can you believe that Dad has such a nice flat and we've been living in the office in Esfahan?' I asked.

'So what? I like the office,' said Rian.

'And anyway, we've stayed here before,' said Cameron.

I was flabbergasted. Late in the summer, my father had brought me up to Tehran on an overnight trip to renew my passport at the US embassy. We had stayed at his cousin Fred's and no one had mentioned this flat.

'I can't believe school's already started. What was so important in Esfahan?' I moaned. And now we're being sent to the American School, the worst school. After what they did to us with boarding school.'

'You're always complaining,' said Rian.

'Why do you always criticise Dad?' asked Cameron. 'If you cared so much about where you went to school, why didn't you figure it out?'

'How'm I s'posed to do that with no phone? You're an idiot,' I retorted angrily.

I could see Cameron's eyes widen at my reaction. I knew my ongoing hyper-analysis of our situation only made Cameron and Rian anxious, but who else could I talk to?

'You're just an SP!' cried Rian.

I refused to ask him what 'SP' meant. I considered the possibilities: spineless, spoiled, silly, stupid, pig, penis, pimple-face . . . Rian had a whole spiel for Cameron: 'You freaky, fat, buck-toothed, French-fried, banana-nosed . . .' I was feeling too fragile to voluntarily open the floodgates to an avalanche of criticism, so I kept silent.

There were few people about at this time of evening. Nonetheless, we found a *kuché* shop and bought *mast* or yogurt, and *paneer*, the local Iranian goat's cheese. At the fruit shop, we chose *zard-alou*, apricots, peachy pink and nectar-scented; *angour*, miniature grapes, far sweeter and more flavourful than large grapes; *albalou*, the tiny, ruby-red sour cherries that most people ate dried, but that we ate fresh; and a large *kharbouzeh*, or Persian melon, the flesh as crisp as cucumber, but sweet as honeydew.

When we returned to the flat, which by now was filled with the familiar fog of cigarette smoke, we sat at the shiny table with its coating of dust and ate, wrapping the crumbly cheese in flat *lavash* bread and washing it down with tea.

My mother's face, usually glistening and golden, was damp and greyish. She laid out the game plan, her eyes tired, and her voice glum: we would all take baths tonight, put out clothes for tomorrow and get to bed early as we needed to be off first thing in the morning.

*

We overslept. The sun, pouring through the blinds, was as thick as honey. We wolfed our bread and butter, and tumbled out to the car with shoes untied and buttons askew.

My mother had not driven in Tehran in more than five years. I had read that Tehran had the highest death rate from car accidents in the world and I didn't doubt it for a second. The tendons in my mother's neck were already standing out and she gripped the steering wheel so tightly her knuckles shone. I sat in front, clutching the dashboard. The boys fought in the back. Gradually I came to the realisation that my mother was driving aimlessly, taking whichever route looked easiest, going up one street and then down another, creeping through a roundabout or surging through a gap in the traffic.

I looked quizzically at Cameron. He leaned forward and asked, 'Mom, do you know where the American School is?'

'Be quiet. Driving here is dangerous as hell,' she replied.

All three of us stared out the window. After a while, I asked hesitantly, 'Mom, do you know where you're going?'

'It's in the north. Your father said to the north.'

I had heard Dad giving Mom directions and Mom saying, 'I know, Malin, I *know*.'

'Did you write the directions down? Want me to read them to you?' I asked.

'For what? Do you see a street sign in English? Do you see a single landmark? Exactly what good would it do to write down directions?' she responded with fury.

I slid over to the window to avoid a horse bite if it was coming my way, but she kept one hand on the wheel while the other held her cigarette. She continued to drive slowly and painfully through the traffic.

'Just make sure we're going north,' she instructed.

Although I berated myself that I should have taken the directions from Dad, my mother was right. It would have been impossible to follow them, for how could we differentiate one building or maydan from another?

'The mountains are north,' piped Cameron. 'You just have to go towards the mountains. We should see Mount Damavand.'

I felt a surge of nostalgia. We had been able to see the Alborz Mountains from the roof of our old Amir Abad flat and I had always thought it romantic that we lived literally in the shadow of Damavand. There were calendars all over Iran featuring the famous volcano.

We craned out the windows but saw no mountains, no snow-glittered peak of Damavand. In fact, a fine haze of smog enveloped the city and nothing was visible beyond a short distance. Every street was the same. It all looked so familiar, although, like almost everything, I could see it was better in memory than in real life. Tehran was filthy and the people on the streets seemed agitated. I had spent five years in Florida imagining Tehran and now the reality was at odds with those nostalgic dreams.

'Um. That "go north" thing's not working,' I finally ventured. 'We need to ask directions.'

My mother was really distressed by now but she refused to stop. She drove and drove and drove. For hours. It was burning hot. The boys were crankily fighting in the back. I had to pee.

'You always need to go to the bathroom,' complained Rian. 'You should stretch your bladder.'

'Oh God, not the whole stretch-your-bladder thing,' I yelped.

For years, I had lived with my parents' admonishments that I didn't need to go to the bathroom on long car drives – that I needed to stretch my bladder. That my father and brothers leaped out of the car, unzipped and let it fly, practically any time and any place they wanted, and that my mother had an adult-sized bladder, were irrelevant. I was the 'spoiled princess' who had to go to the bathroom. Ah, Spoiled Princess. SP.

'I know what SP means,' I gloated at Rian.

'So? It's pretty obvious that's what you are.'

'Mom, please ask someone,' I begged.

'No. What good would it do?'

Finally, though, she stopped the car. 'Well, go.'

I wailed, 'Mom, I barely speak Farsi, I don't drive, and I have no idea where we're going.'

'Go.'

'Oh God! How do you say American School in Farsi?'

'*Madresseyeh Emricai.* Now go.'

I stumbled from one person to the next, asking in my broken Farsi. Whether they didn't understand or whether they didn't know, I couldn't tell. I returned.

'I can't bloody believe I am driving around Tehran on a wild-goose chase for you kids,' Mom said.

She got out of the car, stalked across the street and approached a grizzled man. Her blouse and skirt were wrinkled and wet, stuck to her back and legs. We could see her gesticulating and smiling, and gradually the man smiled back.

'Oh great! He knows,' Rian cried.

Mom returned, lit another cigarette and started the ignition.

'Is it close?' I asked.

She turned to me, 'How should I know? He doesn't know where the goddam school is.'

I sat silent, my face impassive. There was no movement from the back seat. She continued to drive. The streets grew gradually wider and more residential. There were fewer women crouched at the side of the road by the *joob*, washing their dishes and clothes. The air felt distinctly cooler. From time to time we stopped and Cameron hopped out to ask directions, for his Farsi, as he had worked on my father's job site, was excellent.

'I never realised Tehran was so big,' I said.

'There are five million people!' said Cameron. 'And there were only a couple of hundred thousand in Fort Lauderdale.'

We were exhausted by the time we ultimately found the school in the Armenian Jolfa section of Tehran.

'Let's just hope someone's here to see us,' said my mother as she slammed the car door.

The final bell had just rung. We watched as kids called out to one another and ran for their buses. Long, stringy hair and torn, faded blue jeans worn low on the hip was the style for both boys and girls. In some instances, it was hard to tell them apart. Many stamped out cigarettes as they leaped on to the buses. I looked at Cameron and Rian with their short hair and old-fashioned clothes from the Salvation Army and I laughed to myself, remembering my parents ranting on about why we needed to go to boarding school.

'You need discipline. You need manners. You're too soft. You need physical activity. You need competition.'

I gazed at the cramped, dusty playground littered with cigarette butts and gum wrappers, the scrappy two-storey building with its limp American flag, the three or four scraggly trees struggling to survive. Ha!

I waited with my chin resting in my hand. Cameron and Rian continued to fight, hitting each other. I nudged Cameron with the toe of my sandal.

'C'mon, stop.'

He glared at me. His hostility had amplified since living with my father. Whereas my mother had been harsh in stopping him from bullying Rian, Dad, being the elder son who had done the same to his younger brother, felt it was quite natural for them to fight: 'Boys will be boys.'

After the derelict minibuses roared out in a cloud of diesel, shadows crept in and filled the courtyard with cool air. Our mother emerged, accompanied by a man with sandy hair and pink freckled skin who walked with the big, loose-limbed gait of someone who had played serious sports in high school and college.

Her shoulders were up around her ears and her face was tight.

We stood and wiped our hands on our clothes to shake hands.

'Well, OK, guys. Good to see ya. Your mom and I have been trying to figure out what grade you should be in and what classes to put you in. 'Course, it would have been helpful if we had some records from your previous schools, but Mom has assured me that you have actually been in school. Ha ha.'

Our mother shot us a look.

'So, Ashley, you'll start in tenth grade – is that right?'

He looked at me quizzically and I nodded.

'Cameron will go into eighth and Rian will go into fourth. The bus will pick you up on your street – or at least the one your mother thinks you're staying on. There's a junior named Eric who gets picked up there. Keep an eye out for him because the bus driver won't know you're coming. Eric's a big guy – very big. You can't miss him.'

We got lost going back to the flat, but not as badly as getting to the school. My mother must have retained some of the layout of Tehran from the morning's ramblings. We sat quietly, punctuating the silence with questions that Mom answered with a strained expression.

It was clear that the man at TAS had not been impressed with my parents' haphazard approach to education. That most other parents filled in applications and sent school records. That most parents didn't simply show up some days after school began and demand that their children be enrolled – and insist that their daughter, well over a year younger than everybody else, really was in tenth grade. Never mind that she had actually missed half the previous school year. Oh, and by the way, you'll have to wait for payment, we have no bank details, no permanent address, and we don't know where we're staying. Oh, and no, we don't have passports with residence papers.

It was clear that, despite the casual appearance of the kids in the school yard, TAS was a proper school that took itself seriously. But once again, my mother's charm had worked and she had somehow persuaded him.

*

The next morning, after dropping Rian at the elementary school across the street, Cameron and I stood at the edge of the asphalt courtyard, watching all the kids laughing and talking.

'Cam, does my butt look big in these?' I asked. I was wearing my best outfit: a pair of light-blue, high-rise, jumbo bell-bottoms and a duckling-yellow, puff-sleeved top.

'Yea, kinda,' he acknowledged.

Girls walking by eyed Cameron. The bell rang and, clutching the piece of paper with my schedule, I edged my way into the girls' locker room, wedging myself between dozens of laughing, chattering girls. Arms akimbo, elbows bumping, hips clashing, girls were pulling on whatever came to hand: shorts, T-shirts, baggy jeans and sneakers. Not like Fort Lauderdale High School, where we all wore humiliating gym suits. I hovered near the door, hoping nobody would notice me, but also hoping someone would.

'Hi, I'm Lyn.' A girl with a sheaf of hair and a nasal twang approached. 'This is Dolores, Sandy and Robin – they're sisters, Cheryl, Mina, Linda . . .'

I smiled. 'I'm Ashley.'

'Wow, love your name! Where you from?'

'Fort Lauderdale.' I said it like a question.

'Wow! I'm from Ann Arbor, Michigan. Bo-oring!' Lyn exclaimed. 'So, do you need sneaks?' Without waiting, she yelled into the locker room, 'Anybody got sneaks Ashley can wear? Thanks, Sandy,' she said as she grabbed a pair and threw them to me. 'We're playing basketball. Sally, she's the gym teacher, she doesn't really care what we do as long as we're, you know, kinda moving. Isn't it coo-ul that we can call teachers by their first names?'

Lyn's eyes squinted almost shut when she smiled.

I nodded, still silent since Lyn had filled every space in the conversation. I put on the sneakers and followed as everyone piled out.

'Hey, Sal!' Lyn exclaimed as we entered the gym. 'This is a new girl from Florida. Her name is Ashley.'

Without a word, Sally added me to her register, looking up with her eyebrows raised when she needed my last name. Then, plopping down on the bleachers, she examined her nails. We clomped on to the court and girls began throwing balls, dribbling, double-dribbling, fouling and laughing – and only very occasionally taking a shot. If someone actually scored a basket, both teams stopped and stared, as if the hoop had suddenly come alive and snatched the ball out of the air.

'All ya gotta do is throw the ball in the basket and stay out of the key – that little area under the basket,' Dolores whispered. She was wearing jeans and a T-shirt and had soft wispy blonde hair.

Afterwards, hot and sweaty, we flocked to classes in the main building. As we walked, I expected Lyn, Dolores and the rest of the group to dissolve around me, but instead they talked and laughed, including me in the conversation.

We trundled up to second period English with Mrs Wright, who with her bouffant hair, prim outfit and Alabama accent was right out of *To Kill a Mockingbird*. At break, Dolores led me out, almost by the hand, and spoke to me, confiding and almost in my ear, in a way that made me feel special, because it was clear that, from toddlerhood, Dolores had been the pretty blonde girl with whom the other little girls all wanted to play. We gathered next to one of the spindly trees, where I met Cindy, who was as tall as I, with soft brown eyes; a boy named Danny with glossy black hair and a nascent moustache; and Lyn's attractive older sister Deb. I stood shyly, watching and listening as the group laughed and traded plans for lunch, all the while feeling astonished and grateful that Lyn had taken me under her wing. In all my months at Fort Lauderdale High, I'd never been part of a group of kids. After break I went from French to chemistry to world literature.

'Ashley, welcome,' said Mrs Gentry. 'We're discussing *The Epic of Gilgamesh*. I expect you haven't read it, so you can just listen today.'

I had read it, though. Yosy had given me *The Epic* only last year, saying, 'You gotta read this, it is so funny and weird, about the amazing King Gilgamesh of Uruk who is saved by Enkidu, a wild man.'

I was completely engrossed, taking notes breathlessly as she spoke. I hadn't realised *The Epic*'s place in the history of literature. For someone who loved to read as much as I did, it was amazing to think that this story had lasted all these centuries and yet it had been as real to me as a story written that year. Ah, it was good to be in school.

When the bell rang, one of the girls in the class, Maya, short and buxom, swathed in a colourful *shalvar kameez*, smiled at me. 'Want to eat lunch?'

'Uh, thanks.'

I followed her, noting all her accoutrements: rings on her toes; ankle bracelets on both feet; rings on every finger, even her thumbs; earrings; arms a-tinkle with bangles.

For lunch, everything that she took was liquid: soup, yogurt, Coke. 'I'm on a diet,' she said. 'Only liquids and this.' She showed me a foil-wrapped bar of chocolate.

I was surprised because I didn't think Coke and chocolate were diet foods.

'It makes me shit,' she said, laughing, 'a lot.' She held up the bar.

During lunch, I listened, vacuuming up everything. She was from California. Her brother and sister-in-law were teachers at the TAS elementary school.

'Ya know, my parents, they couldn't handle me any more, and my brother and his wife are cool, ya know, so I just came with them,' she said.

'You left your parents?' I asked.

'Oh ya know, too much sex and too much smoking and drinking and marijuana for them. I probably won't see them till I go back for college. It depends if my boyfriend comes over and we travel.' She spoke lazily and matter-of-factly and with little order to her replies. 'Oh God, I miss him so much!'

'Me, too! I miss my boyfriend more than anything. The sex!'

The dark, skinny girl next to her giggled crazily and jumped up and down in her seat. Most of her small breasts were exposed and they too bounced crazily. So much for my parents' concern that I dress appropriately in public, I thought to myself.

'I am so horny I can't keep my hands off myself!'

'I know, I'm dying,' Maya said. 'I don't know if I'm going to be able to last, you know, without a guy.'

'I had to go into the restroom during math today!' said the skinny one, raising her eyebrows knowingly, and wiggling around on the seat some more. 'Mr Wright is so cute!'

They both broke out laughing and rolled their eyes.

'Well, I had to go to the bathroom because I was shitting my brains out, eating all these chocolate Ex-Lax,' said

Maya. 'Believe me, I'd rather be in there playing with myself!'

I almost shot out of my seat, but I kept quiet, hoping they said more.

After a while, asking if I wanted to come along, they sauntered to the smokers' room. I stayed on the bench, looking down at the courtyard. Music blared, boys kicked balls, girls brushed each other's hair, and each group eyed the others. Couples stood locked together, faces glued, eyes tightly shut and hands groping up and down each other's backs. Teachers wandered by, carrying their lunch trays. The couples making out barely budged to allow them past. This certainly was like no place I could have imagined, certainly not Iran.

*

That night around the table in the apartment, my mother was calm, eating bread and cheese, drinking tea.

'So how was it?' she asked.

'OK,' mumbled Cameron.

'Mummy, they've already started doing long division and fractions.' Rian's chin scrunched up in his effort not to cry.

'Well, you'll just have to catch up.'

My mother blamed my father for the boys' poor preparation at the school in Esfahan. My father blamed my mother for the poor schools in Florida.

'My teacher's name is Mr Lett,' he said, 'and he's really strict.'

'You're kidding! I met his sister today at school. She doesn't seem to come from a strict family,' I said. This was the Maya who had eaten Ex-Lax for lunch.

'What about you, Asho?' asked my mother.

'The kids are friendly. I guess because so many American military people are moving here, there are lots of new kids, and they seem really grown up and kind of, I don't know, there's a smokers' room and everybody wears jeans and everybody has long hair.'

I didn't know how to describe the feeling of freedom at the school. The sense that because everybody was out of their normal environment for just a short time, they were going to let loose. And I certainly was not going to talk about my lunchtime conversation.

31

The Problem of the Soosks

*our first Christmas
together in years*

My mother laid out what she wanted. 'A room each for
the children and a guest room for Hugh and Yosy
when they visit. And heat – I can't live through another
Tehran winter without central heat. Not after Florida.'

'Do you know how much that will cost? What about a nice
modern flat downtown?' asked Dad, who was up from Esfahan.
The flat we were staying in had only two bedrooms so we
couldn't all sleep there, but he thought something similar, if a
bit bigger, would be ideal.

My mother was adamant, though: we were living together
as a family for the first time in five years and she didn't
want neighbours complaining if the boys bounced balls or
the dog barked. Every day my parents came back from
house-hunting exhausted and on edge. There was a severe
housing shortage because of all the Americans pouring into
Iran.

'Bloody company housing,' my father griped. 'If someone else is paying for it, they don't *chooneh* to get the best price.'

After days of searching, with my father becoming increasingly desperate to get back to Esfahan, they finally found a house in the Darroos area.

'It's got a pool,' enthused my mother, 'and a big garden.'

'There's an office next to our bedroom,' added my father. 'I can save money by not having an office in Tehran.'

'Is it expensive?' asked Rian, always with an eye on the money.

'Well, I've done a deal, but the rents are ridiculous,' said my father.

As we got closer to the house, I noticed there were no *joobs*.

'Yes, that's one of the government's initiatives, to take the *joobs* underground, putting in sewage pipes in all these new areas,' explained Dad. 'This whole place was built in the last five years. When you were here before, Mummy, this was just *biaban*.'

I remembered that *biaban* in Farsi meant 'wilderness'. The neat paved streets and walled houses were built in what used to be desert, scattered with brush and overrun with feral dogs. Across the street was an empty lot full of rubble, with a scatter of litter clinging to the dry grass. Because Iranians bought most of their food fresh and took it home in plastic shopping baskets, there was surprisingly little litter in Tehran. Generally, the wandering herds of goats nibbled up the fruit rinds, empty cartons and bits of paper. Men pushing wheelbarrows collected tins, paper, plastic bags and cloth to reuse or sell. In the empty lot was a stack of concrete sewer pipes – part of the Shah's initiative to replace the *joob* – that would stay there for the three years we lived at Khiaban Marvedasht.

Our excited mother chivvied us along. 'Come on, come on.'

We followed her through a narrow front garden.

'So this is the front hallway and up the stairs are bedrooms for Rian and Ashley, and a bathroom.' She pointed as she led us into the house: 'Living and dining area. We'll put the TV down there for your father.' She gestured to a sunken, dark area of the sitting room, then led us down a hallway. 'Our bedroom – and your father's office.'

We gazed around. I had never imagined that I would have my own bedroom, a pool, a living room and dining room. We kids looked at each other with a mixture of incredulity and anxiety: this must cost a lot.

My mother flung open a door. 'Do you notice anything about the kitchen?' Her voice was high-pitched and excited.

We studied it.

'No fridge?' I asked.

'Fridge's in the hallway,' she said.

'Mom, I give up.' I couldn't see the point of the guessing game.

'Look at how low the cabinets are,' she said.

I saw they were unnaturally small, only coming up to my mother's hips, and that the sink, too, was miniature.

'Why do you think they're like that?' My mother sounded so thrilled that I thought there must be something extra-specially wonderful about these cabinets.

'They ran out of wood?' guessed Rian.

Cameron wandered out, saying, 'The kitchen was too small to put proper cupboards in?'

I looked expectantly at my mother. Rian's face was shining in anticipation.

'I don't know. I just thought it was interesting,' she said.

'That's it?' I asked. 'Oh Mom! Yeah, really interesting. Fascinating.' I turned to follow Cameron and said, 'They must have built 'em for midgets.'

My mother stared at me. Her face grew still and I thought, oh no, I've done it again – me and my smart aleck mouth.

Instead she burst out laughing, a laugh that sounded like a car starting on a cold day. She laughed and laughed, clutching at her belly, tears streaming out of clenched eyes down her red face, her breath coming in gasps.

'Midgets, midgets,' she squealed, more tears coursing down her cheeks. She clutched at the diminuitive counters.

Her laughter was contagious and soon Rian and I were laughing and gasping for breath. I glanced at my mother to make sure she was really laughing.

Dad came in. 'So what do you think?' He turned to me.

'It's great, it's amazing. Thank you so much, Daddy!' I threw my arms around him and Rian joined in. 'Where's Cameron's room?' I asked.

'Oh, come on!' said Mom. 'That's the big surprise I told you about.' She sounded elated. 'Cam! Cam! Come see your room!' she yelled.

We followed her outside where a small pool festered, half full of algae-green water. Desiccated salvia, like scabs of dried blood, lay in the parched flower beds.

'Just wait till we get this garden cleaned up and get some water on it,' she said as she led us through the little orchard to a concrete shack. 'Ta-dah!' She flung open the door.

I looked into a tiny room with a damp concrete floor. Cracks spread like seaweed all over the walls. A bare light bulb dangled from the ceiling and, despite the baking heat outside, a bone-aching chill permeated.

'Mom, Cameron can't live here! That's crazy . . .' I stared at her, questioningly. Maybe this was a joke like the kitchen cabinets.

Cameron's bottom lip jutted out. He was just thirteen. Pimples sprinkled his face and he had grown almost as tall as my mother.

'What's wrong? We thought Cameron would be happy with this. He's growing up. He needs his independence, right,

Cam?' She smiled at him persuasively. He turned and walked away, his hands in his pockets.

I began throwing out solutions: 'Rian and I can share a room.'

'No, you're too big,' my mother said.

I thought that was ironic, given that she and I had been sharing the same room for the past five years. I knew that Rian and Cameron sharing a room wasn't worth suggesting. It hadn't worked before.

'He can have the room next to yours,' said Rian.

'It's your father's office,' said my mother.

'Dad can use this room. He'll be on the job all the time anyway,' I butted in.

'No!' said my mother.

'Well, all that's left is the area of the sitting room where you're going to put the TV,' I said. 'How 'bout that?'

'No!' said my mother.

'And you've taken the house and paid for it?' I asked.

'Yes. Cameron knows all about this. He agreed.'

I hesitated. 'But, Mom, he hadn't seen it. He didn't realise.'

'No!' said my mother. 'And that's final.'

Rian and I walked over to Cameron, whose shoulders were hunched.

My mother stalked past, saying, 'I've never had a room of my own! Don't you kids realise how lucky you are?'

*

From the time I stepped on to the school bus that meandered all over northern Tehran before ejecting us in Jolfa, to the moment I hopped back off in front of our house, I was happier than I had ever been: I loved my school, I loved my friends, I loved being back in Tehran. It was only once I opened the front door at Khiaban Marvedasht and my mother's complaints began that things began to pall. First, there was the problem of the *soosks*, the big, brown hairy-legged insects that New Yorkers call roaches and Floridians call Palmetto bugs.

'Lin, you've got to do something about the *soosks*! Please! I'm going mad.'

My mother wept and pulled at her face, dragging the skin down so violently that I could see the red lining of her eyes.

I agreed: she was going crazy. She spent hours in front of her vanity mirror, cutting open her face with a needle she sterilised with hydrogen peroxide and squeezing out '*soosk eggs*'.

'I can't sleep, it's terrifying. Do you know what it feels like to have your bed crawling with cockroaches? I hate this goddam country. I hate this goddam house! I'm so cold I'm going to die and now I've got *soosks* in my bed!' My mother's voice was ragged.

My father, barely glancing at her, continued to saw at his meat.

'Genie, if you can show me one *soosk*, if you can wake me up once and show me one single *soosk* . . .'

'They run away as soon as I move. You just lie there, snoring like a great Buddha. Lin, do something. You promised me things would be better this time. You lied again.'

Then there was the cold. Now that winter had arrived and work was slow on the site, my father had brought home from the job a pocket-sized fourteen-year-old orphan, Hossein, who spent his days filling the kerosene heaters. Almost before he had finished going round the house, the ones he had filled first were empty. My mother complained bitterly about the cold and my father complained bitterly about the *naft* bill.

'Put on some more sweaters, Genie,' he admonished. 'Your blood is thin from living in Florida.'

And there was the problem of the food. There were constant

shortages: flour, sugar, rice, meat. From time to time, my father came home with a five-kilo bag of sugar and said, 'There's going to be a shortage soon, so I got this.'

Wealthy *bazaaris*, the merchants who supplied all the food shops, would corner the market on essential foods and then dribbled them out slowly at exorbitant prices. The Shah had imposed price controls on staples, but few shopkeepers abided by them. Of course, the *bazaaris* could have been arrested, but what policeman or soldier, themselves hungry, couldn't be bought off with a few kilos of sugar or meat? Meat was particularly hard to get. As with most things in Iran, knowing someone was helpful, but actually capitalising on the relationship required hard cash. My mother's friends, who could afford it, paid the butcher to save the best cuts of meat for them. For my mother, who was on a tight budget, buying merely edible meat proved a challenge. When she did get some, I spent hours cutting off the bones, tendons and ligaments, and then boiling it to soften it.

Furthermore, there was the problem of money. Mostly there was the problem of money. For the first school parent evening, my mother smiled and chatted with our teachers. When the principal approached her for a quiet word, her face fell. At home that night she went mad.

'Malin, you told me you had paid them.'

'But I did, Genie, I promise. The bank must have made a mistake. I have the paperwork. You can take it in to show them tomorrow.'

With my father, the bank had always made a mistake. Always when my mother asked for money, my father parried: 'I don't have any right now – but I *promise* as soon as this job finishes, as soon as So-and-So pays me, as soon as the bank cashes my cheque, I'll give you some, Genie, I promise.'

When she asked again, he promised again. My father forced my mother into the uncomfortable position of borrowing from her friends to pay for food or heating oil, and then arm-twisting my father, in front of those same friends, into repaying the money.

One evening I asked, 'Dad, please may I have some money to buy a lunch card?'

'How much do you need?' He looked up from the *Kayhan*, the English-language newspaper.

'Two hundred rials, please.' This was $3.

He reluctantly withdrew a 10-toman and a 5-toman note and handed them to me – 150 rials.

'But I need two hundred, please – that's how much a lunch card costs.' I looked at him.

'Sorry, darling girl, that's all I have.'

Next day, I approached the lady in charge of the lunch-room.

'I was wondering if you need help, you know, punching lunch cards? It seems busy and the lines are long.'

Cameron and I became official lunchroom 'checkers' – Cameron during first-period lunch and me during the second – and as payment we got a free lunch. Every day we slipped out of class early to run down to the cafeteria where we quickly added up what people had on their trays and, click-click-click, punched their cards. We could do the maths in our heads and we never let our friends slide through with 50 rials' worth of food and charge only 10 or 20. Not that often, at least. As soon as the line dwindled to a trickle, we rushed through, grabbing food and joining our friends, who couldn't understand why we gave up our precious lunch hour just to earn a few tomans' worth of food.

Once again we were back to the unrelieved pursuit of money. We approached every teacher who had small children and put up a notice at the American Women's Club. Word got out, and soon Cameron and I had a thriving babysitting business six or seven nights a week. Almost every foreign family had a big fridge loaded with food from either the commissary or the Western-oriented supermarkets: peanut butter, chocolate, jam, ice cream – even baby food. I became an aficionado of those lovely little pots of puréed cherries and custard, apple sauce and tapioca, prunes and rice pudding. At 50 rials an hour, it didn't take us long to become financially independent. Cameron and I never again asked for taxi fares, movie tickets or bowling money. As importantly, we rarely ate dinner at home so we escaped the bitter fights, the scraped-together, last-minute meals.

*

It was our first Christmas with our father in five years – longer, given that we hadn't actually celebrated Christmas since I was about six years old. My mother tried her best to make it special: she bought a tree, decorating it with baubles scavenged from her second-hand sales; she wrapped presents, also bought second-hand. On Christmas morning, she orchestrated a family present exchange. We all sat on the floor by the tree, my mother in a lavender-flowered housedress, her hair an atomic mushroom cloud for, unusually, she had been to the hairdresser. Diggie circled manically, toenails clicking on the cold marble floor. We spent as much time taking pictures as unwrapping presents.

My mother as always indulged her tendency to stage-manage events for the photos.

'Brush your hair, blow your nose, lift your chin, pull in your stomach,' she ordered.

If we didn't comply, she refused to take the photo, and any photo, once printed, that didn't stand up to scrutiny under a magnifying glass, she ripped into pieces. She took dozens of snaps and sent copies to everyone: her parents, brothers, uncles and aunts, Yosy, Uncle Hugh and her friends in Florida. For my mother, taking pictures was an act of self-definition. If she had the photos, it must have happened. If we were smiling in the pictures, we must have been happy. That Christmas, she wanted everyone to think that everything was fine – that she had made the right decision moving back to Iran and my father.

*

As spring approached, my mother came to a new decision, though. The happy housewife/happy family thing wasn't working for her. She was almost one year into our new life in Iran and, regardless of what the photos showed, she was miserable. So she was going to get right out and have some fun and she was no longer going to worry about food, heat, cleaning and school bills. At some point I realised I hadn't heard about the *soosks* in a while.

When I asked, she said, 'They aren't in season.'

My father snorted and said, 'You mean they were in your imagination.'

She learned how to play bridge, which now occupied her virtually every day and often in the evenings too. She collected Iranian artefacts and trinkets, and she continued buying foreigners' second-hand goods.

'Gather ye rosebuds while ye may, for this same flower that blooms today, tomorrow will be dying,' she quoted when my father complained about her 'gadding about'. '*Carpe diem*, baby. That's my philosophy. Like it or lump it, baby!'

Because my father never complained, none of us thought much about the huge changes that he had made to his life as a result of our returning to Iran. He had gone from living in his car, with a couple of suitcases in the boot and a jar of Nescafé in the glove compartment, to maintaining a large house and sending three children to school. Despite this, there was nothing he could do to make our mother happy – she complained and fought with him virtually non-stop. He had last lived with us kids when we were sinewy little moppets who adored him. Now we were adult-sized, stroppy teenagers who judged his every action. He maintained his equanimity, however, working, exercising, reading his newspapers, watching US Armed Forces TV in the evening. Nothing could ruffle him.

32

Drier than the Texas Sand

my mother in the 'golden age' of her twenties

The five of us, arms slung over each other's shoulders, wove up Shemiran towards Dan's house, screaming the words of 'School's Out'. Alice Cooper was our *God*. It was Friday afternoon and we were free: free of school, free of parents, free of anything other than 'School's out for summer! School's out forevah!'

Dolores, Cindy, Lyn, Dan and I were the core group, but there were others: Deb, Lyn's sister; Ebbie, an Iranian guy someone had met and become friends with; Chuck, a friend of Dan's who wore an obscenely tight green bathing suit (we tittered when Cindy pulled out the old Mae West line, 'Is that a banana in your pocket or are you just happy to see me?'); Mike, another friend of Dan's; not to mention Anne, Dan's next-door neighbour; and Sandy and Robin, who hung out with us once in a while.

It was amazing; I belonged to a gang; I had friends. We swam at Dan's house. We went to the bowling alley where we all took silly photos in the photo booth. At the Goldis', we watched Peter Sellers in *The Party* and Robert Redford in *The Way We Were*. At the Ice Palace, Dolores and Lyn skated, the rest of us on the sidelines heckling.

As we rollicked down Shemiran, I could smell Dan, a fresh-limey kind of a scent mixed with sweat. I could smell him because his arm was draped over me and also because I was wearing one of his striped cotton T-shirts. All of the girls stole Dan's T-shirts and I had finally gathered enough courage to grab one from the side of the pool and wear it, too. I glanced over at him and he smiled. He had black peach-fuzz on his top lip, and crooked teeth. His hair was black as black could be and, despite the cliché, I thought it looked like a raven's wing sweeping over his forehead. When I said things like that to Dor or Lyn or Cindy, they howled with laughter.

'Oh Ash, you are too funny!' they gasped. 'You are so cute!'

It puzzled me, but I loved the attention. I was their pet – younger, less mature, bookish.

At the pool, we played Marco Polo. Every time Dan and I swam past each other, my insides quivered as his soft hairy body rubbed against mine. I felt sick with delight. Suddenly I sensed him behind me. His arms engulfed me and my whole body was skin-to-skin against him, warm in the cold pool. Oh my God.

'Hey, hey, don't go anywhere, little girl,' he said in his soft Georgia accent. 'I'm not gonna hurt you.'

I relaxed back.

'Hey, look at Dan and Ash!' Lyn called to the group.

Heads swivelled and we separated, guiltily, as everyone

hooted and whistled. Later that day as I came out of the bathroom, Dan reached around the door and pulled me into his room. We stood locked in my first ever kiss. The hair above his lip was prickly and his lips were rubbery, but it was the best feeling I had ever felt in my entire life. I closed my eyes and sank deep.

'OK, OK, that's enough now.' Dan laughed and propelled me out again.

We joined the rest of the gang around the Daleys' kitchen table where everybody tore into *lavash* and drank Coke, chatting with Dan's mom. I propped myself against the windowsill, dazed: Danny had kissed me.

At school the next week, we were bashful, barely glancing in each other's direction. I rested my head dreamily on my hands during class, imagining him and thinking about how good he smelled, how soft and silky his hair was, how cute he looked, how sweet his voice – how nice his kiss.

Now, when I wasn't babysitting, I was out with Danny and the gang. My mother didn't like it. Not a bit. She wanted me working or helping her and she cracked the whip. When I was home, after I had cleaned up, she would call me down from my bedroom to have tea with her and chat. She had started teaching at TAS – first as a substitute and then full time, forced by my father because teachers' kids got to go to TAS for free. She still played bridge, but much less, and she was lonely, craving company. Sometimes I rebelled, preferring to go out with my friends, and we fought. But these were the normal fights of growing up.

Something had happened to our relationship: now we would sit for hours at the dining-room table, noshing on bits of bread and honey, and she would talk. And talk. And *talk*. I knew everything about her friends and her friends' servants, her bridge game, whether 'Pinch and Tickles', the antiquities man, had groped her or one of her friends, what had happened that morning of bargain hunting. She had an infinite supply of stories.

'Can you believe that German woman wanted ten thousand rials for a coat? A coat, Asho!' She was talking about one of her second-hand sales at a foreigner's house.

'Uh-huh.'

'It was worth a thousand.'

'Mom, can we talk about something other than used clothes?'

Hearing me gossip with my friends she had once told me, 'Great intellects discuss ideas; medium intellects discuss events and small ones discuss people.' It made me wonder what kind of intellect a person had who discussed 'objects'. Like her mother Lilly, my mother was obsessed with *things* and the house was jammed with *stuff*.

If I were able to persuade her to get off the topic of stuff, she reverted to her other favourite topic: the golden age of her teens and twenties, when she was the *most* beautiful, the *most* desirable and the *most* popular girl around. I loved these stories; often I wished she told them more rapidly or with less embellishment, but I was completely entranced by her past. I was also relieved that for the first time ever, she seemed to accept me and enjoy being with me. She would never be an easy mother, but at least now I no longer felt that I was balancing on the edge of a razor blade.

Tonight she asked, 'Have I ever told you about Matthew Tandish? I was engaged to him. He went to Yale and wore clear nail polish and clear lipstick.' She paused to draw on her cigarette and then added, as if it was sufficient explanation, 'He was a trumpet player.'

'When was that, Mom?' I asked. 'I thought you were engaged to Joe Green?'

'I was.' She said this as if she were insulted that I would think she had been engaged to *only* one man.

'When? Was it when you went to Gesell?'

She didn't answer, brushing off questions about facts and dates, preferring to focus on the story and the personalities, but I wanted the specifics and the chronology straight.

'No, no! It was after. Joe was long over.'

I couldn't understand how she could have been engaged to Joe, then Matthew, then my father.

'Did you love him?'

'Oh, Asho, I hardly *knew* him! Love? Who knew?'

'Then why did you get engaged?'

'That's what you did in those days.'

'Why would he have wanted to marry you?'

She looked at me as if this were so obvious she couldn't believe I was asking. 'Well, I was beautiful.'

'But, Mom, he wasn't buying a painting – you were getting *married*. How could you have taken it so casually?'

'Asho, I wasn't like you. I didn't think about everything. I didn't have your options. I was just a poor, small-town girl from Connecticut. She threatened to stop so I would beg her to continue. It was a game. As with her youthful romances, she liked being pursued.

'Go on,' I said. 'Please, I beg of you.' I fell to my knees with my hands clasped in front of me as if I were praying. 'Please, Mom, please!'

She burst out laughing, cranking up until she was sputtering. 'You always have to take the mickey, don't you?'

'Please, I beg and entreat you.'

'Well, where was I? Oh, yes, he took me out for lunch, it was a bloody hot day, and you know I could eat, boy, could I eat. After Lilly's food, a meal in a restaurant was something special.'

She paused to light another cigarette, the match head flaring and popping off on to the tablecloth.

'After we had eaten, I excused myself to go to the powder

room. In those days, we all wore these thick, yellow rubber girdles and when it came time to roll that rubber girdle back up, I couldn't! What with the heat and the eating, it was stuck like a rubber band around my thighs.'

'Oh my God, what did you do?' The image of my young mother, sitting on a toilet with a rubber girdle around her knees, was excruciating.

'Well, I tried to get it up – struggling and pulling and sweating in that tiny cubicle until finally I realised there was no way!'

I was laughing uncontrollably now. It was funny but it was also cringingly embarrassing.

'But what could I do? If I didn't wear it, I wouldn't have anything on under my dress and my big belly would be bulging out.'

'Oh my God, Mom. What did you do?'

She stopped again to butter her bread and drip honey on it. This was how she told stories: dribbled out slowly and dramatically.

'Well, I slipped it off and carried it out – flapping like a big floppy fish – under my arm. You know the pocketbooks in those days were too ladylike to actually put anything in them.'

I shook with laughter and she was laughing, too. As always, it sounded like a car trying to start on a cold day and that set me off even more. I laughed so hard my tears wet my shirt. Dad and Rian came running up from the TV room where they had been singing 'I Got You, Babe' along with Sonny and Cher on the US Armed Forces TV.

'Is Mummy telling you one of her stories?' asked my father.

I realised then I had never heard my father laugh. Not a proper laugh. I had heard him smirk cynically, but never a deep, true, belly laugh.

'Dad, laugh, please laugh,' I begged. 'I don't know what your laugh sounds like. Please,' I implored, 'please?'

'You should write her stories down, Asho, as she tells them,' he said, ignoring me. 'You know your mummy has had a very interesting life and she's an excellent storyteller.'

'I've never heard him laugh, either,' said my mother. 'Bloody English sense of humour . . .'

'It's drier than the Texas sand.' I completed her sentence, citing the line from a country and western favourite of Cameron's.

My mother laughed even harder. 'He's drier than the bloody Texas sand.'

'Seriously, Asho, get your mummy to write a book about her life. I think she would be very successful. You know she's looked into it before?' He turned to my mother. 'Genie, why don't you spend some of the time you waste shopping and playing bridge and talking on the telephone doing something useful?'

'You should, Mom,' I said, excited, 'it would be really fascinating.'

'You're damn right it would be fascinating,' she said. 'You wouldn't come out very well, though, you bloody British bastard.' Turning to me, she said, 'And you don't know the half of it.'

My mother told me, once my father had gone off to make himself a coffee, that in Florida she had explored the idea of writing a book about her life. Yosy had been an editor in New York and she still had friends at the publishing houses. Together they drew up an outline and submitted it.

'Do you know what they said, Asho?' she asked. 'They said that it couldn't be true! That so many things couldn't have happened to one person in a lifetime. That no one would believe it.'

33

Carpenter's Dream, Pirate's Treasure

on the runway

A short Iranian girl with a pale complexion approached me in the courtyard at school. 'Ashley, can I speak to you for a moment?'

I hesitated. I was shy about people knowing I spoke Farsi. I just wanted to fit in, to be one of the normal American kids.

'Yeah, sure.'

'My mother is a clothing designer and we are putting on a fashion show in a few months. I was wondering if you would be one of the models?'

I gulped. 'You're kidding?'

'No, why?'

'There are lots of girls much prettier.' I wondered whether this might be a cruel set-up.

She said, 'We would pay you, of course.'

'Uh, how much?'

When she told me, I said, 'Are you sure? Thank you! That would be great. You're sure? Thank you very much.'

That night at the dinner table, I told the family, playing the whole thing down – embarrassed that my brothers might tell my friends and also nervous about my mother's reaction.

My father jumped up from his seat and pinched my bum, saying, 'It must be jelly 'cuz jam don't shake like dat.'

I slapped his hand away, saying, 'Well, they're going to pay five thousand rials per show.'

There was silence around the table.

'Five thousand rials a show?' asked my mother. 'Seventy-five dollars?' She made $20 a day as a teacher at TAS.

'Well, that's how much five thousand rials is. And it's at the Hilton.'

Finally, my mother said, 'Ask them if we can come watch.'

*

Not many days later, my father showed me an ad in the newspaper. 'Wanted: fashion models for new agency setting up in Tehran.'

An American, from the South, judging from her accent, greeted us. I hadn't really thought about what to expect when we entered the air-conditioned office building in downtown Tehran. My vision of Tehran didn't encompass such modernity and cleanliness. It could almost have been Florida and the short, dark-haired woman dressed in black-and-white polyester couldn't have been more Florida. She looked like one of those fat Americans sighted mostly in the aisles of supermarkets.

She explained that she had owned a modelling agency in Alabama.

'We sent a lot of girls to New York – you've heard of Eileen Ford?'

Her husband had been transferred over with the army so she was going into partnership with an Iranian advertising agency.

Iran was at the beginning of an advertising revolution. She said that because most Muslim women wouldn't feel comfortable becoming models, there was an opportunity for Western girls.

'Plus, you know, the Western look is popular here,' she added.

The trend she had observed was definitely correct. All over Tehran there were huge billboards advertising Western goods: Coca-Cola, Mercedes-Benz, Singer Sewing Machines, Tide, Nescafé, Whirlpool and Rolex. Despite the huge duties on imported products, Iranians were desperate for them and would pay for them – or copies of them. There were waiting lists for almost every product; the goods couldn't be unloaded off the ships in Bandar Abbas fast enough. Recently many Western companies had established divisions and franchises in Tehran. Just around the corner from our house was a Kentucky Fried Chicken. Whether it was legitimate or not, we didn't know, but The Colonel graced every red-and-white box.

She was also on target about Iranians preferring a more Western look. Many of Mom's Iranian bridge-buddies had undergone nose jobs, bleached their hair, and had the hair on their faces and arms 'threaded' off. All their clothes came from Europe. Wealthy Iranian women looked very different to poor Iranians or their ancestors or even their children.

'Stand up. Walk. Come here,' the woman commanded.

I towered over her.

'How tall?' She looked up and, at close range, I was surprised to discover how pretty she was, how her eye make-up was carefully applied and that she smelled nice and perfumey.

'Five foot eleven,' my mother said, before I could respond.

'Actually,' I mumbled, 'five foot nine and a half.' My mother thought taller was better.

'That's fine. Weight?'

'A hundred and twenty-five pounds.'

'OK. We start training next week.' She handed me an

address on a piece of paper. 'Bring a bathing suit and some shoes you can practise walking in.'

*

Ciro, the designer, sat cross-legged on the ground pinning the hem; Pharibal, her daughter and my classmate, pinned the waist; and another woman adjusted the bust. They looked me up and down. They pulled me this way and that. They flipped through an album of dresses.

'This one? In blue? In velvet? Longer? Shorter?'

'Try this on.'

'Hold your arm like this.'

'Turn.'

I had eighteen outfits and I took notes on each one's special points. The reality had hit: these women sitting on the floor, sewing these beautiful fabrics, were relying on me to make their dresses look fabulous. Ciro's target market was Iranian women who couldn't afford to go to Europe to buy their clothes but who wanted elegant, Western-style clothes made to order. Each outfit cost hundreds of dollars and required a number of fittings. Ciro imported the wools and cashmeres from Italy, the silks from China and India.

That night I practised what I would do – over and over – in my room. I chose shoes from my mother's cupboard to go with each outfit and marked them on the sole with masking tape. For the first time I was happy about all those trips to the thrift stores and the dozens of suitcases full of shoes and clothes.

On the night of the show, I curled my hair with electric rollers. My mother never used make-up other than the de rigueur 1950s slash of lipstick, but in the weeks before the show she had bought some at the second-hand sales in foreigners' homes. I caught a taxi on Sultanatabad and made my way over to the Hilton. Ciro and her relatives were bringing in racks of dresses while workmen made final adjustments to the long runway in the grand ballroom.

I walked out on to the stage and gazed around the immense room. Mirrors reflected me on every wall. Dozens of tables were laid with white tablecloths and precisely ordered cutlery and glassware. Musicians entered and set up. The master of ceremonies tested the mike. His finger hitting the mesh popsicle made a 'clunk, clunk, clunk' sound. The other models wandered in. I practised walking along the runway, feeling the eyes of the musicians and the MC on me.

'I can't believe I said I'd do this, I can't believe I am such an idiot, I can't believe I actually thought I could do this,' I muttered to myself. One minute my body was freezing and shaky, and the next the sweat dripped off me.

To distract myself, I whispered jokes my brothers had been repeating at dinner.

'You're a carpenter's dream,' said Cameron. 'Flat as a board and straight as a nail.'

'No, she's a pirate's treasure,' Rian chipped in. 'A sunken chest.'

Then, 'Ashley Ashley *nobat eh* Ashley-*eh*.'

It was my turn and Ciro propelled me on stage. The lights were blinding and the chandeliers glittered. The master of ceremonies introduced me in English and Farsi.

'Ladies and gentlemen, our first dress this evening is, *Parvaneh*, "The Butterfly", worn by the lovely Miss Ashley. Ladies and gentlemen, give her a hand!'

For one long moment, I stood poised at the top of the runway and then I was off. Swirling my flowing chiffon 'wings', I felt as if I were flying. Each of my 'little routines' – whether dancing Arabian-style in a crimson sultan's costume, swaying elegantly in a black-velvet beaded dress, or winking at the cameras as I twirled at the end of the stage in a harlequin halter-neck – went off without a hitch. It was as if a fairy had sprinkled magic dust all over me. At the end, the crowd clapped and whistled as I made my way dreamily down the platform in the grand-finale wedding dress. Mom, Dad and Rian, whom

Ciro had allowed to attend as long as they didn't eat, clapped and yelled.

That was the beginning. Soon I was filming TV commercials and appearing on billboards. My picture stared out of newspapers and magazines. I even saw myself during the ad break before the main film at the cinema.

*

I had worried about how my mother would react to my modelling. After all, it was she who was beautiful and who cared so much about her appearance. Like most teenage girls, I was consumed with my looks: did this pimple show? Was this mole ugly? Should I have cut off that half-inch of hair? But by this stage, I was also beginning to get sick of my mother's obsession and the apparent sense of entitlement she derived from her beauty. All her life she had expected special privileges because she was gorgeous, whereas I thought that being stunning should be more than sufficient in itself. And as she aged, it got worse.

'You can't understand, Asho, how it feels to get old when you have been so beautiful.'

Perhaps because I couldn't compete in the beauty stakes; perhaps because we had recently become friends after so many years of antagonism; perhaps because my modelling earned me money and, in our household, money ruled; perhaps because of any or all of these things, she was encouraging.

All the money I earned, I gave to my father for safe keeping.

'Here, Dad, I have a thousand rials for you to put into the bank!'

I proudly presented the cash to him after a busy week of babysitting. After a TV commercial when I made 20,000 rials, or approximately $300, I danced in with a huge wad of bills. My father had convinced me it wasn't safe to leave money in the house, that it was too much of a temptation for the houseboy, and that foreigners' houses were often burgled. When I began modelling, I checked whether I could deposit the money in my Florida bank account, but the costs of exchanging rials to dollars made it untenable. Week after week, between 1973 and 1978, I handed over all my money to my father.

34

Nothing is Simple

my grandparents

Tears welled up in my mother's eyes. A letter had arrived from my grandfather, the writing shaky, as if he had been writing on a moving train, telling us my grandmother had suffered a series of strokes and was in a nursing home.

'Are you upset, Mom?' I asked, incredulous. After listening to my mother's stories of how horrible my grandmother had been to her, I couldn't believe she could be sad.

'Well, she's my mother,' she said.

'At least you've still got your father,' I said cheerily, 'and he'll probably live to be a hundred.'

'He's not my father! How could you think that Willy is my father?' My mother looked at me in disbelief.

'What?' I had no idea what she meant.

'You know that Willy's not my father.'

'No, Mom.' I sat down at the dining-room table. 'What do you mean?'

'Well, why would you think he is?' she replied.

'The reason I thought he was your father is that he's my grandfather and he's married to my grandmother. What do you think?' I said belligerently.

'Get me some tea and some of those nice oatmeal cookies you baked and I'll tell you a story – a very interesting story.' She replied, her eyes glinting.

I brewed the tea and put the cookies, chewy and filled with raisins, on a plate. My thoughts darted around, trying to find some basis for what she was saying, some hint. All I could come up with was that she called him 'Willy'. I had never once heard her call him 'Dad'. I had homework to do, but my mother rarely considered that when she wanted to talk. And tonight, as opposed to plying me with the normal chit-chat about Nounou's servant, she had detonated a bomb.

Hang on, I thought to myself, I had heard her say, 'Ma and Pa'. I was completely bewildered.

When I returned, my mother pried a cigarette from its packet and lit it with a flare of her lighter. She sucked the smoke deep into her lungs and blew it out.

'Well, this is quite a story, quite a story.'

I sat silently.

'You know that Lilly and Willy have known each other since they were kids?'

'How does that not make him your father?'

'Do you want to hear . . . ?'

'Yes, go on, go on.'

'Well, they were from a completely different class of family. Willy came from dirt-poor farmers – good people, but penniless. Lilly, well she came from a better background – her father was a tailor. He worked in New York and he came up to Colchester when he could. Lilly was educated. She finished high school and then she went to normal school. Willy had to leave school when he was in fourth grade to help the family.'

She took a couple of thoughtful drags on her cigarette. I always imagined that the smoke would leak out of her toenails, she drew in so deeply.

'Don't get me wrong, Willy wasn't dumb. His younger brother, Manny, got a PhD and was a teacher in New York. But that's because he was the youngest. Willy, who was older, had to go to work.'

I nodded. I knew all this. She had told me these things many times.

'And Lilly was beautiful – tall, with a rope of golden hair to her waist and bright-blue eyes – and sharp as a whip. She wasn't interested in Willy; she was destined for greater things. He hung around, though, and he was very handsome. She went to New York – and you have to understand this was the flapper era, the roaring twenties. She wanted to be a model, be in show business. She was part of the whole Moss Hart crowd. Every time she came back to Connecticut, there was Willy still hanging around. For some reason, God knows why, she married him. Well, they had no money. It was the depression.'

She stopped to ask me to make some more tea.

'Just top it up with some hot water,' she said. 'It was when Willy was working at the gas station that he fell in love with a woman named Bertha. He didn't want to,' she explained. 'He adored Lilly but she was awful to him. This woman, Bertha, was squat and slovenly, but she was kind to him and God knows he needed a little tenderness. Well, at about the same time, he became friends with an Irishman named Kevin, who was a truck driver for the municipal government. Willy took him home one day and Kevin started mooching around the house when Willy was with Bertha.'

'So was Kevin your father?'

Her face remained unreadable.

'Mom, don't keep me in suspense. What happened? Did you know him? Are you still in touch? What's the story?'

'Oh Asho, Asho, Asho,' she said. 'Yes, I knew him, of course. We lived with him, off and on, for years – in Waterbury and then in New York.'

'How come he and Granny didn't stay together?'

'Well, for one thing, he had a wife and a whole passel of kids hanging around.'

Willy and Lilly continued to live together in Waterbury. Willy shuttled back and forth between Lilly and Bertha, while Kevin did the same between Lilly and his wife. Lilly became pregnant in 1931 and had twins flaxen-haired and blue-eyed: my mother and her brother – in May of the following year.

'They called us "bastards",' said my mother, 'everybody: my grandparents, my cousins, the neighbours – everybody.'

'Mom, are you sure this really happened? Why didn't you ever tell me?' I held my stomach, feeling ill with shock.

'Of course I'm sure! You think I want to be the bastard child of some ne'er-do-well Irishman? Why should I have told you? It's none of your business. This is my life, Ashley, not yours.' Her voice was defiant.

'OK, OK.' I tried to placate her. 'I just don't understand how you could keep something so important a secret for so long. He's just as much my grandfather as he is your father. You have to understand why it's important to me.'

She gave me a withering look.

'All right,' I said, trying to understand. 'When did Granny take Grandpa back?'

'I'll come to that, but first, did you ever notice the scar Willy had across his throat?' she asked.

'No.'

'Don't you remember every time he ate, he would choke?'

'Oh yeah, of course. What was that all about?'

'He cut his throat.'

'Oh God, oh God.'

'He cut his throat and we found him. Let me see, we must

have been about seven or eight years old. My God, it was horrible. He cut his throat all the way across with a straight razor.'

'Oh God.' I rocked back and forth.

'There was blood all over the floor, the bath. Every place. The ambulance came and took him away, and I can still see him on the stretcher, his arm dragging on the ground. There were blood spots on the front steps. None of us wanted to touch them to clean them off.'

She stopped, tears in her eyes.

'Well, poor old man, he never could do anything right. He didn't kill himself and then, when they sewed him up, they didn't get the oesophagus straight or something, because ever since he hasn't been able to swallow properly and he chokes and coughs. After that he and Lilly stayed together. He had no place to go. It was just too difficult for them to do it on their own. My God, what a life that man had. Miserable. Boy, did he make it miserable for us, too. He could never forgive us for being Kevin's. He beat us, my God, he beat us.'

'That's horrible. Poor you. Poor Grandpa.'

'So you see, Asho, nothing is simple. He may not be my father, but he raised us. Despite everything. No matter how hard he had to work. No matter how awful Lilly was to him, Willy was the one who left the house every night in the freezing cold to go work his guts out for us.'

35

Joanie's College Fund

*my mother as a
young teacher*

'A sho, Asho honey, come feed the dogs with me.'

My mother called from the bottom of the stairs to my room where I was sneaking in some homework. Even if I begged her to let me study because I had a test or a paper, she always needed help with some task and she always wanted company.

The dogs, Diggie and Ivan, an enormous Alsatian my mother had been given recently, ran in circles around us, growling and barking at the shadows of cats both real and imagined. They were hungry. We broke off chunks of raisin cake and threw it to them. She hadn't been to the bazaar for the cow and sheep lungs, intestines and feet that she bought in large squidgy bags and then boiled for hours, the stench crawling wetly through the house. Nowadays my mother was mostly too busy to go to the bazaar, since she was teaching again and Hossein had gone back to the job. Often I would find her, as I did tonight, sitting on the edge of the balcony, feeding the dogs bread, leftover beef stew or cake, a cigarette resting beside her.

'Asho, have I told you about the little boy in my first-grade class?' My mother always enticed me away from whatever it was I should be doing with stories from her past.

'No, Mom. I really do have homework to do, you know.'

'Just sit with me for a few minutes, honey, while I feed the dogs.'

I didn't particularly want to hear about her little student, but I did want to get back to Lilly and Willy. I tried a couple of questions.

'Mom, why did they get back together and why did they stay together since they clearly hate each other?'

'God knows, Ashley. They've been together for decades so they're used to each other. But really, honey, you have to understand how poor they were. They had no one to turn to and four kids to raise. Divorce was difficult and it wasn't common. Bringing up the kids together was the only way and, even so, it was back-breakingly difficult. You know, we mothers, we women, we do things for our children.' She trailed off.

'I still don't understand why you have no desire to track down your real father – to see what happened to him.'

'Well, I don't!' she said curtly. 'In any case, I know what happened to him. He lives in Florida, close to where we used to live. And Lilly and Willy saw him not that long ago. He stopped for a visit and Lilly said she couldn't understand what she had seen in him – he was a dried-up old emphysemic.'

'So that's who you get your cigarette addiction from!'

She laughed ruefully as she took another drag. 'OK, get to bed and don't stay up all night studying.'

I went upstairs, stopping on the way to fill a can with kerosene for the hot-water heater. I always found lighting the heater scary, dropping the match into the dripping *naft* and seeing the flame whoosh up. All over Iran there were people horribly disfigured by burns when their stoves malfunctioned.

I was badly shaken by my mother's revelation about her parentage. She couldn't understand it, having the attitude that it was her story and her concern, not mine. What I found distressing was not the fact that my grandfather might not have been my grandfather biologically, but the cavalier way my mother had kept secret something that was so important.

*

'Now back to my story,' said my mother.

I was not going to escape the tale of my mother's first-grade pupil. I had become her confidante and she delighted in her Scheherazade role. It was the next evening and we had been gorging on bacon, sausage, blood pudding and eggs, because my father had just come back from Karaj. Muslims considered pork *najess*, but an Armenian Christian family had established a pig farm and processing plant in Karaj. Once or twice a year when my father drove through there, he would buy all his favourite treats from childhood and we would all feast.

'You know that when I finished college, I taught for a year in Connecticut?'

I nodded.

'Well, I had a little boy in my class, a sweet boy – big, a big kid for five – an only child from a Greek family. There were lots of immigrants in the area and they were real peasants.'

Her eyes became dreamy as she mentally revisited her small classroom twenty years earlier.

'The mother was young, still only in her twenties, but middle-aged before her time. She came and stayed with him the first few days of school to get him settled. He didn't speak a word of English.'

She went on, after many dramatic pauses and tension-building asides, to say that often she would find the toilet in her classroom unflushed and each time she would ask which child was responsible. When no one 'fessed up, she would remind them and then forget about it until the next time, when a little girl or boy burst out of the bathroom, crying, 'Someone didn't flush the toilet!' Finally she kept an eye out and she discovered that it was this little farm boy.

'OK, Johnny,' said my young mother, 'I'm just calling him that because I can't remember his name right now; it will come to me,' she told me, 'you can't leave that bathroom until you flush the toilet.' She laughed. 'Well, I was busy, and hours later, when another child finally had to use the bathroom, I thought, my God, Johnny is still in the bathroom!'

'Mom, don't, please! I bet I know where this is going and I don't want to hear any more!' I was already laughing.

'Well, there was this kid covered in pee and shit, red in the face – he had been trying to push it down the toilet.'

She hesitated to let the image of the sight and smell sink in. 'No, Mom, please . . .'

'Hours, Asho, hours he was in there, pushing the shit down the toilet – *he didn't know how to flush*!' she continued. 'He was just a poor farm kid who had always used an outhouse. My heart bled for him. I'll never forget that child.'

Although I was still laughing, I felt a flash of shame and pity for the little boy. I had come to realise that many of my mother's stories had a moral. She wasn't a teacher by accident and she wanted to impart to me, her only daughter, as much as she could.

'What did you do?'

'I took that child and cleaned him off and then I taught him how to use a toilet.'

I knew how sensitive my mother's stomach was and how little it took to make her vomit, so I understood how big a gesture this had been.

'Mom, I still find it amazing that you, just a poor farm girl – not that different from that little boy – after teaching only a year, simply jumped on a ship and went to Pakistan. You'd never even been on a plane or a ship; you'd barely been on a train. The furthest you had been was Washington on your school trip.'

'Well, we planned it. We didn't just jump on a ship. We thought the whole thing out.'

It took me more than a few seconds to absorb this. We. We. We.

'Just a minute!' I sat up. 'You never told me you went with somebody else. Who'd you go with?'

Somehow I knew, almost instantaneously, that it hadn't been just a friend. My whole body was shaking. Hearing the Willy and Lilly story had made me wary.

'With Ben, my husband,' she answered.

I could feel my face flush. It was immediate.

'Your husband?' Tears scorched my eyes.

She nodded, keeping her own wide and empty. 'Yes, you know, Ben.'

'No, I don't know. Not Dad?'

'No, not Dad.' Irritated, she mimicked me with a high squeaky voice.

'You had another husband?' My tone was accusatory and I leaped out of my chair. 'I can't believe you lied to me! First about Grandpa and now about this!'

'I didn't lie! I've never told you I *wasn't* married before!'

'No, but how many times have you told the story of how you went to Pakistan? Every *single* detail: how you had read the *National Geographic* about India when you were five years old and it had been your dream all your life; the name of the captain and how much he was in love with you; the route; how you were stuck for fifty-seven days because the Suez Canal was closed . . . blah blah blah. I practically know what you ate at every meal, but somehow in all that you never mentioned that you were married and had gone there with your husband.'

I stalked around, unable to sit still.

'If I did something like that, you would say I was lying. If I took drugs or drank and then just "forgot" to tell you, you would say I was lying. You've never told me you haven't taken heroin ... Should I assume you have? You've never told me you haven't got a PhD should I assume you do?'

I was on a rant.

'*Who are you?* First your father's not your father, now you suddenly have another husband. And anyway, it figures – I never understood how you had done all those things on your own.'

'It's my life,' she said, 'not yours.'

'But how many times have I heard the whole song and dance? Somehow, *somehow* the fact that you went with *your husband* never came up. I would call that lying. Anyway, if it's your life and not my business, why are you telling me now?'

'Sh, be quiet, your father will hear.'

'The *husband* part, Mom.'

'Well, your father wouldn't let me tell you.'

'Mom, we were separated from Dad for five years. None of us ever thought we would see him again. You're lying.'

'No, it's the truth; he said he would divorce me if I ever told anyone.'

'So what? You've just told me. What's changed? Is he going to divorce you now?'

'I just try to tell you a simple story, and you're making it into a big song and dance. I thought you would be interested. Everything with you is a federal case, Ashley.'

'OK. OK.' I wasn't going to let her get off-track. 'OK, so what was his name again?'

'Ben. Benjamin.'

'Oh my God!'

I suddenly remembered that when we were in the bazaar in Esfahan my father had asked, out of the blue, whether I liked the name Benjamin.

'Mom, I told you about this in Esfahan. I told you that Dad had asked if I liked the name Benjamin and you played dumb. You lied to me then, too.'

'Really?' She ignored my accusation. 'He asked that? I never thought your father was capable of jealousy. That he had the emotional capacity for it. Hm.'

'Why do you go on and on with all the stupid unimportant stories and lie to me about everything that is important? How many times have I heard about the *stupid* turtle farm and the *stupid* blueberries and the *stupid* holes in your socks, and here with something so important, just like with Grandpa, you somehow forget to tell me?'

'Do you want to hear the story or not?'

'You just constantly lie to me . . .'

'Do you want to hear?' She was angry now.

'OK, OK. Go on.'

She started at the beginning, gearing herself up. She told me how when she finished high school at Bacon Academy in 1950, one of a class of twenty-three small-town kids, she had dreamed of becoming an air hostess, of travelling the world wearing a light-blue Pan American uniform with a pert little cap. Her parents thought that air hostesses were whores, though, and told her she could become a nurse or a teacher and nothing else.

'But why did you listen, Mom?'

'What did I know?' she said. 'I was so naive. I didn't have your opportunities – any of the help you've had.'

She was too squeamish for nursing but she couldn't become a teacher because she was left-handed and in those days teachers had to be right-handed. Teachers College of Connecticut, Willimantic, accepted her on the condition that she changed her writing hand.

'Mom, I know this stuff – you've told me a million times. What about the husband part?'

Please, just get on with the story, I thought to myself.

'Anyway, I needed fifty bucks for my tuition and Lilly and Willy refused to lend it to me. After all the work I did. You know why? They wanted to buy a television.'

I nodded.

'So I worked to save money for college at Gurian's Drugstore and, lovely man that he was, Harry Gurian, he put a coffee can on the counter with a sign on it: "Joanie's College Fund".'

'Mom, please . . . How did you meet your first husband, Benjamin?'

'OK! OK! One day I was serving behind the counter and a man came in. I had no idea then what he would become in my life. He asked for a maple walnut ice-cream cone.'

'So was that Ben?'

I knew that maple walnut was her favourite and that would have been an instant topic of conversation. The young pretty girl behind the counter, the man who had asked for the cone . . . I could imagine it perfectly.

She ignored me, engrossed in her memories. 'Well, he saw the sign for the college fund and he asked if I was Joanie and then he put a dollar tip into the can. A dollar! An ice-cream cone in those days was a nickel. A whole dollar.'

Twenty years later and my mother was still impressed by the tip.

She went on to tell me that he came back to the drugstore every evening on his way home to his mother's house, where he lived. He was a Yale graduate, a civil engineer, working on a Levittown-type housing project in the area. He was stocky, shorter than she was and had thick, curly brown hair. Every day he put a dollar into the can. Soon Harry Gurian joked that he would put the can away and Ben could just send the money

337

straight to the college. It didn't take very long before Ben asked her out on a date.

'What about Joe Green? What about Matthew Tandish?' I asked.

She shrugged them aside. By then she was living in the dorm, with a bunch of giggling girls – girls who rolled their hair on beer cans, wore skin-tight dungarees and bobby socks with saddle shoes, and danced together to the 'dreamy' music of Frank Sinatra and Dean Martin.

'Nancy, Nance!' She came in breathless with news one Saturday night and flung herself on her best friend's bed. 'I've been pinned.'

Ben had fastened his Yale pin on her baggy college sweater. Then, not long after, she burst into the dorm to announce, 'Girls, girls! I'm engaged!'

They were married in December 1952, just a few months after they met. She was twenty.

'Gosh, that was fast. Did you love him?'

'He was a good man. A professional, with a good job, well educated. And he loved me, Asho. He adored me. He worshipped the ground I walked on.'

'That's not what I asked.'

'It always has to be this way with you, Ashley. I tell you a story and you have to jump all over me.'

'Oh please, Mom, if he was so wonderful why didn't you stay with him?'

She shook her head. 'I was young. I was beautiful. I was full of life.'

I had listened to enough for one night. As I went up to bed, she stayed at the table, smoking her cigarette pensively. 'Don't tell your father I told you.'

'Why, Mom? He knew you were married, didn't he?'

'Just don't tell him or the boys. Or I'll never be able to trust you with a secret again.'

I didn't turn on the light in the hallway as I climbed the stairs. My legs felt as if I had climbed up and then down the Alborz Mountains behind Tehran. I didn't stop in the bathroom to brush my teeth. I didn't tidy my pile of books. I didn't load up my school bag. I didn't put out my clothes for the next day. I didn't put on my nightgown. I simply pulled off my jeans and fell into bed.

Benjamin. You could have been my father. Benjamin. My mother says you were a lovely man. One of the kindest people she ever met in her life. That you were brilliant, that her nickname for you was 'Gen' – short for genius – and that was why my own father called her Genie, except he was being sarcastic. That you were cultured, well read and beautifully mannered. That you grew a beard because she thought it would make you look 'distinguished'. That you bought lifts for your shoes so you would be taller. That you changed your whole wardrobe – and hers, buying her beautiful clothes for the first time in her life. That you learned to dance. That you collected antiques because she loved old things. That you lived in a cottage on a lake. That you left your home, your beloved mother and sister, your well-paying job, to follow her dream of going to India.

I lay in bed, my bedspread pulled up to my chin, the moon shining through the curtains, and thought to myself: now I understand those beautifully organised and annotated photo albums of the Pakistan years. Benjamin, Ben: you had done them. You were the bearded man in the pictures. So much made sense now.

If you had been our father, we would have lived in a proper house and gone to school, and had enough money to buy food and clothes. You would have helped with my homework and bought me a bike. You would have loved Mom and supported her. She wouldn't have lost her teeth because we didn't have enough money for the dentist; she wouldn't have lost two babies because of poor medical care; she wouldn't have had to work as a waitress, getting varicose veins. She wouldn't have almost died from some 'female infection'. You weren't the kind of man who would have allowed that for your wife and family. You could have travelled together and my mother would have had her dream of seeing the world.

I would have been short, though. And had a big nose. I placed my index finger and thumb over my nose. But the rest. The rest. Benjamin, you could have been my father.

Then I realised, with a jolt: maybe they had children? If they were married when Mom was twenty, then they had been married for five or six years. *Five or six years?* That was a long time. Mom had described it as if it were just an adolescent phase she had gone through. She had five children in fewer than five years with my father. My mind churned away: could she have had more? I was horrified at the thought I might have brothers or sisters I didn't know about.

But, no, after a few minutes, I calmed down. The *only* thing I knew with absolute certainty about my mother was that she would never abandon any child of hers.

36

Fanning the Flames

on a bed!
with a man!

We were plummeting through the night on the deserted new highway to the west of Tehran. I crawled towards the cabin of the joobhopper and began to pound on the roof over the driver's head, holding on to the side so I didn't fall out. My hair whipped my face and my eyes watered in the wind. The driver ignored my banging and screaming – if anything, he drove faster. He swerved from lane to lane, swinging us from one side of the van to the other. The highway, still under construction, was absolutely empty. We were the only vehicle on it. I leaned over the side, holding on with one hand, to slam the small back window. I could see a grim smile on the driver's face. Diane, Danny's little sister, began to cry.

'Ri, hold on tight,' I yelled, worried that he would be

thrown out by the driver's wild swerving. *'Agha, vaysa!'* I screamed.

There was definitely something going on here, something that fitted in with a pattern that seemed to be emerging more generally. The Iranians, more and more, seemed to hate Americans – to hate us. To hate me. Men regularly jeered at and pinched me on the streets. Not many days earlier, one had spat on me after handing me a flyer of a woman fellating a man. Everywhere I went, I could tell from the taunts, the looks, the touching, that Iranian men thought we American girls were dirty and slutty. Tehran was a changed place and any friendliness that Iranians might once have felt towards Americans had now turned into antagonism.

I thought about the assembly we had in school recently.

'All classes gather in the gym immediately,' someone yelled into the megaphone in the courtyard below.

We poured out of our classes and filed into the gym. A distraught-looking man stood at the mike.

'You know our son, Paul,' he said, 'and I know a lot of you kids, too. Hi, guys.' He greeted the members of Paul's basketball and football teams. 'And so do the Iranian police.'

The bleachers were silent. Paul's dad told us that the Iranian police had caught Paul with heroin wrapped in tin foil, stashed in his shoe. *Heroin in his shoe.* That small detail shocked me. It was so premeditated. The punishment for possessing heroin in Iran was death *if you were an adult*. Paul was big and tall, with a fuzzy moustache. But he was only seventeen, technically a child. The police insisted he was an adult, though. His parents tried to prove his age, using his passport and birth certificate, but the Iranian authorities would accept neither of these documents.

'You can buy a passport in the bazaar for four hundred dollars,' they argued. They threatened execution, the standard punishment for drug dealing.

In jail, meanwhile, Paul and another inmate fought off other prisoners. He witnessed convicts have their heads shoved down toilet holes full of excrement and beaten with rubber hoses. The police showed Paul photos of himself and his friends – my classmates – in the bazaar, in the parks, on the streets, buying heroin and hashish.

'The drug dealers work for us,' the police told him. 'We know everything you do. Every place you go. We watch you Americans every minute of every day. You do not belong here. You are not welcome here.'

Paul's parents, meanwhile, were trying to prove he was seventeen. The authorities would accept only an X-ray that showed his bones were still growing. They went from one doctor to the next, but each, fearing reprisals, refused to scan Paul. Finally, they found one willing to take the risk, who produced the necessary X-ray showing he was still growing.

'So we're leaving Iran, all of us. Paul wanted me to come and tell you that they know everything and that you need to stop. You need to stop now.' Paul's dad choked. When he finished speaking, most of the girls in the gym were crying and many of the boys looked shaken.

By now, Lyn, Cindy and I were slamming the roof so hard our fists ached, the wind swallowing our screams as we raced along. I was sure we would crash. Finally the highway ended and we entered an area with more traffic in the south of Tehran.

'He's slowing down, guys, we can jump out if he stops,' Lyn yelled as we pulled up behind a car.

We all piled out, falling on to the side of the road. The driver leaped out and grabbed me by the arm, screaming, '*Pool bedeh, jendeh!*'

It took me a second, but then I understood: 'Give me my money, whore!'

Men gathered, pressing themselves on us, shouting and shaking their fists. The sidewalks of Tehran were always crowded – mostly with men – strolling along, passing the time.

If there was a fight or an accident, a noisy throng gathered in seconds. This mob that had formed around us felt threatening. The fact that a Muslim man used the word *jendeh* with teenage schoolgirls was the ultimate sign of disrespect.

'Just give him some money,' Rian yelled.

Another incident flashed through my mind and I drew Rian to me. Only recently, the tall black hero of our football squad had died in an anti-American knife fight. I grabbed money from Lyn and Cindy. The crowd pressed against us, angry and yelling.

I could hear Lyn screaming in front of me, '*Nakon!* Stop it!' She was swinging her arms out in front of her to fend the men off. 'Ouch! I can't believe it, he pinched my boob.'

The men imitated her high-pitched shriek as they reached to grab and pinch her again.

'*Estop eet!*'

'*Estop eet!*'

The men parroted Lyn, laughing and plucking at her breasts.

I thrust the money at the driver and seized Rian. The crowd hemmed us in. We couldn't move.

At dinner a few nights earlier, my mother had told us a story about a storekeeper who had kidnapped an American boy. It had taken days before his parents got him back and that was only after paying both the police and the kidnapper. Apparently, though, the storekeeper hadn't done it for the money, but because of his fury about Americans being in his country. The American family immediately left Iran, abandoning their jobs, their possessions and their car, which they left parked on the street.

'Guys, find a taxi!' shouted Cindy.

She was tall and had a big voice. She waved her arm frantically and a taxi skidded to a stop. As we crammed into it, fighting our way through the crowd, some men yelled to the driver not to take us. I begged him in Farsi, '*Borro, Baba, borro!*' babbling that we hadn't done anything, that we would pay him, that the joobhopper driver had taken us to the wrong place. He turned the key in the ignition, the engine faltered and he folded his arms. He was not moving until we either got out of the car or paid him.

We pulled money from our pockets and thrust it at him. '*Borro, Agha, lotfan, borro!*'

I implored him to go but he waited, his arms crossed, while men battered the windows and leered at us, shrieking, '*Estop eet!*' The car was rocking from the weight of the crowd. Finally, reluctantly, he inched the taxi through the crowd of furious, screaming men.

All the way to Goldis Cinema, Lyn repeated, 'He pinched my boob, they pinched my boobs, they touched me,' until finally we began to laugh and the incident became something we could talk and giggle about.

I told my parents the next day. Despite having Rian there to verify all the details, my father made light of the incident. 'You're imagining it,' he said. 'Iranians would never do that.'

'Dad, she's not, it was really scary,' confirmed Rian.

'Don't be silly – why would anyone do that?' asked my father, still reading the newspaper.

I wondered the same thing. Could anyone realistically have kidnapped a whole group of us? And why?

'Maybe he thought it would be funny to frighten us,' I said. 'He seemed really angry. Maybe he thinks Americans shouldn't be in his country. That we should be wearing chadors. He called us "*jendeh*".'

'Just be careful,' he said. 'Things in Iran are changing.'

That social unrest was rampant was obvious to teenagers like us who spent a lot of time just flowing around the city without much to do. Despite the fact that the Iranian middle class had doubled in size during the Shah's regime, the vast majority of the country was still so poor that they lived hand to mouth. By the 1970s, Iran had one of the worst income distributions in the world, as well as one of the worst infant mortality rates and doctor–patient ratios. Most Iranians did not have electricity, piped water, transportation or medical care. In fact, the women at my mother's bridge parties joked that it was lucky that there were a few Indian doctors in Iran because all the Iranian MDs had emigrated to New York City. The term 'brain drain' was first used with reference to Iran. Almost three quarters of all adults were illiterate. Meanwhile the Shah was in a spending frenzy: on defence systems, intelligence and information networks, missiles, helicopters, jets, tanks – never mind the Mercedes, the palaces, the private planes.

We had seen a highly visible example of the Shah's extravagance when we visited Persepolis. Adjoining the magnificent ruins was a tent city built for the 2,500th anniversary celebration in 1971. He reportedly spent $200 million importing Baccarat crystal, Limoges china, Porthault linens, as well as thousands of bottles of wine and champagne. At the time, anti-Shah protestors attacked banks, assassinated police officials, blew up movie theatres and threatened to target Persepolis. The Shah's secret police, Savak, reportedly arrested hundreds. The cost of Savak and the police state in itself was enormous. Everywhere battalions of soldiers tromp-tromp-tromped the streets to the rumbling accompaniment of tanks and convoys of outsized military trucks. However, this might couldn't blind the Iranian people to what they were observing: that all around them were people living high on the hog, driving glittering foreign cars, holed up in marble-clad mansions that were protected with barbed wire, broken glass embedded in concrete and round-the-clock guards – and that many of them were Americans.

Even I, with my modelling, was fanning the flames by advertising expensive foreign goods in a sexualised way. One of the ad campaigns I did, for Whirpool air-conditioners, caused a furore, with newspaper editorials bristling because, for the first time in a national advertising campaign, a foreign woman was photographed half dressed on an unmade bed with a bare-chested Iranian man. The clash between the actual way of life for most Iranians and that of *farangi* like us led to unquenchable anger. We teenagers, who were on the streets all the time, bore the brunt of it.

37

The Whole Story

*my favourite picture
of my mother*

Mom was going on about her bridge group and the three no-trump bid she and her partner had successfully manoeuvred but I wanted to know more about Benjamin.

'Mom, how come you and Benjamin, Ben, never had kids?'

'We just never did.'

'But why? You had me ten months after you married Dad and you've told me that the reason you had five kids in four years was because you didn't know about birth control. So why did you and Ben not have any?'

My mother looked uncomfortable and her response was stiff. 'We didn't have that kind of relationship.'

'What do you mean, you never had sex?'

'Sh, Asho. Don't talk like that.'

I was almost sixteen, kids in my year were being jailed for using heroin, and my mother couldn't even use the word 'sex' in front of me.

'Seriously, Mom, what are you saying?'

'Well, that was part of our problem, he could never, um, you know. He needed someone softer. I heard later that he married an Asian woman – Vietnamese or Thai. That would have been better for him.'

'So you're saying that you made him impotent?'

'Asho! Please don't say things like that!'

'But you never had children?'

'No. That was one of the reasons I married your father, because I thought he would make good children.'

'Huh! He might have made good children, but Ben would have been a better father!'

She nodded.

'And husband.'

She nodded again. 'He was a wonderful husband. I'll never have a better one.'

'I s'pose you've thought about the fact that if you had stayed with him, you could have travelled and had a better life? Really Mom, I just don't get you, how you make the decisions you do.'

She nodded again. 'Asho, it wasn't that simple. Some day I'll tell you the whole story and you'll understand.'

'Oh God, there's more?'

'Oh yes, there was grand passion, romance, love at first sight.' She raised her voice in a dramatic flourish. 'But I'm going to take a bath now, Asho. Another time.'

Of course, with my mother, the story was never simple. One version she subsequently told me had it that when Ben proposed to her, he told her that he was impotent. My mother claimed that she didn't know what that meant so she said 'Fine.' It was only after a few years of marriage that she realised. That's one story.

Another story was that my father was ashamed to marry someone who wasn't a virgin so he instructed my mother to tell people that her marriage to Ben had never been consummated. And of course there was the version she told me originally, they they were unsuited sexually. My mother told me variations of all the stories at various times.

What I do know, having pored through the thick album of cards, pictures and newspaper clippings of her courtship and wedding to Ben, is that she went into it in a big rush. On the first page of the album, on a card decorated with red roses, she has the chronology: they met on 27 June and married on 21 December. In that same album, scribbled on the back of her wedding shower menu, are some notes between her and a friend, who asked if she were certain she should marry so quickly. My blithe young mother's scrawled response was that, if things didn't work out she could, 'Divorce! Divorce! Divorce!' So even as she planned the wedding, chose her gown of 'Chantilly lace and nylon tulle', bought their cottage and a new car, as well as taking and passing her end-of-term exams, doubt had already crept in. Whatever the reason, they never had any children.

*

'Ow,' I cried. Mr Hamill, the school guidance counsellor, had bustled into my classroom and, in front of everybody, grabbed me by the ear and pulled me into the hallway. 'Ow, ow, what have I done?' He wasn't trying to hurt me; he was just doing this for effect, so I overreacted, just for effect.

'What have you done? After that article, you ask me what you've done?' he said.

I had written an article in the school newspaper, damning the school guidance office for not giving seniors sufficient help getting into college.

'Mr Hamill, I'm sorry. Really. Please let go of my ear.'

I was sorry. He was a nice man and it wasn't his fault that when I asked half-baked, inarticulate questions, he wasn't able to help me.

'What kind of college do you want to go to, Ashley?' he had asked.

'What do you mean?'

'State or private? Large or small? Engineering and science or liberal arts? Academic or non-academic?' I could tell he was trying to be patient.

'I don't know. What are the differences?'

'Where do you want to go? What state?'

'I don't know.'

'Listen,' he said. 'Go to the library, read the books about colleges, talk to your parents, and come back to me when you have some thoughts.'

Reading the material confounded me. City or suburban? Small or large? Liberal arts or technology?

When I spoke to my parents, the response from my mother was, 'No bullshit Bachelor of Arts degree – get a Bachelor of Science like me, a real degree.'

From my father I got, 'Don't look into it any further, I'll write to my tutor at Cambridge and you can go to Trinity.'

Neither had any insight into the questions Mr Hamill had asked me. In any case, I had learned my lesson on the school front. It had been just two years since the boarding-school debacle and I didn't trust them for a minute. I went back into Mr Hamill again. And again.

He let go of my ear. 'Come on, come on. I have someone to introduce you to – you're going to thank me for this. And let's see if you put any articles in the paper saying how great I am.'

We entered a small office and he said, 'Ashley, please let me introduce you to Miss Elizabeth Vermey.'

Mr Hamill did a slight mock bow.

'And Miss Vermey, please let me introduce you to the young woman I was telling you about, Miss Ashley Dartnell.'

He said, 'young woman' as if he really meant young scally-wag or young mischief-maker. He put a stress on 'Miss' in a slightly patronising way.

A tall stately woman with a well-groomed sweep of hair, held back with a headband, smiled at me. She had crinkly brown eyes and freckled skin. Gracious. Strong-willed. Independent. Friendly. Intelligent. These descriptions came to me before she even said a word. She dominated the room, encompassing it in a powerful and positive way. It was fair to say I had never met a woman like her. I was wearing jeans, desert boots and an embroidered smock top from Pakistan. My hair hung to my waist, and I had fifteen or twenty silver bangles clinking on my arm. I sat down, bewildered.

'Have you heard of Bryn Mawr College?' asked Betty Vermey.

'Uh, no.'

'The Seven Sisters?'

'Uh, no.'

'The Ivy League?'

'Uh, no.'

'Harvard? Yale? Princeton?'

'Oh yes, yes, definitely.'

'Well,' she explained, 'Bryn Mawr College is one of the Seven Sister colleges, the female equivalent of the Ivy League colleges. Like Radcliffe and Barnard and Wellesley, it is an all-women's first-rate, liberal-arts college.'

'Oh.' I was impressed.

'Mr Hamill said you might be interested in applying. That you are the one young woman at TAS graduating this year who might be right for Bryn Mawr.'

Young woman! No one had ever before called me a young woman and this was the second time in a few minutes. My father would laugh if he heard.

'Well, I haven't heard of Bryn Mawr, but if it's as academic as you say, there are lots of girls in the class who have much better averages and scores.'

She smiled.

'And also, my mother says I should get a proper BS, not some silly BA degree – that's what liberal arts means, doesn't it? And besides, I'm not really interested in going to some namby-pamby school where a bunch of girls sit around under trees, sewing all day.'

She burst out laughing. 'Young women. And hardly sewing.'

She described Bryn Mawr and showed me the course catalogue, printed on beautiful thick ivory paper and bound in a rich nubby cover. She repeated how exclusive it was, how difficult to get into, how independent and strong-minded the students and how bright the prospects of the graduates. She cited statistics about how much better young women performed in a single-sex environment, how it helped prepare them for the competitive world of graduate schools and careers. She told me she was in Iran for a meeting with advisors of the Empress Farah Diba who were hoping to establish a university for young women. She even asked me my opinion on this.

I was so shocked that I stumbled before saying, 'It would be great for the girls of Iran. They're treated like second- or third- or zero-class citizens. The danger is that it would become a bastion of the rich because the only people who could afford to send their daughters are the elite.'

She nodded.

'And also you could be endangering the girls – young women – by giving them all these highfalutin liberal ideas because they would still have to live in this repressive society. They could become unmarriageable.'

'But how else can a society change?' she asked, her face glowing and her voice eager.

'I don't know! I don't know how to change my own life, never mind the lives of all the women in Iran.'

'The answer is the same,' she said. 'Through education. For yourself. And the women of Iran.'

'I hope so. Something has to change, doesn't it?'

Too soon, she left. I sat and read the catalogue from beginning to end. Then I reread certain sections. I missed my next period and went back into Mr Hamill's office for a note for my teacher.

'Well, what do you think?' he asked.

'It's amazing, but I would never get in.'

'Just apply.'

'There's no point, I'd never get in.'

'Just apply.'

I took the catalogue home and showed it to my parents. Dad read it, putting on his glasses and turning each page slowly and thoughtfully. He and my mother thought it would give me ideas, though.

'Oh, you'll just become one of those artsy-fartsy liberals who can't do a proper day of work,' said my mother. She thought liberal arts and communist were almost synonymous.

'And it's *kheyli geroon!*' said my father, using the Farsi for 'very expensive'.

I put the application aside.

'Have you applied to Bryn Mawr?' Mr Hamill asked me a couple of weeks later.

'No. I'd never get in.'

'Just apply.'

Some time after that, he called me into his office. 'I'm disappointed in you. I put myself on the line recommending you and now I hear you haven't applied.'

'That's because there's no point. Who told you, anyway?'

'Betty Vermey. She and the president of the college are coming back here to visit the queen and talk about the

354

university. They want to meet you and your parents, but she wants to make sure you're applying.'

'Are you sure?'

'Just apply.'

He shook his head, bored with the discussion.

38

Men are Bastards

*my mother with Pakistani
village women*

The house was suddenly grey. Late afternoon was always a strange, downhearted time, those few minutes when everything moves from Kodachrome to black and white. Cameron was at football practice, Rian at Boy Scouts, and Dad away on the job.

I drizzled batter and made designs: a heart, a question mark, an 'A'. While the pancakes cooked, I stirred maple and vanilla extract into a pot of boiling water, adding sugar to make home-made 'maple' syrup, or 'sweetie' as we called it. Its sugary smell filled the air. My book was propped against the kitchen cabinet and I read as I cooked. I had finished *Catcher in the Rye*, and was now on to *Franny and Zooey*, getting to know the Glass family: Seymour, Buddy, Boo Boo,

Walt, Waker, Zooey and Franny. I loved them. I adored them. I wanted to be a Glass. I was in love with Seymour. It was hard for any high-school boy – in fact, any male – to measure up to the witty, brilliant, urbane Seymour and, truth be told, the high-school boys who liked me were nowhere close.

'Mom, would you or Nounou like some pancakes?' I called from the kitchen to the dining area where the two of them sat with their cups of tea cooling and their cigarettes smoking.

'I'll have a couple,' said my mother, always game when it came to food.

'No, no!' said Nounou, as if it were poison I was offering. She was, as usual, on a 'regime'. Nounou was the kind of Sophia Loren-like woman who jiggled when she walked and she didn't like it – never mind that men loved her voluptuous figure.

After delivering Mom her stack of pancakes and topping up her tea, I sat reading in the kitchen, alternating bites of pancake with sips of steaming tea. My mother and Nounou sounded like two pigeons cooing on a windowsill. No matter how much they saw each other, they never ran out of things to say and their conversation inevitably veered between hysteria of one sort or another: either laughter or tears. Today their natter was low and intense, like a car working its way up a medium slope. I looked up from my book. The light was like dishwater outside the kitchen window.

'Yoo-hoo! Asho! Asho darling, can you make me one of those – what do you call them?' Nounou's trill interrupted my thoughts.

'Pancakes.'

I walked through to the dining room, still holding my book. Around Nounou, I felt big, adult and solemn, despite the fact that she was eighteen years older than I and living with a man who was old enough to be my grandfather. Old enough to be *her* grandfather.

Nounou raised the cover of my book to see the title and

357

then let it fall, uninterested. Hell, I thought, she was married by the time she was my age – and I had barely kissed a boy. Yet in many ways, I was more serious than both these grown women.

'Ah, yes, pancakes. I like the way you have done the, you know, the designs.' She fell back laughing.

I raised my eyebrows at my mother.

'Can you make them with letters? Can you make me one with a K?'

Her brows were artfully painted and her hair formed glossy golden petals. When I was little, Nounou had jet-black hair and geisha-white skin. Then she had transformed herself into a redhead and she had since become a sun-kissed honey blonde.

'Sure.'

I turned to go. I had no idea what was so funny. Really, I was more interested in the Glass family than my mother and Nounou's silliness. For years, they had fascinated me and I had skulked around, trying to eavesdrop. Now their constant dramatics seemed ridiculous.

'No, no, wait!' She held her finger theatrically to her cheek in a parody of someone thinking hard. 'Make it with a B for bastard.'

She laughed uproariously. I found it embarrassing that when she laughed she actually made the sound 'heeheehee'. I found it even more embarrassing that my mother, joining in, laughed so hysterically that she was reduced to tears.

'I can just make the whole word "bastard" if you want – if you can eat that much.'

My face felt stiff and I felt very strait-laced.

'Bastard!' Nounou gulped and tittered, giggled and sputtered.

'Men are bastards . . .' My mother choked.

None of it seemed at all funny to me but with these two it was always as if I were on the outside of an inside joke.

'Bastard!' Nounou repeated. Then the laughter ended abruptly. She began to cry, huge glugging sobs. 'But I love him. *This* one I really love . . .'

My mother gestured me out. I made two pancakes: one with a K and one with a B, and took them to Nounou. She sniffled and snivelled, dabbing at her eyes, her small satiny face still perfect except for the streaks of black mascara.

'God damn him! How can he do this to me?' she cried, flinging her arms about dramatically. 'Asho, don't let men do this to you!' She clutched my hand. 'They are bastards, they really are.'

When she left I asked my mother what was going on.

'Well, Nounou has fallen in love, completely head-over-heels, crazy, mad in love. She's going to ruin her life if she's not careful, silly bitch.'

'What about Nasser?' I asked.

'Him? She's never loved him. This is the real thing. She's mad about this one.'

'*This* one? Have there been that many?'

'Well, you don't expect her to be with just Nasser, do you?'

I understood that, for my mother, 'be' meant 'have sex with'. In the same way that she had expected me to realise that she couldn't possibly have stayed with Ben, given her beauty, she was implying that Nounou couldn't possibly be faithful to Nasser, given his age and her desirability.

'Well, Mom, why does she stay with him?'

'Oh, Jesus, Asho, why do any of us stay with the bastards?'

I ignored her anti-husband rant; I had heard her blame the failure of her life on my father way too many times.

'How did she meet this guy?'

'On a plane. Flying back to Iran.'

'And they fell in love and started having an affair just from that? Wow! She works fast.'

'Ashley, don't be ridiculous. She loves him. Have some sympathy,' Mom snapped.

'Well, if they're so in love, she should just leave Nasser.' I began ticking off the reasons on my fingers: 'He's way older than her, they're not even married, they don't have kids and they're both rich.'

'It's not so simple, Ashley.'

Suddenly I realised those words sounded so familiar. I had heard them not so long before.

'You always think it's so simple, Ashley.'

When had I heard those words? Those exact words? They were an echo. Not so simple. Like an itch on my brain: not so simple, not so simple . . .

I stood at the dining-room table across from my mother, thinking. Then I remembered.

'Mom, when you told me about Ben that it wasn't so *simple*, that you left him for the love of your life, you didn't mean Dad, did you?'

'Your father?' She looked at me, a funny expression on her face. 'Your father, the love of my life?' She gave a rueful laugh. 'Hardly.'

I slowly made my way around the table and sat down. 'So who was it?'

'I've never told you?' she asked as if this were one of her many regular stories.

'No, Mom, you know you haven't.'

Oh God, not another one of her secrets. She had told me about every high-school boyfriend but not 'the love of her life'.

'I haven't told you about Waahid?' Her eyes grew darker and she smiled. Her voice dropped a few registers and grew perceptibly warmer. 'I haven't told you about Waahid? Waahid Ali?'

'No, Mom, you haven't.'

'I have!'

She was indignant, even a bit coquettish, as if this man I had never heard of – this Waahid Ali – had suddenly appeared in the room and she was flirting with him.

'You know when I was in Pakistan and got malaria? Well, the doctor who treated me was Waahid Ali.'

'The one you said was an "angel"?'

I remembered the story now: the rapturous way in which she told it: 'He was amazing! He *saved* my life. He was an angel, an angel.'

'Yes. Waahid Ali was the love of my life. *Is* the love of my life,' she said, not dissimilarly to the way I crooned to my friends when I had a crush on someone.

'I should have realised it wasn't Dad,' I said wearily. I didn't understand why I was upset. It wasn't as if I had thought she adored my father, but she was *so* dismissive of him.

She wasn't at all interested in talking about him. Now that the cat was out of the bag, she wanted nothing more than to tell me, with her normal, grand, storytelling flourishes, the tale of meeting and falling in love with Waahid.

'When I got malaria, my fever raged. I flitted in and out of consciousness. For days, I didn't eat, I didn't drink. They thought I would die. The only thing I was conscious of was the beautiful face above me and the soft cool hand on my fore-head. I thought to myself, God has sent an angel to me. Well, he saved my life. You should have seen him, Asho. He was beautiful. Slim and with the beautiful face of—'

'I know,' I interrupted, 'an angel.'

'Yes.' She looked at me to see whether I was being sarcastic.

'He was a Kashmiri prince from one of the most prominent Pakistani families. He was well educated; he knew all the classics – *The Iliad*, *The Odyssey*, poetry; he loved music – Tchaikovsky, Bach, Schopenhauer; he rode like a dream . . . He was beautiful. We fell in love. We planned to start again in Canada.'

'Well, what happened?'

I just wanted her to get on with it. I felt so bone-shatteringly exhausted by her stream of revelations. I couldn't imagine what would come next or when. I stood up and walked around the table, twitching the mats into place, straightening the salt and pepper shakers, brushing crumbs into my hand. All I could feel, rising like some distasteful fishy burp, was irritation.

'Neither of our parents would allow it,' she answered.

'*What?* Mom, that's crazy. You were in your twenties, a married woman, and he was a grown man, a doctor. If you wanted to marry, you didn't need your parents' permission. And what about Ben? You know, Ben your husband?'

'We did! It was the 1950s!' Her voice was teeth-grittingly high-pitched, like a drill. 'Lilly wrote me I could never marry a "nigger" – that it was against the law. You know in most states in America they still had all the Jim Crow laws until the sixties, don't you? Can you believe how uneducated and stupid they were that they thought Pakistanis were negroes?'

'Mom, that's not the point! Even if he were black, so what? That's why you left America, to get away from that kind of small-minded thinking. You didn't need to ask permission! You were just cowards. Look at all your friends – they all married foreigners: Theresa, Lisa, Maureen. There are tons of Western women married to Pakistani men.'

'It wasn't so simple.'

Not again.

She continued, 'He came from a princely Kashmiri family, and as a doctor he was essential to Pakistan. Don't forget, they needed every professional they had. There was a brain drain. He was a national asset and they wouldn't let him go. He was brilliant, Ashley.'

I thought bitterly: of course, Mom couldn't fall in love with a normal man; she had to fall in love with a national asset – the country's crown jewels.

'We planned and schemed. He hid a horse. He was going to ride to the border and escape.'

I shook my head. No, naturally he couldn't leave by the normal channels – nothing as mundane as a car or a train or a plane or a ship.

'But his family found out so they stopped him at the frontier. They got the army out to stop him at the frontier.' She kept repeating the word 'frontier' as if it had magical properties: frontier, frontier, frontier.

I couldn't bear it any more and I burst out, 'Mom, you're kidding, right? They got the army out?'

'No, why would I be kidding?' She drew on her cigarette, animated by the talk of her angel, her eyes a-glitter, her hair in wisps around her ears. Talking about her Waahid, she exuded energy and happiness.

'Which country was he going to escape to: Afghanistan? China? India?'

I summoned a mental map of Pakistan's border.

'On a horse? How many hundreds of miles was he going to travel on a horse?'

'Well, why not? We were close to the Afghani frontier and he was an excellent horseman. In fact, he was dazzling at everything he did. He was perfection. There was nothing he couldn't do: he was a fantastic squash player, a musician, a poet; he was intelligent, well read, cultured.' She began the whole litany again.

'I know, I know! He was an angel.'

All her superlatives about Waahid held implicit a criticism of my father and, by extension, me.

'Well, he may have been all those things, but he was a coward,' I said. 'If he *really* loved you, if he *really* were your "soulmate", getting stopped at the *frontier* shouldn't have thwarted him. Look at Dad: at least he showed some mettle and followed you to America. Say what you want about him, he's got guts. You can't tell me that you couldn't have made it work if you had really loved each other. If *he* had really loved you.'

'It's true, Asho, it's true. They stopped him at the frontier! They put him under house arrest. They confiscated my letters.' She was crying, not in great big hysterical sobs like Nounou, but small bitter tears that forced their way out.

'Mom, please *stop* with the frontier!'

Despite her whole, fantastical tale, it was her repetition of that one outmoded, over-emphatic word that made me edgy.

Her shoulders shook and she began to cough in an effort to control her sobs. I rubbed her back and poured her tea.

'Mom, I'm sorry to say this, but if he loved you, he's had twenty years to come find you.'

Her shoulders shook harder and the sad, reluctant tears continued to run down her face.

'I know, Asho. Some day, I know he'll come and get me. Believe me, I wonder, each time I move, how he'll find me. As long as Lilly and Willy lived at Halls Hill Road, I knew he could. Now they've moved, it will be more difficult, but I know he'll do it. I wait for him to come so that I can go back to him, to Pakistan . . .'

I felt tenderness towards her creeping through my annoyance. She had lived with this dream for so long. I kept rubbing her back. She was always so tense. I was only sixteen years old, but I knew that Waahid Ali was never, ever, not in a hundred million years, going to ride up on his trusty steed, gather my mother up in his arms and thunder off with her to the frontier.

'Ouch! Ouch! God dammit, stop that!' She flicked my hands away.

'Mom, if he came, would you just leave? Just like that?'

'I don't know, Asho, I don't know what I would do.'

'But what about Dad? Did you ever love him?'

She shrugged. 'Oh, I don't know, Asho, nothing is simple, is it? I *wanted* to love him, didn't I? He was different when I met him – charming, dashing, handsome. Look at how hard I've tried, for him, for you kids . . .'

Once again, after an evening of Mom's revelations about yet another secret, I dragged myself upstairs to my bedroom to ponder what she had told me. The house was quiet. Cameron and Rian had long come in, eaten the pancakes I had made and gone to bed. The dogs were outside, running up and down the length of the roof, barking and snapping as the cats taunted them. I lay in bed, trying to figure it all out.

So first my mother had 'gone out with' Joe Green and they had been engaged. Then, while she was still in high school, or the year she had worked at the drugstore before going to college, she had been engaged to Matthew Tandish and maybe even others. Then she had met Ben and, within a matter of months, married him. After living in Connecticut for a year, they had gone to Pakistan where she met both Dad and Waahid. She had fallen in love with Waahid and they had planned their great escape. When it hadn't worked, she had fallen back on Dad. All by the age of twenty-five.

I re-created the scenario I had played out not so long before with Ben. What if Waahid Ali had been my father? Would we have lived in Pakistan, which was even poorer and harsher than Iran? Would we have been immigrants in Canada, living in a cold climate that my mother would have hated?

I thought about my own father.

He was not her first choice, nor even her second choice. He was no choice at all. She had never wanted him. That was what she said now.

I couldn't let the conversation slip away, though, and pretend nothing had happened. I started in on it again the next evening.

'Did Ben mind that you were "seeing" all these men when you were married?'

'Oh, Ashley, it wasn't like that! Ben always hoped I'd end up with Waahid. And he warned me to keep away from Dartnell. He respected Waahid, you see. Whereas your father, he recognised him for what he was.'

'Why was he so involved in arranging your next marriage?'
I was belligerent.

'Don't be ridiculous.'

'And what exactly is so wrong with Dad anyhow?' I asked,
defensively.

'You *know* what he is.'

Although I was furious, I understood what she meant. Of
course Ben hadn't known specifically that my father would
toil, year after year, in an unforgiving environment, constantly
cheated by his partners and suppliers, undercut by his compet-
itors, taken advantage of by his customers. Ben could not have
predicted that my father would go bankrupt, be thrown into
prison, barely escape amputation in an Iranian hospital after
being hit by a truck, almost freeze to death on a mountain
pass, go hungry and be forced to eat offal because he couldn't
afford proper food, live apart from his wife and children for
five years while pursuing an ephemeral dream. Ben would have
seen that my father was a dreamer, though, a man who cared
more about being independent than anything or anyone else.
A man who was prepared to watch his wife suffer desperately,
lose babies, almost die giving birth, become ill, working herself
into such a nervous state that she couldn't function. A man
who was prepared to watch his children grow thin, stop attending school, live without heat – not because of famine or war
but because he wanted to be his own boss.

39

As the Romanians Do

in Tehran

'Ashley,' said Betty Vermey, 'this is Harris Llewellyn Wofford, president of Bryn Mawr College.'

We were having breakfast at the Hilton. I was familiar with the hotel from the fashion shows I had been doing there over the past few years, but I hadn't eaten there since the tea with Farah Diba with Nounou when I was eight. My mother brought up this tea, much to my chagrin, when President Wofford and Miss Vermey talked about the queen and the new women's university that they were planning. The conversation ranged from my father's and Harris Wofford's Welsh heritage, the part my father played in building the hotel, and Wofford's work with John F. Kennedy and his role in establishing the Peace Corps, to the human rights practices in Iran and the stability of the political situation.

'Oh, the Shah is a fixture. His position is one hundred per cent stable,' affirmed my father.

'Yes,' chimed in my mother, 'the Iranian people love the Shah and Farah Diba.'

I watched the adults closely. I knew my parents didn't believe what they were saying. It seemed to me that Harris Wofford and Betty Vermey knew more than they were revealing – that they thought what was happening in Iran was wrong and dangerous, and that its citizens were being abused. It was clear that they would help establish this new university only if it were the *right* thing to do. They believed that the Quaker, liberal-arts tradition of Bryn Mawr College would benefit the young women of Iran. They weren't doing this for the money, the kudos, or the privilege of working with the queen. They were completely different from any of the foreigners I had met in Iran who were advising the Shah, building oil refineries, or training Iranians to fly helicopters or set up satellite systems. Those people were here for the money and only for the money. In the case of Harris Wofford and Elizabeth Vermey, they were trying to decide whether there was the opportunity to try to transform the country for ever. Phrases like 'educating the future leaders of the country', 'sowing the seeds for a more tolerant society', and 'changing perceptions of women' flowed naturally and unaffectedly.

They asked about the recent amendments to the Family Protection Law that gave women equal rights in divorce and custody of children. My parents acknowledged that little had changed in actual practice.

'All the husband has to do is say, "I divorce you, I divorce you, I divorce you," and walk away,' said my mother.

'What about the reports of human rights violations? The lack of freedom of speech? The repression of the press?' President Wofford asked my father.

'It's the price you have to pay to exert control,' said my father. 'You can't expect people with no history of democracy to handle freedom. They need a firm hand. Democracy has to come gradually.'

It was clear that neither Mr Wofford nor Miss Vermey agreed, but they moved on to the subject at hand.

'Why haven't you applied to Bryn Mawr, Ashley?' asked Mr Wofford.

I cleared my throat and tried to look at him squarely. He was the single most accomplished man I had ever met, yet he was having breakfast with me. I didn't feel I deserved it. More to the point, my parents not only didn't have the money but they ridiculed the liberal-arts curriculum and 'left-wing, touchy-feely', liberal Quaker ethos.

'We would very much like Ashley to attend Bryn Mawr,' said Mr Wofford, addressing my parents.

'Yes,' said Betty Vermey, 'she's exactly what we're looking for and it will change her life – make her the woman she could be.'

My parents stared at me as if meeting me for the first time.

Outside in the car, I felt regret. Harris Wofford and Betty Vermey were exceptional. Bryn Mawr was amazing. It *would* change my life to go there. Why hadn't I studied more? I shouldn't have babysat every night. I should have done better on my SATS. I should have stood up to Mom when she pulled me out of ninth grade. But it was my own fault that I wasn't good enough and I knew it.

'Well, they are certainly *hessabi*,' said my father, using the Farsi word for 'substantial', as in having value.

'Yes, they certainly are,' agreed my mother. 'I like that Betty Vermey. I think if we lived near each other, we would become friends.'

I was surprised by this and a bit jealous. They had bonded over smoking, both of them admitting their passion for cigarettes and their vehement addiction. I overheard my mother saying, 'There is nothing I love more than my cigarettes,' and Betty Vermey replying, 'Me too, but I don't have children.'

I marvelled again at my mother's extraordinary ability to charm. My friends doted on her, as did all her colleagues from school, the kids in her class, the parents: everybody loved her. I was surprised that she liked Miss Vermey, though, since she was both unmarried and childless, and who, although highly attractive, was decidedly unglamorous, with no jewels, a toothy smile and career-oriented clothing.

'So are you going to apply?' asked my mother. 'I think you should.'

'You might as well,' said my father.

'I think as soon as they see my records and my scores, they'll realise I don't belong there . . . Also it costs a lot.'

My parents' about-face didn't surprise me. They were clearly just as susceptible to the powers of President Wofford and Miss Vermey as I was.

'She's seen your grades and scores,' said my mother.

'How could she? I haven't sent them.'

'Pete Hamill gave them to her.'

Since my mother had been teaching at the school for the past couple of years, she knew all the TAS staff on a first-name basis.

'Anyway, she said your grades and your scores were excellent. Just apply, Ashley.'

'If they want you,' said my father, 'they'll find you the money.'

I stayed up late a couple of nights and wrote the application. Unexpectedly, my father read and edited it. I sent it as well as my other applications out myself, and this time I made sure that they were actually posted, routing them via the father of a friend who worked in the embassy.

*

My mother adored her new 'houseboy', an esteemed and educated Sri Lankan doctor, driven to Iran and this demeaning position by the civil war and resulting poverty in his own country. His real name was the length of a sentence, but we all called him 'Ganesh'. My mother and Ganesh sat together in the kitchen, discussing Sri Lanka's relationship with India and Pakistan, the Tamils, tea production, Hinduism, medicine, nutrition and vegetarianism. When the Hindu Ganesh began working for us, he did not eat meat. Within a day or so, though, I saw him ploughing into an enormous plate of my mother's beef chilli.

'Isn't the cow sacred?' I asked him, shocked.

'Oh my goodness, this is very delicious, missus.' He moaned with pleasure.

'But, Ganesh, I thought you were vegetarian?'

'But you know, miss, I have always been of the philosophy that, when in Rome, you must do as the Romanians do! *Ha ha ha!*'

He laughed and laughed. Our entire family joined in and his 'When in Rome' expression became part of our family vernacular.

The fact that Ganesh ate beef chilli despite his strong religious beliefs seemed to my mother just an indication of how starved he was. Over the next few weeks she made it her mission to feed him, clothe him and nurture him. His skin and hair became glossier and his belly became rounder until he looked like a plump, ripe blackberry. He sat at the kitchen table, poring over books my mother bought him, while I washed dishes and cooked, Cameron scrubbed the floors and Rian filled the stoves. He laughed constantly. We all loved him.

Regardless of how beloved he was in the family, though, he imperilled our existence, for he, like my father, was an illegal alien. My father had never recovered his passport, never bribed the right officials, never paid whatever debts and taxes he needed to pay. He had undergone sixteen long years of never having a holiday, never seeing his childhood friends or family, never visiting the country of his birth.

Somehow, despite the fact that every foreigner in Iran was so visible that my classmates' photos were in albums at Evin Prison, our family continued to live and work 'under the radar'. Our position was very straightforward, though: the police could ask for our papers, arrest us and either throw us into jail or deport us on the next plane. If we left the country, we couldn't re-enter it again. When the school asked Cameron to participate in an athletic competition in India, he was forced, reluctantly, to turn it down because we didn't know whether he could get back into Iran. It was somewhat ironic because my father was building a dam for the royal family in Kalaleh, near Gorgon.

If it was dangerous for us to have the charming, intelligent, highly carnivorous and now pot-bellied Hindu Dr Ganesh in our house, the problem was compounded by my mother's soft heart when it came to Pakistanis, Indians and Sri Lankans generally. Every night at about nine or ten, shadows slipped quietly through our gate – painfully thin, ragged men from the Indian subcontinent, all illegal, who were in Iran working on construction sites for a pittance. They could barely feed themselves, never mind rent a place to sleep. Initially only my mother knew that Ganesh was sneaking his friends into the house, as we were all upstairs in bed or out babysitting when they arrived. Soon there were so many of them, though, that there was no hiding it. Men curled up at night on the bare concrete of Ganesh's floor and, if we ran into them, they mumbled, 'I thank you very much, sir. I thank you very much, madam.'

In the beginning, my mother fed them leftovers, sending in Cameron or me with a big pot and a fistful of spoons. Then she started cooking extra and finally she began buying piles of bread and making huge pots of soup, stew or chilli each night especially for them. She asked her friends for old clothes and bedding. When she went to the foreigners' second-hand sales, she bought all the old stuff for a few toman and gave it to the men.

Dad became increasingly concerned. 'You're going to land me in jail, Genie.'

My mother, finding it difficult to turn the men away, begged Ganesh, 'Please make sure the policeman doesn't see them.'

It was hard to imagine how they would avoid that, for there was a policeman on the corner of our street, and of most streets, in Tehran. So when I baked, she plied the policeman with fresh cake and we kids regularly took him cups of tea. Every time my father went out, he slipped him a couple of hundred rials. However, he would certainly have received more if he had turned us in for harbouring a whole room full of illegal Sri Lankan men. Day after day, night after night, Dad argued: fire Ganesh and get rid of the men. Mom responded, 'Get your passport in order so we don't have to worry.'

But my father was anxious. The situation in Iran for foreigners was daily becoming more dangerous and the repercussions worse still. He knew the grotesque torture that took place in the Shah's prisons and was frightened by having the men in the house. My father's nagging continued and finally my mother spoke to Ganesh and the men stopped coming, although Ganesh himself stayed.

*

'Dad, have they come yet?' I asked my father each day.

Many of the other kids who had applied to college had already heard back.

'No. Maybe you'll just have to stay home and make me raisin cake every day next year!' He smirked and danced around the dining-room table. 'You can stay, work and make some money for your tuition – how's that?'

Despite my begging, he had not completed the financial aid forms; he was unable to, not having paid tax for many years. The issue of how we would pay for my college fees was unresolved.

'Oh, Lin, don't be stupid. Tell her.'

My mother sat at the table, circling the second-hand sale ads.

'He picked up your letters at the PO Box days ago,' she continued, looking up from the paper. 'He just didn't want to give them to you.'

'What? But why?' I ran over to my father and pummelled his chest. When would I ever learn? Why was he so manipulative? He had done the same with the boarding schools. 'I didn't get in, did I?'

'Well, you got into the best university,' he said.

'I got into Bryn Mawr?'

'You got into FIT and that's where you should go,' he said, suddenly serious.

Florida Institute of Technology was my last choice. It was a weak nod to my parents who felt only a technical degree was worth getting and it was in Florida, 'our home state', so it was cheap and convenient.

'So I didn't get into Bryn Mawr?'

I had known I wouldn't get in from the start, but the encouragement from Betty Vermey and Harris Wofford had allowed me to dream.

'But, Asho darling, FIT is excellent. You can stay with Yosy during the holidays and she can find you work,' said my father.

Despite encouraging me to apply to Bryn Mawr after meeting Mr Wofford and Miss Vermey, once out of the orbit of their influence my parents had swiftly reverted to their original opinions on the value of a liberal-arts degree and its horrifying financial costs.

'Well, I won't go. I won't go to FIT. There's no point. I'll wait and do some work and improve my SAT scores and reapply next year to Bryn Mawr.'

'Lin, give her the letter.' My mother's voice was harsh.

'Why do you want to go to *that* school, Asho?' my father

asked, as if he were discussing a dissolute nightclub, not a top university.

'You're kidding? Did I get in?'

I looked from one to the other, my mother's face small and tight, my father's red and guilty-looking.

'What's going on? Tell me,' I begged. 'Give me the letters.' I waited. 'Please,' I added. 'Please.'

'Your father wanted to throw away all your letters except FIT. He thought you wouldn't notice. I wouldn't let him,' said my mother.

'So I did get in?' I felt sick.

'You got into some at least.' My mother stalked around the table, wisps of hair escaping from her French roll and sticking out around her forehead.

'Mom, I know about FIT, but please tell me, did I get into Bryn Mawr?'

She nodded at my father.

'Dad, please tell me.'

But my father had turned to my mother and, atypically for him, raised his voice. 'Stay out of this, Genie! This isn't your business!'

My mother leaped towards my father, and shrieked, 'Just give the child the letters!'

He handed me four envelopes addressed to me, all neatly opened. I flipped to Bryn Mawr's envelope and pulled out the letter.

'Yes, yes! I can't believe it! Cam, Ri, I got in!' I screamed and raced outside to tell the boys. They cheered, whooping and whistling.

'But you wouldn't choose Bryn Mawr over FIT, would you, Asho?' asked my father, when I returned.

There was no offer of financial aid from Bryn Mawr but I had known there wouldn't be since my father hadn't completed the forms. He thought Bryn Mawr would waive my fees just because they liked me, without my even asking.

'Dad, I can't believe you hid the letters just to get me to go to the cheapest school. That you were lying to me.'

'Why not? Why shouldn't you go to FIT? Anyway, what would you have done?'

He was right. I would have had to book a call from the telephone exchange or write, by which time the deadline for acceptances would have come and gone. As it was, because he had hung on to the letters, I risked being too late.

'Just so you know, Dad, even if I hadn't gone this year, I would have reapplied. I told you before, I'm not letting you dictate where I go to college.' I lifted my chin defiantly. 'Why do you think you deserved to go to Cambridge and Mom to Yale but I don't deserve to go to a good university?'

I went over to my mother and hugged her. 'Thanks, Mom.' She looked old and tired. She had saved the day by forcing him to show me the letters. Now we had to persuade him to pay.

40

A Change in the Weather

*convocation
ceremony*

'To everything there is a season, a time for every purpose under the sun.'

My voice rang out. From the podium, I could see the familiar faces of my high-school class. It was the night before graduation and I was reciting Ecclesiastes at the convocation ceremony.

Shortly before graduation, the principal had called me in. 'Ashley, you don't seem to have enough credits to graduate. You're missing a whole semester of ninth grade.' My stomach plummeted.

But after a flurry of meetings, he decided that if Bryn Mawr had accepted me without enough credits, TAS could graduate me.

With my hair gleaming in a glossy pageboy, my eyebrows plucked into thin crescents and wearing a dress and heels, I called out earnestly, 'A time to be born and a time to die; a time to plant and a time to pluck up that which is planted.'

I could see Rian, wearing a proper sports jacket, sitting next to my mother. Cameron, next to him, looked forlorn; his girlfriend, Pam, who was a senior, was also graduating. My mother wore a primrose jersey knit. Dad was spread-legged in his light-grey suit, smiling his lopsided smile. Lyn and Colleen were crying and some of the basketball players stared at their hands.

Tehran American School: my first group of friends, my first boyfriend, my first kiss. I thought back to the three years I had been here. In just over a thousand days so much had happened. From Florida and Tom Glenn to Iran and my father. From bottle collecting and working for Uncle Hugh, living with Yosy and my grandparents, to living in a big house as a family. Becoming friends with my mother and learning her secrets: about my grandfather, Ben and Waahid.

What would the next phase bring? Bryn Mawr College. Seeing my family just once a year. Living in America, on my own. Learning, becoming the kind of woman Betty Vermey had described. How would Iran change as I grew up and matured? I wondered whether I would come back, settle once more and work. Would my parents grow old here? I couldn't believe it was all over.

Before that, though, there was the not so trivial question of how to get to America. In fact, there was no problem with my actually leaving Iran, but because my father was still illegal, once I left I couldn't return without applying for a visa. Making that application would potentially reveal Dad's status.

My parents went back and forth on the issue. Should my mother and we three children go to a neighbouring country such as Kuwait for a 'holiday' and use the opportunity to try to renew our tourist visas? This had the advantage of being relatively cheap, but it was risky – for what if the visas were denied and none of us could get back into Iran?

The other option was that I simply go to college and stay with Yosy during the holidays. As a short-term solution this was fine, but not in the longer term. My mother didn't want to be trapped in Iran while I was prevented from entering the country. In any case, in just two years we faced the same situation with Cameron.

My parents fought relentlessly about how to resolve the situation. 'This is not what I struggled so hard for, Lin,' said my mother. 'I want to be able to see my own children.' Finally, we took the risk and, leaving my father behind, we departed that summer for America.

During Freshman Week, I fell in love: with Bryn Mawr and with a boy, a tall merry soccer player. Betty Vermey had been absolutely correct. I loved the atmosphere of intellectual exchange, the strong sense of tradition, the subversive sense of humour. Many of us wore T-shirts proclaiming the words of Bryn Mawr's first president, M. Carey Thomas: 'Our failures *only* marry'. We had posters on our walls declaring, 'A Woman Needs a Man Like a Fish Needs a Bicycle.' Bryn Mawr was exactly the kind of liberal, feminist, egalitarian place that had so worried my parents.

*

My father certainly did not show his normal sang-froid at the sight of something he hadn't seen since the summer of 1958, almost two decades earlier. I was jumping up and down, saying, 'Can you believe you're here after all these years? You're out of Iran. Does it look the same? Does it look different? What do you want to do?'

After all those years, I was standing near the Baker Street tube in London, en route from my freshman year at Bryn Mawr to Iran for the summer, where I had a series of modelling 'assignments' already booked. I had gone from barely been kissed to barely being a virgin. I had survived academically, despite being frighteningly unprepared. Miss Vermey may have been right about my spirit, but I was correct about my academic readiness – all those years of missed school did matter.

'Asho, look!' Dad's excited face was reflected in the plate glass. 'Come on!' He dragged me in by the hand. 'We'll have the one with the strawberries in the window, and the cream.' He almost groaned saying 'cream'.

The Turkish waiter brought us each a small strawberry tartlet.

'No! No! No! The other one!' My father bounded up to show him.

'You want that?'

'Yes, yes. With Nescafé.'

When the waiter brought us the whole tart – the one that was supposed to serve six – he and the other waiters gathered around to watch and when we polished it off they clapped. My father leaned back, patted his stomach and, withdrawing something from his jacket pocket, tossed it across to me.

His face in the photo in the passport, dated 10 May 1977 and issued by the British embassy in Tehran, was smooth, the scar on his chin barely visible. He gazed out into space and his hair was neatly cut and combed. He was wearing a fine Glen plaid suit with a tie I instantly recognised: navy with lighter-blue ovals, like a fan of feathers. There was no trace of the man who had been living illegally in Iran, working without papers, driving without a licence, uninsured, unregistered by any government anywhere, never mind one of the most repressive regimes of the twentieth century.

I stared at his photo and thought about the aplomb with which he had travelled around Iran doing his business and the sound sleep he enjoyed every night, despite the risk. I wondered whether he felt relief when he was handed that slim navy UK passport with its gold lion and unicorn crest.

'Wow! That is amazing, Dad! How did you get it?'

'It was all down to your mummy, so I'll let her tell you.'

*

A few days later, sitting in the dining room of a different house – they had moved out of our old one at Khiaban Marvedasht while I was at Bryn Mawr – my mother told me what had happened.

She and the boys had been able to get back into Iran after they dropped me off at Bryn Mawr – whether it was just luck or because my father had actually paid off the right people, she didn't know. She resumed teaching at TAS and within short order was called in to see her principal to be told that she was getting a very special pupil – someone politically extremely sensitive to the Iranian and US governments: the son of General Nematollah Nassiri, the head of Savak, the Shah's secret police, the single most hated and feared man in Iran. Nassiri had both designed and reigned over Iran's network of repression since 1965. A close friend of the Shah, he had personally delivered the warrant for the arrest of the popular prime minister Mohammad Mossadegh in 1953. This was a man who could have slammed my father straight into Evin Prison.

When the TAS administration told my mother this, she weighed her alternatives. If she refused to teach Mehdi Nassiri, she would lose her job and our residence status might be revealed. If she did teach him, Savak and probably the CIA would investigate her as part of a security check and our residence status would come to light. She was stuck.

'Why didn't you get this straightened out years ago?' she screamed at my father.

'What bad luck,' groaned my father, 'what bad luck.'

When Mrs Nassiri was chauffeured into the parking lot of the Lavizan campus of TAS one fine sunny day to meet her little Mehdi's new teacher, my mother, now forty-four, stood waiting next to the principal of the Elementary School. Mrs Nassiri was elegant and lovely. Mehdi, a quiet, pale boy, had been wretched at his previous school and joined my mother's class for a trial run. She chatted with him in Farsi and included him in all the class activities, making him happy in school for the first time ever. Mrs Nassiri said she had never before come across such an exceptional teacher. Almost immediately, my mother confided, woman-to-woman, in Mrs Nassiri, who arranged a meeting between my parents and her husband.

'First of all, Ashley, I have to tell you how many layers of security we went through. How many barbed-wire fences and high walls,' my mother said. 'When we finally got there we had to walk down a long hallway while a soldier pointed a machine-gun at our backs. My skin crawled.' She paused for effect. 'There he was in an enormous room with white marble floors and a huge desk. He looked tiny behind it.'

I interrupted, 'Was Mrs Nassiri there?'

'No, this was a business meeting,' she replied. 'Well, I told the general what your father had been doing for the past ten years and General Nassiri just nodded his head. You know, he's an old man, Asho, to have such a young child.'

'Mom, stick with the story.'

'Well, he turned to your father and said, "Mr Dartnell, do you realise that what you have done has never been done in our country? It is a historic event. There is no man ever who has lived illegally in Iran for over a decade."'

'Was Dad nervous?'

'Nervous? My God, we were both terrified. The head of Savak. *The head of Savak.* And he was completely stony-faced while your father told his story.'

She stopped to light another cigarette, pour some tea and straighten the tablecloth – again all for dramatic effect. 'He said it was historic,' she repeated.

'Mom, I know it must have ended well or I wouldn't be sitting here in this house with you, and Dad would be in prison. Tell me what happened.'

'Well, he said that Mrs Nassiri had told him that Mehdi needed me as his teacher, so that meant your father had to stay here. That he may be a powerful man, but if his wife was unhappy, it was more than his life was worth. Of course your father made a snide comment about men being under their wives' thumbs.'

'And that was it? After all these years and he gets his papers like that?' I snapped my fingers.

'Yes, after all these years, I got your father his papers.' She smiled.

I couldn't believe how it had all worked out. A little boy had liked his teacher: as a result a grown man wasn't thrown into jail and his family could stay in a foreign country. If the little boy hadn't liked his teacher . . . Well, it didn't bear thinking about.

*

My father was lucky he got his papers that year. Twelve months later, after my sophomore year at Bryn Mawr, I prepared in June 1978 to go to France for summer school. I had no premonition that anything in Iran would change. Cameron, who had just finished his senior year of high school and was preparing to go to America for college in the autumn, was getting up before dawn to work on a Westinghouse satellite system. My mother was 'gadding about', playing bridge, Rian was swimming with his friends and my father was on the job. But world-changing forces were at work.

Graffiti emerged across the city and there were student demonstrations boiling up all over the southern districts, especially around the university. Troops armed with rifles patrolled the streets, and tanks and armoured cars rumbled around, cutting through traffic, and scattering children and goats. My father came home tired and frustrated after being stuck in the resultant traffic snarl-ups that lasted for hours. There was never a mention in the newspapers the next day. Where we lived, in the northern foothills of the Alborz Mountains, all was glassy and still.

Under pressure from the US to improve Iranian human rights practices, the Shah fired General Nassiri as the head of Savak and demoted him, sending him to Pakistan as the Iranian ambassador. The Shah scrambled to maintain control in a country that was imploding around him: communists, nationalists, modernists, traditionalists, the poor, the wealthy, the uneducated and the intellectuals – each group was fomenting. The US, which had spent the previous twenty-five years supporting and arming him, abruptly changed strategy. President Carter created a Special Office of Human Rights that sent the Shah a 'polite reminder' of the importance of political rights and freedom. From just outside Paris, Ayatollah Ruhollah Khomeini, who had led the 1963 fundamentalist revolt against the Shah's White Revolution, orchestrated demonstrations within the country, promising freedom and an elected government if the Shah was toppled. Anger was growing at America's influence over the Shah and the American presence in the country.

My father took me to the airport. As we drove, we saw a group of young men, bearded and wearing jeans, excitedly yelling, pushing and shoving. I didn't realise what was happening, but my father, who by now had seen other similar groups, scanned the road, trying to avoid them.

Spotting we were foreigners, the men rushed the car, chanting and banging sticks. '*Farangi*, go home' and '*Marg bar Shah*' – Death to the King,' they screamed hysterically, their mouths huge.

'Get down and don't meet their eyes,' ordered my father. 'Show them respect.'

I cowered in the foot-well, my back and shoulders scrunched, my knees up around my ears. The men, their faces distorted, pounded against the windows with rocks, sticks and fists. One of the side windows cracked. My father simply stared ahead. I peered out from under my elbow. Suddenly the students surged off. When I scrambled up, I could see they had left to join a larger crowd of demonstrators near by. My father didn't get out to examine the car. Cutting across the traffic, he drove rapidly away.

Shaking, I asked him what was happening.

'Nothing, darling. The Shah arrests the people involved and it blows over.'

'It's so sad that they'll all be put in jail,' I said. 'Why doesn't the Shah change? He should give some of the oil money to the poor. And stop buying so many tanks.'

'Not only will he not do that, he will stamp down harder,' said my father. 'They'll arrest these guys and then the next group will rise up and walk into the firing squad.'

'How long will you be gone on this trip?' I asked. 'Is it safe for Mom and the boys all alone?'

'Of course,' he scoffed. 'No one would ever hurt us.'

Airborne at last, I looked out at the wispy desert clouds and wondered once more whether this would be my last sight of Tehran. I said a silent, fervent prayer that nothing happen to my family. I didn't believe my father that no one would hurt us. The men pounding our car had been filled with hatred.

*

I should have realised, as animals do before a hurricane, that a change in the weather was imminent. That autumn of 1978, the violence erupted. My mother remained in Florida, waiting for the situation in Iran to 'cool down', while Rian went back to school in Tehran and lived with Dad. Cameron started his freshman year at Georgia Tech. I carried my cartons up to my new dorm room and pinned my posters of Iran on to my walls. As the summer came to a close with a brilliant burst of warm weather, I read the newspapers at the library: the Shah was desperate, attempting to tighten control; 100,000 troops patrolled the streets of Tehran; martial law was imposed in twelve cities; and student protesters at Tehran University were shot at and jailed.

My mother moved back into the little house she owned in Fort Lauderdale and complained bitterly about how uncomfortable it was living with Yosy and her son. I laughed, remembering that, when my grandparents and the Glenns were there, eight of us had crammed into it. Once again, my mother was on her own with no means of support, having left Iran with two suitcases for a summer holiday. The brutal circularity of the situation did not escape us: my father and Rian in Iran with the company of only the family dogs; my mother in Florida, older, but no better off.

*

Early in my junior year – before the onset of the winter cold, because she couldn't abide anything other than balmy weather – my mother visited Bryn Mawr. She loved the 'hotel' aspects of my college life. I had borrowed my friend Nina's room for her, she was eating heartily at the cafeteria, and my friends sat at her knee while she told them romantic versions of her early years. It was one night while she was telling her stories, and I was studying in my room, that I heard a sudden shriek. Nina came bounding in and grabbed me, literally pulling me from my chair in her excitement.

'I didn't know you were Jewish! I can't believe you never told me! You're my best friend and I never knew!'

'What are you talking about?' I said.

'Your mother told me!' she crowed. Nina was sparking with glee. 'She told me that her mother was Jewish and if her mother is, then she is, and if she is, then you are.'

I walked into the room where my mother sat holding court, the kids from the hallway gathered around her on the floor, eating pizza and eagerly listening.

'Mom, what is Nina talking about?'

'Oh yes, honey! You knew that, didn't you?'

I looked at Phil's chubby face, staring at me expectantly, at Chris softly playing the guitar in the corner, at Sal fastidiously manoeuvring his slice into his mouth, and I walked out.

Later that evening she came and sat on my bed, saying defensively, 'You must have known. Willy's last name is Goldberg! Lilly always used words like "schmuck".'

'Mom, it doesn't matter to me whether they are or they aren't, but how would I have known? You and your secrets! Your maiden name was Grayson. I didn't know their name was Goldberg and, even if I did, I didn't know it was a Jewish name. Other than Nasser, who had an Iranian name, I don't think I ever met a Jewish person until I came to college! I had no idea what all those words Granny used were. Her parents were Austrian; they sounded German to me. I thought we were Anglican. I was christened and confirmed. We went to church every Sunday of our lives. What was that all about?'

I glared at my mother. Once again, why had she lied about something so important?

'Ashley, honey, I don't understand why you're so upset.'

'I'm upset because you have lied to me about everything that is important in my life. And now this.'

'But you must have known—'

I broke in, 'Mom, every letter I ever wrote to Granny and Grandpa was addressed to "William and Lillian *Grayson*" so I must have gotten that from somewhere.'

I jumped up to get my address book, which indeed had their name under 'Grayson'.

'I can't believe you would lie to me about something so important. Again,' I cried.

Suddenly she was angry, her voice low and hard. 'Understand it from my perspective! Do you know how it felt when I was babysitting and the family took me to the lake and the sign said "No dogs, No Jews, No niggers"? You know why I didn't become a stewardess? Because I was a Jew.' She said the word 'Jew' as if it were a curse. 'Do you know how it feels, baby, to have every door slammed against you because you're a Jew?'

I shook my head.

'No, you don't! The reason you don't is because I made damn sure I married someone with the name "Dartnell", someone with an English accent, and I got you christened and confirmed, and I made sure you went to this fancy college.'

Each time she said 'I' it was like a nail-gun slamming a nail into the wall.

'And by the way, your lovely father? He said he wouldn't marry me unless I hid the fact that I was Jewish. That his parents wouldn't have let me into their house. Wouldn't have served me food. Wouldn't have even let me eat at the same table. So much for your father.'

'I don't care, Mom! Half the kids here are Jewish! So what if Dad said that? You are what you are. But at least you know what you are!'

'You can say that because you are what everyone wants to be!'

*

Still we didn't realise. We thought it would all go back to normal. That the Shah would wrest control and next summer we would all regroup back in Tehran, that my father's jobs would resume, TAS would reopen, and I would go back to modelling, and Cameron to his job at Westinghouse.

Preoccupied with heartbreak – my first love, the boy I had met and spent virtually every moment with since the first day of freshman orientation, had dumped me – I barely registered my parents' despair or the situation in Iran. I retired to the library and burrowed into my work. Over Thanksgiving weekend, I was sulking in my room. The dorms were deserted, when suddenly I heard laughter and voices.

'Come on, Asho! We're off then!'

Sal, a new friend from down the hall, swept into my room, mimicking my mother's 'British accent'. He, Michael and Richard bundled me into their car and took me to south Philadelphia and an Italian-American Thanksgiving. From that point forward when I came back from the library in the evening, I sang in the hallway to Donna Summer's 'I Feel Love' and on the weekend I would dress up in my Iranian tribal dresses and go dancing at the Black Banana in Philadelphia.

But soon I couldn't ignore the situation in Iran. A strike by 37,000 workers at the oil refineries reduced production from 6 million barrels per day to about 1.5 million barrels. Foreign workers poured out of Iran, literally leaving with nothing but the shirts on their backs, using any mode of transport that was available. Iran plummeted into anarchy. I called my mother.

'Mom, tell Dad to get Rian out!'

Still they stayed. I had no contact with my father, getting all the news from my mother: his assets had been seized; his work had come to a standstill; no one was paying him, although he had to pay his workers; he was close to bankruptcy. Again.

For Christmas 1978, my father brought Rian out of Iran and we all met in Florida. He told us that 2 million people had taken to the streets of Tehran at the beginning of December, demanding that the Shah step down. The next week, over 5 million had staged a countrywide protest. My father didn't say this, but it was clear he had left Iran because he felt the situation was unsafe for him and Rian. Subdued, with big bags under his eyes, he told me how he had tried to save his company, scuttling from one government office to the next. The hard work of the prior decade, those terrible years recovering from the tunnel disaster: everything he had achieved was slipping away.

Rian, about to turn fifteen, told us that soldiers armed with machine-guns had guarded his school bus and patrolled the roof of the school. He had lived alone with his two cocker spaniels, Munchie and Missie, while my father went from job to job and site to site. Rian was distraught that his Iranian friends, with whom he had played football on our street for years, had thrown stones at him when he had walked his dogs. Fires burned all around their house. Shots rang out near by, so close, in fact, that on one occasion as Dad skipped rope on the roof, bullets whizzed past him, barely missing.

It was a subdued Christmas we spent together.

*

On the way back to Iran, my father stopped in Washington. During high school, Cameron's girlfriend was a classmate from TAS and the daughter of the head of the US Armed Forces in Iran. He and my father had become friendly. The Colonel had arranged for my father to meet with US officials to give them a first-hand account of the situation in Iran. He took the train up afterwards to visit me for the first time at Bryn Mawr. We held hands as we trotted around the campus and he gazed with delight at the science labs and library.

'It looks like Cambridge,' he said.

He chatted with my friends and feasted on the food in the cafeteria. 'This is not like Cambridge!' he said, laughing.

Before he left, I gathered my courage, for my father hated being asked for money, and I asked him once again to transfer to my bank account the money I had earned over the previous years. I had asked him many times before and he had always put me off.

'What do you need it for, darling girl?'

'I have *no* money, Dad, none.'

He had promised me funds, but, because of the unrest in Iran, he had been unable to transfer any out or pay my Bryn Mawr fees that year.

'Dad, I want my money, please.' My voice was desperate.

'Why?' he asked, a sly smile already playing on his lips.

'Well, to pay for things now and I'm going to graduate. I'll need a place to live, things to put into it, sheets, pots and pans, y'know.'

'Well, we'll do it then,' he responded. 'You don't need it now and you don't want to be tempted to spend it, do you?'

'Dad, it's my money. Please just give it to me. Please.'

I was concerned that the situation in Iran would get worse and he wouldn't ever be able to get the money out – even if he wanted to.

'How much do you think you have?' His hands were thrust into his pockets and he was no longer smiling.

I pulled out the little notebook in which I had written the amounts each time I had given him money and which I had painstakingly added up.

'You've kept track?' he asked, surprised to see my rows of dates and the amounts next to them.

'I have two thousand and six hundred dollars plus the interest I've earned.'

I started to ask whether I should calculate the interest or whether it would have just been compounded in the account, but he interrupted, truly stunned: 'No!'

'Well, Dad, look. I kept track of it – see: 3 June, babysitting – three hundred and fifty rials; 9 June, fashion show, five thousand rials . . . You can check my addition,' I handed him the book, 'and my exchange rates.'

He glanced at it, stuck it in his shirt pocket and said, 'You have nowhere close to that, Ashley. You're mistaken. I thought you had been contributing to the family. I can't believe you're claiming this money back. What about me? How much money have I given you for your food and school?'

'But, Dad, you're the father,' I said, genuinely shocked. 'Plus I've paid for all my extras since I was in high-school – lunch, cinemas, taxis . . .'

'Well,' he said, 'I thought you wanted me to have the money.'

He said this jokily, with his crooked half-smile – as if I were talking about a few hundred rials, not the money I had spent hundreds of hours earning over the past five years.

He had simply pocketed it.

I turned away. All that work. Night after night babysitting instead of going out with my friends. Working every lunch hour of my sophomore, junior and senior years of high school. I should have just spent it. Mom was right. *Carpe diem*, baby. Spend it. Enjoy it. She had told me, so many times, 'Don't trust your father.'

I was suckered, snookered, swindled, stuffed, scammed.

*

When I saw the news on my father's fifty-second birthday, 16 January 1979, that the Shah and Farah had left for Egypt, I realised the situation in Iran had finally and irrevocably changed. As his final act the Shah bent to pick up a clod of Iranian earth, knowing he would never be returning.

'I can't believe the Shah would just leave like that,' I said to my mother. 'How could he abandon his country when the chips are down?'

'He did it before,' she said. 'He knows when to get out, unlike your father, who should have left years ago.'

In February, the well-known, defining events of Iran's current history unfurled: Ayatollah Khomeini returned in a blaze of glory. Within ten days, the army had stepped aside, allowing him to establish a government. My father's assets were nationalised – they now ostensibly belonged to the Iranian people. Since the religious hierarchy had subsumed the entire Iranian judicial and administrative system, my father was negotiating with mullahs for the return of his property. He went from one cleric to another, paying people off, begging, pleading and arguing, in order to wrest back some of his hard-won assets of the previous ten years. It was no use. Everything my parents had worked for – my father's company, his equipment, his contracts, all the precious things my mother had collected, all those photos she had taken, her years of teaching at TAS – gone.

The huge American community in Iran disbanded. First through official channels, and then as the situation deteriorated they escaped through Turkey or Kuwait. Much later, I discovered that my father had played a role in getting some of these last Americans out of Iran. Sometime in the spring or summer of 1979, my father helped the Colonel who had been charged with evacuating the armed forces. They established safe houses to hide American military and embassy personnel until they could get safe passage out of the country.

I learned this years later, at Cameron and Mary Ann's wedding, when the Colonel pulled me aside and asked, 'Do you know that your father is a very brave man?'

He told me how my father had helped a number of Americans escape and about one incident where my father risked his life. My father was with a group of Americans in a safe house and, as dawn seeped over the rooftops, the person keeping watch saw soldiers carrying machine-guns unload from their jeeps and begin searching the houses along the road. The soldiers kicked down any door that wasn't answered promptly. My father, fluent in Farsi, met the soldiers at the door and delayed them long enough for the Americans to get away, clambering from rooftop to rooftop.

Later, when I asked my father about it, he said, 'Oh, the Colonel gives me far too much credit.'

*

That summer, after my junior year ended, I worked at Bryn Mawr, earning money and sharing an off-campus apartment. I lived on granola and tuna fish. Cameron alternated going to school with working as a diesel mechanic because my father was unable to pay his fees or send him money. He too was on a restricted diet: a jar of peanut butter over a couple of days, alternating with a can of beans.

My phone conversations with my mother and Rian were gloomy: she was frantic and furious with my father. His dedication to throwing all that he earned back into his business meant that he didn't possess a single penny outside Iran to support her or Rian. They were living on my mother's savings.

She would stay on the line with me, until I would say, 'Mom, please, I've got to sleep.'

'*Jayeh shoma khali-eh*, Asho. Your place is empty. *Jayeh shoma khali-eh*.'

Her voice was plaintive, but there was nothing I could do to help her.

*

My relationship with the Bryn Mawr bursar became more troubled in my senior year and I dreaded the messages left in my cubbyhole. I barricaded myself in my dorm and in the library, piling on credentials: a double major in Economics and Psychology, a minor in French. I interviewed for every job available, practically begging the Philadelphia banks to accept me into their training programmes. By then the crisis in Iran had forced the US economy into freefall. Oil prices were at a historical high of almost $40 per barrel. Inflation leaped into double digits and unemployment doubled to over 10 per cent. Gold hit $900 per ounce. I took my turquoise bracelet and a gold chain that my parents had given me to a pawnshop and left with them still in my pocket. The amount I could get for them was derisory, despite the gold prices.

This was definitely not a good time to be graduating and looking for a job. There wasn't much call for liberal-arts graduates from an elite women's college. Maybe Dad had been right; I should have gone to FIT and studied for a technical degree.

'Convince me you really want to be a credit officer,' urged a recent college graduate at one of the banks. 'I want to know you really, really want this job.'

Looking around the grubby, grey-carpeted cubicles and the grey-suited, grey-faced people hunched over their calculators, with the rain whipping the sidewalks outside, I pleaded, 'I really, *really* want this job – no, I really, really *need* this job – please.'

I taped all the 'Sorry we have no positions available at this time' letters to the wall of my room until I ran out of wall space. I had never really thought that I would return to Iran to live and work, but I would never have predicted that I couldn't return.

My final year was dominated in every way by the situation in Iran and the impact on our family. My friends' concerns – boyfriends, graduate exams, final grades, applying to med school, drunken beer bashes, soccer tournaments – seemed far removed and I isolated myself, eating virtually every meal alone and rarely going out. One night I was horribly awakened by two large roaches crawling on my face and my overreaction of panic and disgust reminded me of my mother during the period the *soosks* overran her bedroom. I felt as if nothing in my life was right, just as she had.

*

Rain beat relentlessly on the streaked windows of my room in Erdman, the modern 'Scottish castle' designed by Louis Kahn and built at the south end of the campus. A call from the career counsellor, a quiet grey-haired lady with round spectacles, interrupted my work.

'The CIA is coming to campus and would like to interview you.'

Knowing my situation, she alerted me whenever there was a potential job.

We were in the middle of the American embassy hostage

crisis. A few months earlier, a group of Iranian students had seized sixty-six Americans and were holding them hostage in the US embassy, located right in the middle of Tehran. It was where we had celebrated the Fourth of July with hot dogs and fireworks.

'They are looking for Farsi speakers, people familiar with the country. Shall I sign you up?'

'Uh, yes, yes, of course.'

I was so thrilled at the prospect of an interview that I automatically said yes. A job. Money. My final year Bryn Mawr bills covered.

Then when I reflected, I decided I was scared of all that cloak-and-dagger spy stuff, the torture in Evin Prison. Imbued with Bryn Mawr's philosophy of Quaker tolerance, my liberal tendencies well nurtured, I had neither the guts nor the morals for it. Most importantly, though, I would be spying against Iran – the country of my birth and the country I considered home. How dare they ask me to do such a thing?

I stopped by the careers office and crossed my name off the sign-up sheet.

*

'Hello. Is this Ashley Dartnell?'

For once it was not the bursar. I was immediately distrustful.

'Yes.'

'This is XXX from the Central Intelligence Agency and I was hoping to interview you today.'

*

My father called me, for the first time in many months, to say, 'I've only got a minute. Your mummy tells me that you are in discussion with "the Black Organisation". Do not pursue these discussions, Ashley. Trust me, they are an evil force. Do not talk to them.'

'But, Dad, I need a job. I need to pay my school fees.'

I didn't want to work for the CIA, but I was desperate.

'I'll get your school fees. I promise. Don't throw your life away. Do not join that terrible organisation.'

His voice was serious. Very serious.

41

In the End

my irrepressible mother

My father came through for me in the end. It was excruciatingly difficult but, by hook or by crook, he paid my final year's school fees. I turned down the CIA and, after Bryn Mawr, I scrambled around for the summer trying to get work. Completely randomly, I ended up landing a job on Wall Street. One of the hundreds of letters I had sent out during my senior year had mouldered in someone's in-box and they called me months after the recruiting season.

A classmate's mother lent me $500 for my apartment deposit. Uncle Hugh on a visit in the autumn paid for half a winter coat. My mother sent me boxes of old pots and pans and sheets – some left over from those we took from Lilly on our trip down to Fort Lauderdale in 1968. She was working at a museum of archaeology, and she and Rian were living in an apartment in Fort Lauderdale. My father stayed in Iran, trying to salvage what he could. Cameron persevered at Georgia Tech.

398

While I joined the ranks of young graduates ascending the elevators of Wall Street's investment banks at dawn, Iraqi forces invaded Iran in an attempt to seize control of the oil-producing province of Khuzestan and govern both sides of the Shatt al-Arab Waterway. By this time the hostages had been held for over a year and American hatred of Iran was so strong that I was advised by a colleague not to wear an Iranian necklace to work.

It was the beginning of the rock and roll years on Wall Street. I was swept up in the gruelling exhilaration of working as a foot soldier on a number of what were at the time record-breaking deals. My mother visited regularly. She would lie on my sofa bed, her head just a few feet from mine, resuming the conversation we had begun on those long evenings in Tehran when I was in high school. Her parentage, her Jewish antecedents, her marriage to Ben, her love affair with Waahid – she wove her tales night after night. At some point over those years, she revealed another secret, one she swore she never would: her IQ. Inexplicably, for I never thought to ask, she mentioned it in conversation. Her IQ was indeed higher than mine – but not so earth shatteringly that it warranted her reaction when I told her mine those many years ago in Florida.

Meanwhile my father remained in Iran. The war with Iraq brought tremendous hardship. Tehran was shelled and his life was in danger. Food and fuel shortages were severe. He toiled trying to recover his assets. When things periodically heated up to the point that even he felt it was unsafe, he would make his way to Florida. My mother wasn't happy at all about being used as a hotel.

'This is no marriage!'

There was no solution, though. She couldn't return to Tehran; he wouldn't realistically get a job in Florida – and she probably wouldn't have wanted him to in any case.

When I shared a van to move up to Harvard Business School, my mother said, 'Who woulda thunk it, my daughter at Harvard?'

I too found it unbelievable. Here was a bookish *farangi* girl, who had missed almost as much school as she had attended, going to Harvard. I met Bruce there, the man I would eventually marry, and we moved to New York after graduation.

My parents divorced in 1986. My mother was fifty-four and my father fifty-nine. After all those years of childhood anxiety about them divorcing, when they finally did, I was a 'grown-up'. As it happens, it didn't improve either of their lives. Neither ever remarried or had another relationship. My father, never especially attached to anything, was even more adrift. My mother, who was so sociable, suddenly joined the ranks of all the divorcees and widows in south Florida, losing whatever social standing she had.

The government finally ejected my father in the spring of 1989 (a decade after the Revolution), when Iran and the UK broke off diplomatic relations following Ayatollah Khomeini's fatwa against Salman Rushdie. My father had survived the revolution, the Iran–Iraq war and the bombing of Tehran, bankruptcy, jailing and deprivation. That the end of his thirty years in Iran was signalled by a soldier with a sub-machine gun banging on the door of his flat and telling him to get the hell out was an appropriate finale. All because an Indian writer living in England had published a book. He gave his plants to his neighbour and locked the door, expecting he'd be back in a couple of weeks. He showed up on our London doorstep, where we ourselves had just landed, suitcase in hand, and slept on the carpet.

'Who the hell is this Salman Rushdie man, anyway?' he asked me.

I had seen my father only sporadically in the prior decade.

The evening before my Harvard graduation, Bruce and I had returned to my room to find him lying on my couch.

'Didn't expect to find me here, did you?' he quipped. He had done essentially the same at our wedding, turning up like the prodigal son at the last minute.

For the next six years, our home was his base. When he was in London he dropped me off and picked me up from work, and I baked him raisin cakes. The special bond that we had when I was a little girl was re-established and we became close friends. Being with him was easy, so long as I didn't mind that he never filled the car with petrol or tell me when he would be home – and I didn't. My father's inability to accept that people might be bad or ill-intentioned or wish to take advantage of him was the outcome of his relentless optimism. He was always looking forward. If someone did him a wrong, he just moved on – as he did with his business partners, my mother, and the Iranian authorities who stole his assets. It was his ability to get on with things, his positivism, that made him such a grand companion. We were always off on our next jog or drive to see this woodland or that new concrete-pouring technique.

When he died of a heart attack in Zimbabwe in 1995, I was gutted. He had been running a division of a UK construction company and shortly before he suffered severe chest pains, his finance director heard him on the phone, screaming at someone in Farsi. He was still trying to recover his assets. For thirty years my mother had said that Iran would kill him, and maybe it had. He died that night in a Harare clinic. When I spoke to the doctor a few days later, he told me that my father had been in marvellous shape for a man of fifty-eight – 'really quite breathtaking'.

'You mean sixty-eight,' I said.

'No, fifty-eight,' said the doctor. 'It said on his passport that he was fifty-eight.'

I laughed. I knew that my father had replaced a managing director who had been forced to take mandatory retirement at the age of sixty-five. My father was sixty-eight at the time so he had simply lied about his age. After all those years of not having a passport, when he died he had two: his real one with his actual age of sixty-eight and a counterfeit one, with his age shown as a decade younger. Those many hours of skipping rope and jogging meant he looked wonderful. Too bad about his congenital heart defect.

My mother did not cry when we called to tell her that our father had died. Neither did she attend his funeral. Until her dying day she blamed him for almost everything wrong in her life. She found safe harbour in a tall white condominium in Fort Lauderdale where security guards patrolled the halls twenty-four hours a day and video cameras scanned the garage. She worked and supported herself, remaining friends with Uncle Hugh, Yosy and her whole Florida gang.

As far as I know, she never saw Martin again. He remarried within months of breaking off with her and lives in Iran. Tom Glenn died of alcoholism in his early fifties after remarrying and, through the wonders of the internet, Dana and I are again friends.

Waahid never came to find my mother. When she was in her mid-sixties, friends of hers visited Pakistan and at her request looked him up. They discovered that my mother was a myth in his household: the beautiful blonde foreigner Waahid had loved. He had written poetry about her, which he read aloud. He sent my mother a picture of himself, dressed in his Pakistani military uniform.

'I don't see anything of Waahid in him, Asho,' she said plaintively. 'Maybe when I turn it upside down, something in the mouth.'

The picture showed a genial portly man in his sixties. She was expecting an angel.

At about the same time, she decided to find Ben.

'I want to tell him that I'm sorry if I hurt him. To tell him I was young, impetuous. That I never meant him harm.'

She located him in Sarasota, Florida, and, gathering her courage over many months, called him. He was so stunned he barely spoke and he never called back. It had been forty-two years. At my mother's request, Rian approached the guard at his gated community a short time later, only to find he had died. My mother cried bitterly.

'He was so kind, so kind.'

His benevolence had even seeped down to us. It was Ben's generosity that helped get us started in America when both my father and Martin had abandoned my mother in 1968. When we landed in New York that June day, we had only $28, which we paid the limo driver. I had never questioned how she had enough to support us that summer in Colchester, to buy Jessie and drive to Florida. She told me years later that when they had split up, Ben had given her $5,000, which she had banked in Connecticut, hidden from my father.

Perhaps, in completing our stories, least surprising of all is how my mother ended hers. For years I had expected her to die of cancer. Regularly I dreamed about her death, even throughout my adulthood. My anxiety stemmed from her hospitalisation when we were living in Florida, which had never been explained, until one day years later, when Yosy referred to it.

'What was it, though?' I asked.

'She had peritonitis because her IUD punctured her uterus.'

'But what about the tumour – you know, the tumour she had?' I asked.

'Oh no, she didn't have a tumour,' she said. 'She just made up that whole story so people wouldn't know she had an IUD.'

When I asked her, my mother confirmed the infection

had been the result of an IUD. At the time, of course, she couldn't admit to having one because it would have meant acknowledging she was having sex with Tom. Why the secrecy when, a few years earlier, in a Muslim country as a married woman, she had lived with Martin in our Amir Abad flat? Was it because we children were older? Because we had neighbours? Because her parents were living with us? Did she not want to acknowledge that she was sleeping with Tom because she somehow hoped that Martin would reappear?

What my brothers and I had predicted, of course, came true: cigarettes killed our mother. By the time she was fifty, her life was quite curtailed by emphysema and, by the time she reached sixty, she suffered severely. By this time, she and I had been best friends for decades, speaking on the phone daily. One day in November 1999 she called at an unusual time – mid-afternoon on a weekday when my house was frantic, with six-year-old Dylan and four-year-old Kyle having tea and sticking bits of food into baby Cara's mouth.

'I told you, didn't I, that I had a pain in my back?' she said.

'No, Mom. Tell me.'

I had a terrible sense of foreboding – as I had so many times before.

There was a tumour in the upper lobe of her lung. Her body was already ravaged by the effects of forty years of smoking. There was no cure, only palliative treatment.

Over the years, as her condition had worsened, she had tried to make me promise that, if she deteriorated to a certain level, I would 'put her out of her misery'. Of course, as her health declined, that level changed. First it was, 'If I am ever like that,' and she pointed to a woman with an oxygen tube; then it was, 'If I am ever in a wheelchair'; and finally, 'If I get cancer.' In the end, she fought to stay alive as hard as she had fought to raise us kids. For almost two years, I commuted to Florida from London with baby Cara and took care of her through her painful radiation and chemotherapy treatments.

During this period, she lay on a couch in the living room, telling and retelling her stories while directing me to do this or that. In the final months before she died, she became preoccupied with making an inventory of all her possessions and divvying them up between us children She remained obsessed with 'things'. She would ask me to find such-and-such or dig out this and that.

One day she sat up straight and, gasping, said, 'Oh dammit, I have to find something . . . something I haven't seen in years.'

Instantly I knew. 'Mom, don't worry, I've already read them.'

'You have?' She looked at me, her blue-grey eyes glittering. 'What?'

'Martin's letters.'

'You have!' Her eyes were now flashing. 'When?'

'When you were in the hospital.' I thought for a minute to figure out the date. 'In 1970.'

'You've known all those years?' She regarded me with grudging respect.

'Yes, I've known,' I said. 'I knew.'

She fell back on to the couch, resigned. 'So you knew.'

It was while clearing my mother's home after she died, that Yosy, who remains extremely close to my brothers and me, inadvertently helped untangle a mystery. We had just come across Martin's letters to my mother. Yosy took me aside and, whispering so that Cameron and Rian, who were sorting through my mother's knick-knacks, wouldn't hear, said, 'Well, from what your mother told me about Martin, the sex stuff was pretty powerful. The first time they "did it" was in some chicken coop on your father's job and she was all scraped up.'

I collapsed on to the sofa.

'That's how she got all scraped up? Having sex with Martin, not falling down a mountain?'

I remembered instantly the whole episode with my mother: the run down the mountain, the uncomfortable drive with my father's workers, the medic and my father questioning her wounds. Over three decades ago and yet it was as fresh as the day it had happened. Even the physiological response was the same: my breath grew shallow and my stomach clenched. The memory hadn't changed, softened, or transformed into a softer, fuzzier, happier one. It remained shrapnel sharp, piercing tender emotional flesh.

Yosy and I puzzled together over the events that began in Khomsar when I was just eight years old. The night before 'the fall', my mother and Martin had met in the wooden shed where the cook housed the chickens. There was no place else to go. My father was close by on the site or in the office, poring over the accounts until the early hours. Brigitte and Mikey were but a short distance away in their little cement cube. We children were fast asleep on the thick quilts laid out on the floor, tumbled together like bear cubs. I remembered the chicken hut well, for my brothers and I gathered there many afternoons as the cook sharpened his axe on a stone. With apron flying and shoes flapping, he dove straight on to the screeching chickens as they raced around. Sweaty and breathless, he would capture a struggling brown hen and whack off her head. We kids would shriek with nervous laughter as the headless chicken ran around and around, stumbling and falling, until it fell lifeless, ready to be plucked, for the *khoresht eh morgh* he prepared for dinner.

In their passion, my mother had been scraped – presumably by the rough wood of the henhouse. She had hatched a plot to explain the mysterious wounds: she would stay in bed late, avoiding my father and breakfast, and then orchestrate a fall that we children would witness. That night, the tale would be told, the injuries explained and hopefully never closely examined. My run for help and the subsequent public revelation of her scrapes had spoiled the plan. Both my father and the medic had realised something was suspicious: that the wounds had scabbed over, that there was no blood, that there was no dirt or grit – hence their pointed questions. As a child, of course, I had no idea my mother and Martin were having sex in a chicken coop only yards away from where we slept. At the time, it was inexplicable to me why my mother had sulked for days, ignoring my father and me as if it were the two of us who had thrown her down the mountain.

Sitting on the couch in her flat in Florida, mourning her death, I wondered how my mother who was so fastidious had dealt with the smell of chicken shit and how they had kept the chickens from clucking and awakening the cook. I wondered whether Brigitte and my father had suspected even then. Mostly, though, I felt tremendous relief that the firestorm of anger she had showered on me had nothing to do with me. And, truth be told, I felt grudging admiration for her. Despite the unhappiness and uncertainty in her life, she had found love and ardour in a chicken coop.

'Oh,' Yosy added, 'there was another thing she told me. Do you remember when you were visiting a remote mountain village and she got lost and Martin found her? She had started her period, so she went and squatted on a rock in the middle of a river and got trapped there in the dark. She told me that it was then that she knew they had a special connection: your father couldn't find her, but Martin tracked the smell of her menstrual blood through the woods.'

I was deluged with yet another cascade of 'what ifs'. In the same way that I had thought about what would have happened had she stayed with Ben or Waahid or Tom. I pondered what our lives would have been like if my mother and Martin had married. They were well suited in their love of the outdoors, their energy, their sense of adventure. They would certainly have had more children – in the letters he mentioned this repeatedly. I wonder whether my mother would have had more fun with Martin and known more contentment.

After she died, I put the neatly bundled letters in my underwear drawer. For years I didn't look at them. I wasn't sure I wanted to be reminded of the complex emotions they would dredge up. Finally I read them, though – and it took hours.

There were a dozen, all written between July and December 1968, and each one consisted of pages and pages of single-spaced typing. Interestingly, there were letters missing; some that I remember reading in 1970 were no longer there. Despite English being his second or maybe even third language (after Dutch and Farsi), Martin expressed himself beautifully. I was moved to tears by his passionate love of my mother. He worshipped her and was heartbroken that he was not with her, jealous of my father (and any other male who might glance her way), and intent on getting his divorce from Brigitte, while trying to make enough money to join her in Florida as soon as possible.

Upon rereading them, I learned more, though, about my father, his debts and the disastrous episode of the tunnel. Martin, my father and his two partners were linked to each other, as well as to others, in a chain of liabilities. As a result, my father was arrested and jailed when Martin, with a gendarme, tracked him down near the Caspian, demanding repayment. Martin also owed my mother. Some of the money she had borrowed from friends had gone Martin's way as well as my father's. I discovered that, of course, my father had known about 'the affair' and was deeply hurt and angry. Martin on the other hand, was adamant my father had to honour his obligations to him despite the fact he had stolen his wife. In his letters, Martin was anxious that my father might somehow get back his passport and papers, which would allow him to follow my mother to America. Martin repeatedly urged my mother to proceed rapidly with a divorce and he became agitated when she appeared to be dragging her heels.

It became clear from the letters that the big surprise my mother had promised us, that first Christmas we were in Florida, was Martin's arrival. All her homey touches – the tree, the presents, and the lights that she spent back-breaking hours repairing and then nailing to the eaves of the house – had been in anticipation of this. Christmas in 1968 fell on a Wednesday. School probably ended the Friday before on 20 December. On Wednesday the 18th or Thursday the 19th at the latest, my mother came home from her job at Sears Town where she had been on her feet, working as a waitress, for at least eight hours – maybe more if she had been able to get the overtime. In the mailbox there was a fat letter. Would my mother have put the letter into her bag to read after we had gone to bed or gone out Christmas-carolling with Uncle Hugh? Would she have read it straight away? Ultimately, she did read it and what it said would change everything, for ever.

Martin addressed the letter, begun on 9 November 1968, to 'My Miraculous Princess!' On page three of the single-spaced letter, it said, 'I LOVE YOU MORE THAN MERE WORDS COULD EVER SAY!' On page five, he talked about the children they would have together. But by page seven, which was dated two days later, on 11 November, the euphoric mood had plummeted: he called it quits, he told her he loved her but that it couldn't work. Then he slept on it for eight days, and on 19 November he wrote, as if she had been arguing with him, that he was dead serious and there were too many things that didn't fit. It was over. Nevertheless, he hesitated. Finally, he scrawled in pencil in big letters on 23 November that he was going to burn all her letters and photos. The letter was stamped at the Fort Lauderdale Seminole Annex post office on Tuesday 17 December.

'So,' Yosy explained when I discussed the letters with her, 'Christmas 1968 didn't turn out the way she had expected. You gotta remember she'd left her husband, her friends . . . As your mother would say, she was working as a bloody waitress in a goddam coffee shop and the man she was in love with had dumped her.'

In her final months, during one of our many conversations, I told her, 'Mom, I wish so much your life had been happier – that you'd married someone you really loved, that you could've lived in Pakistan, that you hadn't had to work so hard – that you had tons of money.'

'Yes, tons of money would have been nice.' She smiled. 'But don't cry for me, Ashley, I made my choices and what I wanted most was an interesting life – an exciting life – filled with travel, and I've had that. I wanted life to be fascinating and unusual. It would have killed me to be a small-town housewife in Connecticut. In my own way, I did love your father although, God knows, he led me a merry chase. And I have you kids and you know how much I love you. The only thing I regret is losing those two babies.'

As she lay dying in the hospital, I spent many hours at her side. Despite the 'no children allowed' rule, the nurses let me wheel Cara in every day. In fact, she became a favourite of the patients and nurses, who handed her around and crooned to her. I would sit at the side of my mother's bed, drinking tea from Styrofoam cups, and we would talk and talk and talk. It seemed our conversation could go on for ever.

One afternoon, watching Cara nurse at my breast, my

mother said, 'How wonderful to be held like that – with such love. In my entire life no one ever held me like that.'

I got up, placed the baby in her pushchair, gathered my mother in my arms and held her.

Acknowledgements

This is a work of non-fiction. I have changed some names and personal details to protect the privacy of those involved. Although I have relied largely on my memories, I had hundreds of letters and photographs as well as access to many of the people who lived through these years with me. I have reconstructed the dialogue in this book as faithfully as possible.

I have received a great deal of help while writing *Farangi Girl* for which I am very grateful.

To my publisher, Lisa Highton, thank you for including me in the opening salvo of the Two Roads imprint and working with me to hew this book out of the immense original manuscript. Helen Coyle edited the book with great delicacy and Valerie Appleby helped throughout.

Thank you to David Meller who introduced me to my agents, Luke Janklow and Claire Paterson, and to Luke and Claire themselves, a big thank you.

Michael Zur-Szpiro provided great insight when I was choosing a title for the book for which I thank him.

I have had extraordinary teachers: Susan Elderkin, Martina Evans, Maggie Gee, Lavinia Greenlaw, Jackie Kay, Blake Morrison and Ali Smith and I thank them.

My Goldsmiths writing group has provided me with unstinting feedback and friendship and I am grateful to them all: Sara Grant, Bronia Kita, Emily Jeremiah, Vinita Joseph and Sandra White.

Thank you to Tina Fateh and Noushin Danechi who corrected my Farsi and to Maike Braun who translated the German.

Both Colleen Brand and Lubka Gangarova helped tremendously with the photos.

Rebecca Dobbs and Michael Wood spent their much-deserved holiday reading an early draft and giving me very valuable suggestions.

My dear friends Darrill Anderson, Bonnie S' Capes, Mary Ann Dartnell, Stan Harrison, Cynthia King, Melissa Leet, Margot Steinberg, Lee Vance, Deborah Winshel, Joanna Wise and Lisa Wolfe were early and generous readers.

To my wonderful friend Suki Smith, thank you for the many turns around Regents Park talking through every dilemma and triumph.

Thank you to my god mother, Rosemary Jones, who has shared her love of reading and writing and has worked with me every step of the way on this book.

Finally, thank you to my beloved family, Bruce, Dylan, Kyle, and Cara for engaging in this book wholeheartedly and lovingly.

TWO ROADS

stories ... voices ... places ... lives

Two Roads is the home of fabulous storytelling and reader enjoyment. We publish stories from the heart, told in strong voices about lives lived. Two Roads books come from everywhere and take you into other worlds.

We hope you enjoyed *Farangi Girl*. If you'd like to know more about this book or any other title on our list, please go to www.tworoadsbooks.com or scan this code with your smartphone to go straight to our site:

For news on forthcoming Two Roads titles, please sign up for our newsletter

We'd love to hear from you

enquiries@tworoadsbooks.com   Twitter (@tworoadsbooks)